BARBARIAN TIDES

TimeFrame 1500-600 BC

THE MEDITERRANEAN: ETRUSCANS, GREEKS, AND PHOENICIANS

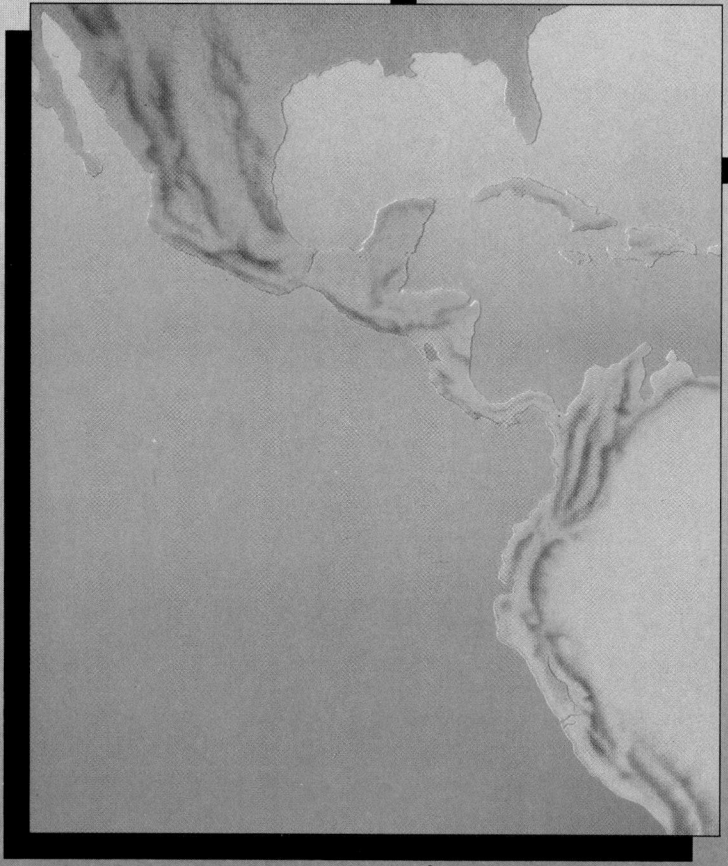

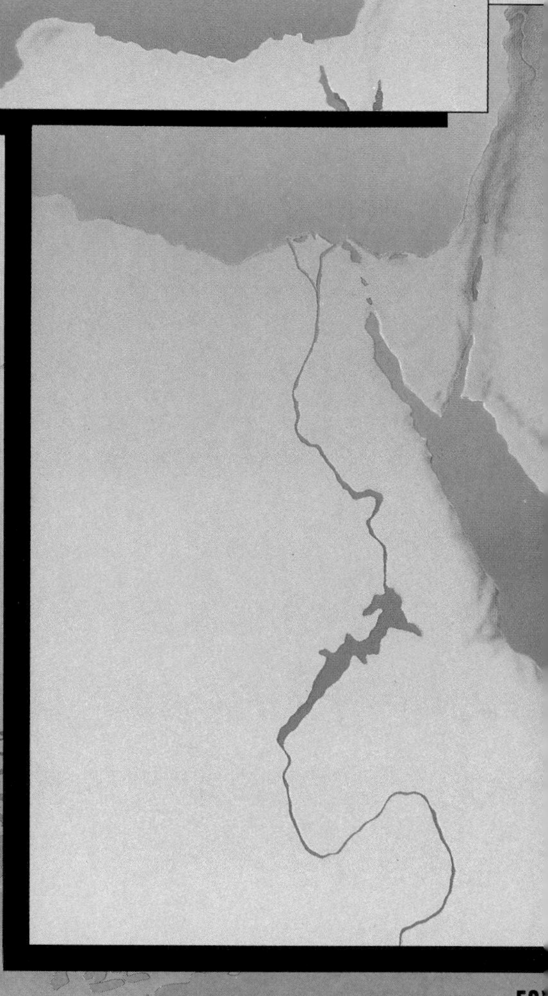

THE AMERICAS: OLMECS AND CHAVÍN

EG

Time Frame: 1500-600 BC

THE MIDDLE EAST: HITTITES, ASSYRIANS, AND BABYLONIANS

ASIA: ARYANS AND CHINESE

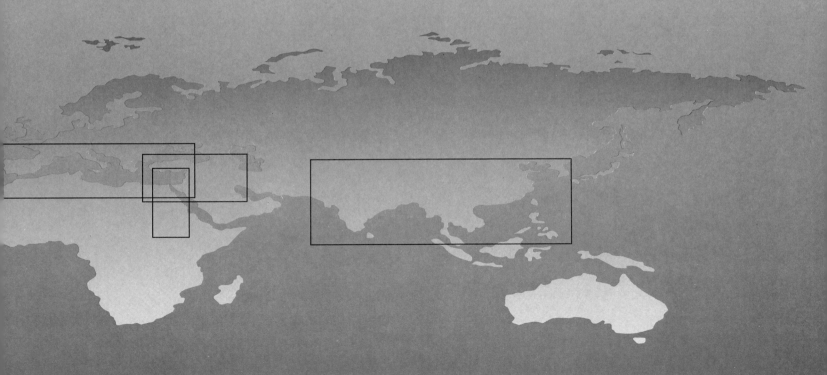

TIME® LIFE BOOKS

Other Publications:
MYSTERIES OF THE UNKNOWN
FIX IT YOURSELF
FITNESS, HEALTH & NUTRITION
SUCCESSFUL PARENTING
HEALTHY HOME COOKING
UNDERSTANDING COMPUTERS
LIBRARY OF NATIONS
THE ENCHANTED WORLD
THE KODAK LIBRARY OF CREATIVE PHOTOGRAPHY
GREAT MEALS IN MINUTES
THE CIVIL WAR
PLANET EARTH
COLLECTOR'S LIBRARY OF THE CIVIL WAR
THE EPIC OF FLIGHT
THE GOOD COOK
WORLD WAR II
HOME REPAIR AND IMPROVEMENT
THE OLD WEST

For information on and a full description of
any of the Time-Life Books series listed above,
please call 1-800-621-7026 or write:
Reader Information
Time-Life Customer Service
P.O. Box C-32068
Richmond, Virginia 23261-2068

This volume is one in a series that tells the story
of humankind. Other books in the series include: *The Age of God-Kings.*

BARBARIAN TIDES

TimeFrame 1500-600 BC

BY THE EDITORS OF TIME-LIFE BOOKS

TIME-LIFE BOOKS, ALEXANDRIA, VIRGINIA

Time-Life Books Inc.
is a wholly owned subsidiary of
TIME INCORPORATED

FOUNDER: Henry R. Luce 1898-1967

Editor-in-Chief: Henry Anatole Grunwald
Chairman and Chief Executive Officer:
J. Richard Munro
President and Chief Operating Officer:
N. J. Nicholas Jr.
Chairman of the Executive Committee:
Ralph P. Davidson
Corporate Editor: Ray Cave
Executive Vice President, Books:
Kelso F. Sutton
Vice President, Books: George Artandi

TIME-LIFE BOOKS INC.

EDITOR: George Constable
Executive Editor: Ellen Phillips
Director of Design: Louis Klein
Director of Editorial Resources:
Phyllis K. Wise
Editorial Board: Russell B. Adams Jr., Dale
M. Brown, Roberta Conlan, Thomas H.
Flaherty, Lee Hassig, Donia Ann Steele,
Rosalind Stubenberg, Kit van Tulleken,
Henry Woodhead
Director of Photography and Research:
John Conrad Weiser

PRESIDENT: Christopher T. Linen
Chief Operating Officer: John M. Fahey Jr.
Senior Vice Presidents: James L. Mercer,
Leopoldo Toralballa
Vice Presidents: Stephen L. Bair,
Ralph J. Cuomo, Neal Goff, Stephen L.
Goldstein, Juanita T. James, Hallett
Johnson III, Carol Kaplan, Susan J.
Maruyama, Robert H. Smith, Paul R.
Stewart, Joseph J. Ward
Director of Production Services:
Robert J. Passantino

Editorial Operations
Copy Chief: Diane Ullius
Editorial Operations Manager:
Caroline A. Boubin
Production: Celia Beattie
Quality Control: James J. Cox (director)
Library: Louise D. Forstall

Correspondents: Elisabeth Kraemer-Singh
(Bonn); Maria Vincenza Aloisi (Paris); Ann
Natanson (Rome). Valuable assistance
was also provided by: Mirka Gondicas
(Athens); Bing Wong (Hong Kong); Marlin
Levin (Jerusalem); Caroline Alcock, Chris-
tine Hinze, Caroline Lucas, (London);
K. K. Sharma (New Delhi); Elizabeth
Brown, Christina Lieberman (New York);
Ann Wise (Rome); Lawrence Chang (Tai-
pei); Dick Berry (Tokyo); Traudl Lessing
(Vienna).

TIME FRAME

SERIES DIRECTOR: Henry Woodhead
Series Administrator:
Philip Brandt George

Editorial Staff for *Barbarian Tides*
Designer: Elissa E. Baldwin
Associate Editor: Marion F. Briggs
(pictures)
Text Editors: Jim Hicks, David S. Thomson
Writers: Stephen G. Hyslop, Ray Jones
Researchers: Paula York-Soderlund (text);
Jane A. Martin, Connie Strawbridge
(pictures)
Assistant Designer: Alan Pitts
Copy Coordinator: Vivian Noble
Picture Coordinator: Renée DeSandies
Editorial Assistant: Patricia D. Whiteford

Special Contributors: Ronald H. Bailey,
Richard Billings, Champ Clark, George
G. Daniels, Donald Dale Jackson, Charles
Phillips, Bryce Walker (text); Henri Grossi
(research)

CONSULTANTS

General
JOHN R. McNEILL, Assistant Professor,
Department of History, Georgetown Uni-
versity, Washington, D.C.

The Americas:
JILL L. FURST, Adjunct Professor of An-
thropology, State University of New York,
Albany, New York

PETER T. FURST, Professor of Anthropology and Latin American Studies, State University of New York, Albany, New York

GORDON F. McEWAN, Assistant Curator, Pre-Columbian Studies, Dumbarton
Oaks, Washington, D.C.

Assyria:
ROBERT D. BIGGS, Professor of Assyriol-
ogy, Oriental Institute, University of Chicago, Chicago, Illinois

China:
ROBERT THORP, Professor of Art History
and Archeology, Washington University,
St. Louis, Missouri

Egypt:
ROBERT S. BIANCHI, Associate Curator,
Department of Egyptian, Classical, and
Ancient Middle Eastern Art, Brooklyn Mu-
seum, Brooklyn, New York

ALESSANDRO ROCCATI, Professor of
Egyptology, Rome University "La Sa-
pienza," Rome, Italy; Curator, Museo Egi-
zio, Turin, Italy

Etruria:
LARISSA BONFANTE, Professor of Clas-
sics, New York University, New York,
New York

Greece:
GEORGE MYLONAS, General Secretary,
Greek Archeological Society; Professor of
Archeology, University of Athens,
Athens, Greece

JOSIAH OBER, Professor of History, University of Michigan, Ann Arbor, Michigan

DEMETRIOS SCHILARDI, Visiting Profes-
sor of Classical Archeology, University of
Ottowa, Ottowa, Ontario, Canada; Cura-
tor, Archeological Museum, Delphi,
Greece; Director of Excavations, Paros,
Greece

India:
SHIVA BAJPAI, Professor of History, Cali-
fornia State University, Northridge,
California

GREGORY POSSEHL, University of Pennsylvania Museum, Philadelphia,
Pennsylvania

Phoenicia:
PIERO BARTOLONI, Instituto per la
civiltá Fenicia e Punica, C.N.R., Rome;
Director of Excavations, Monte Sirai,
Sardinia, Italy

P. KYLE McCARTER, William Foxwell Al-
bright Professor of Ancient Near Eastern
Studies, Johns Hopkins University, Balti-
more, Maryland

**Library of Congress Cataloging in
Publication Data**

Barbarian tides.
  Bibliography: p.
  Includes index.
  Summary: Describes the historical events and
the various civilizations that flourished through-
out the world, with emphasis on the Mediterra-
nean area, from 1500 to 600 BC.
  1. Europe — History — To 476. [1. Europe —
History — To 476. 2. World history]
I. Time-Life Books.
D62.B37 1987   930   87-17961
ISBN 0-8094-6404-7
ISBN 0-8094-6405-5 (pbk.)

CONTENTS

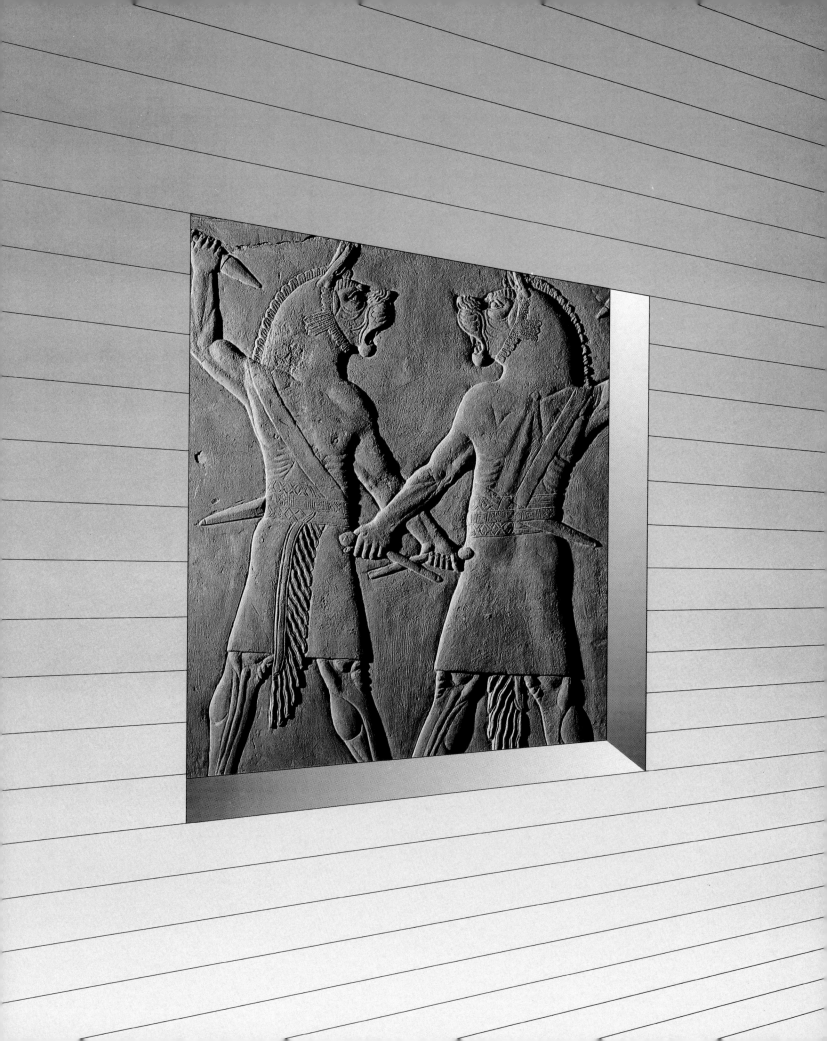

THE AGGRESSIVE EMPIRES

1 Human beings always have been a restless species, making their way from mountain to plain, from valley to valley, from one corner of the planet to another in search of better hunting, greener pastures, someone else's cattle, richer ores, more water, wealth, a chance to get in a fight, freedom, an opportunity to exploit other people, or any of dozens of other goals that have inspired individuals, families, tribes, or whole nations to pack up and move. Although this peripatetic spirit has characterized life in most ages, rarely has it been more evident, or more consequential for developing civilizations, than during the era that began early in the second millennium BC.

On the great Eurasian landmass, two major groups of peoples were on the move during this period. At the time, they were not identified as two groups — simply as many different tribes, each with its own name. Much later, scholars would sort them out by language characteristics, which probably indicated racial relationships as well, calling one group Indo-European speakers and the other Semitic speakers. In their own day, to the already-settled peoples whose lands they invaded or infiltrated, they were probably known by whatever local epithet approximated a mix of contempt, fear, and enmity. In a later age, the Greeks would pack these same emotions into a word that they coined for foreign-speaking strangers: barbarians.

Neither the Indo-Europeans nor the Semites left any obvious clues as to why so many of them spilled out of their homelands into new regions during this era. Migrating was not a novelty to either group; each had been finding new places to roam or settle as far back as the beginning of the third millennium BC, although not in such numbers as now. Both had the same general impetus for seeking more amenable environments: Indo-Europeans came from the harsh, semiarid Eurasian Steppes and Semites from somewhere in the deserts of Arabia and North Africa. Both possessed the means of mobility that encouraged migration: horses for the Indo-Europeans, asses and camels for the Semitic peoples.

But just why the trickles of population movement swelled to a flood would remain a mystery. Perhaps a disastrous drought on the Steppes forced Indo-Europeans to seek fresh grass for their cattle. Maybe a long string of bountiful years in normally marginal desert lands had inspired an increase in the Semitic population, which then needed new places to support itself. Or perhaps tougher people simply moved in and bumped the Semitic or Indo-European groups out of their territories, setting off a chain reaction like billiard balls clicking one another into motion on a baize-covered table.

Whatever the reason, they moved, and from about 1500 to 600 BC, few civilized parts of the world failed to feel the tremors that resulted. Probably only in South and Middle America were there advanced civilizations so remote that they were not influenced by the migrations of the Indo-Europeans or Semites; there, the Chavín culture in the Andes region and that of the Olmecs in Mesoamerica achieved high levels of artistic and organizational refinement, undisturbed by the momentous changes taking place on the other side of the world. Even far-off northern China, home of a long-established civilization that grew and flourished during this period despite the violent overthrows of two successive ruling dynasties, probably was indirectly affected. The Chinese had to contend with roving barbarians on their own borders — barbarians who may well have been on the prowl because they had been bumped by other peoples, who had been jostled in turn by Indo-Europeans.

At the European end of the landmass, the migrations of the peoples from the Steppes made a much deeper impression on the shape of the world. Indo-Europeans who would come to be known as Mycenaeans moved into Greece and created a dazzling Aegean civilization that replaced the lost world of the Minoans. They were followed to the region by other Indo-Europeans, whose settlements would become the spawning grounds of classical Greek culture. To the north and west, Indo-European peoples — Celts and Germans, Balts and Slavs among them — were to penetrate almost every inhabitable area of the European continent and to cross the waters to Britain and other offshore lands. Some who settled on the Italian peninsula, most notably a people called the Latins, would eventually eclipse the Etruscans — whose civilization was one of the crowning glories of this age — by building an even greater civilization for a later era: Rome.

At the height of its power in the seventh century BC, the Assyrian empire stretched in a great 1,400-mile arc from the Persian Gulf through the Tigris and Euphrates valleys, westward across Syria to the Mediterranean, and then down the coast to include Palestine and Egypt. During the centuries-long conquest of this realm — which embraced the Middle East's most fertile lands and valuable trade routes — the powerful armies of a succession of Assyrian kings overran territories previously controlled by other strong peoples: the Aramaeans, Hittites, Kassites, and Mittani.

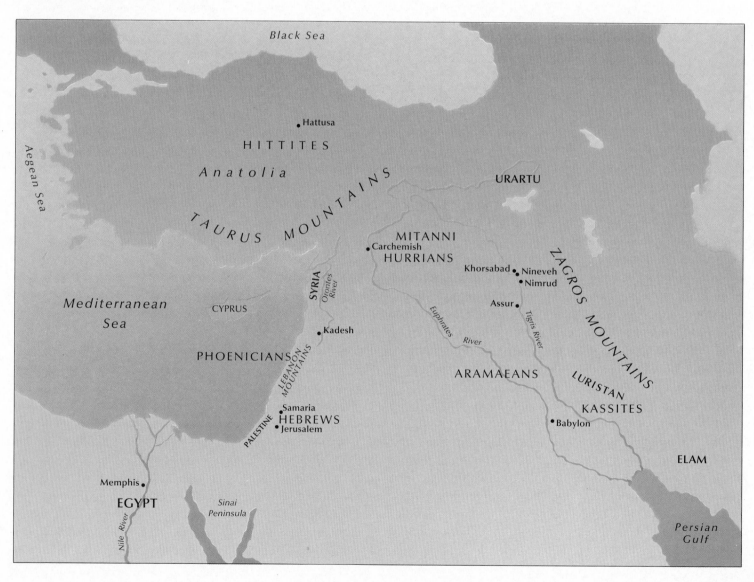

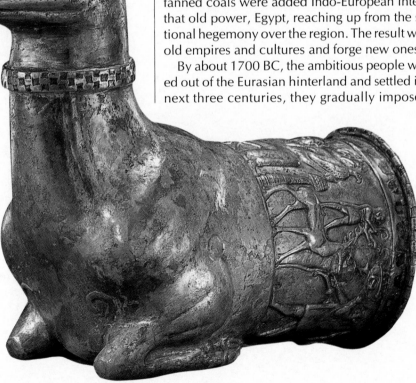

This silver ceremonial drinking cup in the shape of a stag was crafted by Hittite artisans about 1200 BC. Living in mineral-rich Anatolia, the Hittites were for generations the finest metalworkers of the ancient Middle East. Their skill is especially apparent in the delicate frieze, depicting a religious ceremony, that runs around the cup below its lip *(right)*, as well as in the stag's checkerboard-patterned collar, which deftly conceals the seam where the head and body, made in two parts, were joined.

Other Indo-Europeans, among them a people who would be called the Hittites, came from the Steppes to Anatolia, the mountainous land protruding between the Black Sea and the Mediterranean Sea like the head of a huge rhinoceros standing in Asia and glowering at Europe across a narrow stretch of water. In those mountains the Hittites would found a mighty empire. Others went from the Steppes to the Iranian plateau, and from here some groups trekked east over the Hindu Kush mountains to north India. These people, the Aryans, would bestow their social institutions on the Indian subcontinent and spawn a unique spiritual culture, Hinduism.

But for all those sweeping, large-scale shifts of peoples across the breadth of Europe and into south Asia, nowhere were the effects of moving populations more visible — or more violent — than in the relatively small region that encompassed the Middle Eastern birthplace of civilization, Mesopotamia, and the adjacent lands along the Mediterranean's eastern shore, later known as Syria and Palestine. In this area resided tribes and nations that had been fighting territorial battles for centuries. Here, too, were storied cities large and rich and tempting enough to lure ravening armies from afar and set small kings to dreaming about large empires. Here were prized Mediterranean ports and overland trade routes that could provide untold wealth for those who seized control of them. And here, finally, was where Indo-Europeans pushing down from the north collided not only with settled populations but also with Semitic peoples thrusting in from the south and west.

Most of the established inhabitants of the region were Semitic, among them the Assyrians, who had first wandered in from the desert and settled along the Tigris River in northern Mesopotamia around the beginning of the fourth millennium BC. The constant hostility and conflict that marked relationships among local tribes was exacerbated in this period by the pressure of more recently arrived Semites, including Chaldeans, Aramaeans, Phoenicians, and Hebrews, who were trying to carve out territories for themselves in the crowded neighborhood. To this bed of continually fanned coals were added Indo-European interlopers encroaching from the north and that old power, Egypt, reaching up from the south in an attempt to maintain its traditional hegemony over the region. The result was a furnace roaring hotly enough to melt old empires and cultures and forge new ones.

By about 1700 BC, the ambitious people who would be known as Hittites had drifted out of the Eurasian hinterland and settled in Anatolia. There, over the course of the next three centuries, they gradually imposed their rule as a warrior elite over the inhabitants, who called their land Hatti, from which came the name Hittites. There as well, among the bleak, snow-clad mountains, they established their capital of Hattusa, a storm-swept citadel that stood on a plateau 3,000 feet above sea level.

The Hittites were a short, stocky people with hawklike noses, whose men, commonly bearded, wore earrings and frequently arranged their long hair in pigtails so thick that the purpose may have been to protect the neck in battle. Women and men alike dressed themselves in tunics, shoes with pointed, turned-up toes, and, when the weather demanded it, long robes made of wool.

Their culture was notable for its energy and adaptability. They shared many of their gods with other Indo-Europeans. And although the Hittites inscribed monuments with their own hieroglyphs, they enthusiastically adopted the cuneiform writing of the Babylonians, using it to record voluminous myths, hymns, royal edicts, and records of state. Yet the Hittites were also impressive innovators. Their art was highly imaginative. They promulgated a remarkably humane code of law, and they were pioneers in the craft of diplomacy, generally choosing to extend their domain through negotiations and treaties rather than by force of arms. Within the velvet glove, however, was a heavy fist, strengthened by fiercely valiant Hittite warriors and by a mechanical innovation: the Hittite battle chariot.

The typical battle chariot of the day was far different from the clumsy vehicle that had been employed by the Sumerians a millennium before. This new machine, developed by Indo-Europeans for steppe warfare and quickly adopted by Semitic armies, boasted slim, racy lines. In place of heavy, solid wooden wheels were spoked wheels, light but strong. With the axle positioned well to the rear, the chariot was highly maneuverable, capable of snapping around sharp turns without toppling over. Drawn by horses specially bred and schooled for combat instead of the scarcely tamed onagers used by the Sumerians, the new chariot could charge into battle at high speed.

But the Hittites had made some improvements of their own. Whereas most other battle chariots carried two warriors — a driver and an archer — the larger, heavier Hittite vehicle carried three: a driver, a spearman, and a shield bearer. What the Hittites lost in speed and maneuverability they more than gained in the shock value of massed chariot charges, particularly against enemy flanks. Moreover, because Hittite crews carried both offensive and defensive weapons, they were far better equipped for close-in fighting than the occupants of smaller, faster chariots, who usually showered the enemy with arrows from a prudent distance.

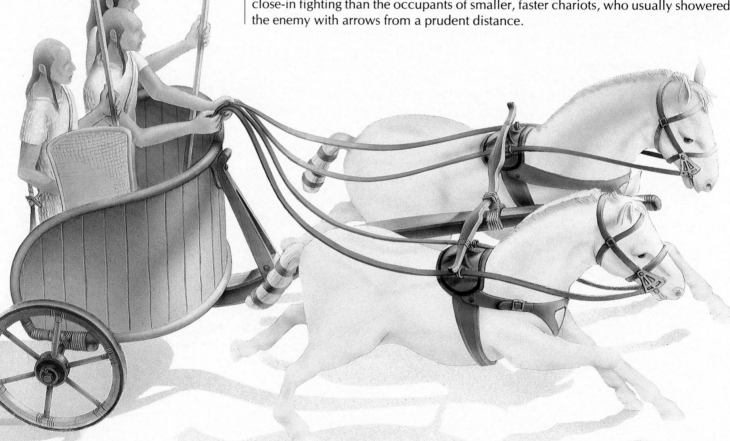

Despite such an advantage, the Hittite rise to imperial power was a twisting, erratic climb. An early king known as Mursili I marshaled a large army and marched it 500 miles down the Euphrates River, where he successfully stormed Babylon. But he immediately turned around and marched back to Hattusa, possibly because of reports from home of unrest within his own family — he was assassinated by a brother-in-law upon his return. His conquest of Babylon had little advantage for his own nation: It merely opened the way for a successful takeover there by other Indo-Europeans, Kassites who had migrated into Babylonia from the western plateau of Iran.

The Hittites, preoccupied with palace intrigues, royal murders, and usurpations, remained in the shadows of their mountain fastness for more than two centuries, until 1372 BC, when a sure-handed administrator, diplomat, and warrior named Suppiluliuma became king. Upon ascending the throne, Suppiluliuma found his land beleaguered by foes on all sides. Especially threatening was a warlike Indo-European tribe called the Mitanni, which ruled a powerful northern Mesopotamian state. Suppiluliuma was a patient man. Only after twelve years of strengthening his defenses and reorganizing his army did he turn his hostile attentions to the Mitanni.

Suppiluliuma's first expedition ended in failure, but in 1366 BC his Hittite army crossed the Euphrates and marched southward to attack the enemy from the rear. Surprised and cut off from his allies, the Mitanni king fled and was subsequently put to death by disgusted members of his own court. The Mitanni became Hittite vassals. The victorious Suppiluliuma then recrossed the Euphrates into Syria, where he conquered eight small kingdoms. Among them was the city-state of Kadesh, whose ruler was brave and foolish enough to challenge the Hittites in battle. He was easily vanquished.

By 1353 BC, the Hittite empire was rivaled in size and power only by Egypt — and in that year Suppiluliuma received an astonishing message from Egypt's young Queen Ankhesenamen, the widow of Tutankhamen, who had recently died at the age of eighteen. "My husband has died, and I have no sons," she wrote plaintively. "They say about you that you have many sons. If you would send me one of your sons, he could become my husband."

The Egyptian, who lacked political support within her own country, probably wanted the security that a Hittite prince's army would provide. Such a marriage might have altered the course of international politics in the region for decades to come. Suspecting trickery, Suppiluliuma cautiously dispatched an emissary "to find out," as his chronicles put it, "what truth there was in the matter with the woman." The emissary, apparently, was not tactful. The queen replied that she was "insulted" at having her motives questioned. Nevertheless, she renewed and even strengthened her offer: If Suppiluliuma would send her a son, then he would "be my husband and king in the country of Egypt." Still the Hittite monarch delayed, dragging out the negotiations for almost a year until, satisfied at last, he sent a son to accept the hand of the Egyptian queen. But it was too late. By then, an Egyptian courtier-priest named Ai had preempted Ankhesenamen's throne. Upon his arrival in the land of the Nile, the unfortunate Hittite prince was seized and put to death.

But the Hittite realm continued to prosper and expand until, by the time Suppiluliuma perished of a pestilence in 1334 BC, it encompassed 260,000 square miles, stretching from the Aegean Sea south to the mountains of Lebanon and east to the headwaters of the Euphrates. And Hittite political, religious, legal, and military institutions were firmly established in a manner that befitted one of the mightiest empires in the world.

A Hittite war chariot with its six-spoked wheels was light enough to be drawn swiftly by two horses. It was also stable enough that one of the warriors on board could use a bow or javelin while the vehicle was in motion; it was strong enough to stand the jolting of a cross-country attack. Widely copied by other Near Eastern empires, such chariots dominated warfare for several centuries. About 900 BC, they were superseded by cavalry and massed infantry.

Hittite power was of course founded on military prowess, which in turn was based on Hittite chariots. The chariots needed constant maintenance, and both the warriors who manned them and the horses that drew them required rigorous training. In fact, good war-horses were considered more valuable than men. The Hittites used a military manual that set forth in meticulous detail a schedule for equine care and training — when to wash a horse and when to rub it with oil, when to cover the animal with a blanket, how to prepare the horse's feed, and how to exercise the beast each day.

So much did Hittites rely on the chariot that the vehicle in a sense shaped their society. There evolved a powerful class of charioteers, whose aristocratic leaders, in order that they might devote full time to their belligerent calling, were awarded estates by the king. The result was a feudal system. At the pinnacle stood the monarch or "Great King." He was at once the head of state, the commander in chief of the army (which he was fully expected to lead into the field), the supreme judicial authority, and the master of his own household, right down to such details as the straining of the royal water. Palace discipline was rigorous. On one occasion, a servant named Zuliya was executed for permitting a hair to appear in the king's pitcher.

Taking precedence over all else were the ruler's obligations as high priest. Religious duties were so important that Hittite kings occasionally were compelled to suspend military operations in midcampaign so they could preside over religious observances at home. Whenever the Hittites suffered a reverse in war, it was taken as a sure sign that they had somehow displeased one or more of their diverse collection of gods. At such moments of crisis, the king would repair to the roof of his palace and enter into a prayerful discourse with the deities over two tables laden with sacrificial bread. "I have taken refuge with the storm god," the monarch would intone. "Save my life. Walk on my right hand. Team up with me as a bull to draw the wagon."

The storm god thus petitioned was Teshub, often depicted clutching a lightning bolt as he rushed about the mountaintops in a chariot drawn by two sacred bulls, Sheri and Hurri. He was chief of the Hittite pantheon, a rowdy, even earthy lot, endowed with all manner of human frailty. They feuded among themselves; they lied and cheated; they lusted and were consumed by jealousies.

Yet if their gods were exceedingly unruly, the Hittites themselves were of notably lawful mind. Although all legal authority stemmed from the king, judicial responsibility was delegated to local elders, along with provincial military commanders who, as the king's representatives, had strict orders to "do what is just."

Hittite law was remarkably free from the mutilative cruelties of the earlier Babylonian code or those of the later Assyrian empire. To be sure, defiance of the king's authority met with draconian punishment: The offenders' homes were "made into a heap of rubble," and the criminals themselves were stoned to death — along with all members of their families. Other than that, the death penalty was mandatory only for bestiality and for rape, where an odd distinction was made between seizing a married woman "in the mountains," which was a capital crime, and attacking her in her house. In the latter case, if the woman could not be heard crying out for help, she would be put to death — apparently on the theory that she had willingly committed adultery.

The basic principle of Hittite law was one of restitution instead of retribution. For example, arsonists were required to replace the property they had burned, and even murderers could go free after remunerating their victim's heirs, generally by payment of silver, slaves, land, or a house, along with burial costs. For the Hittites, the rule of law extended even into foreign relations, and their empire was in fact a web of states

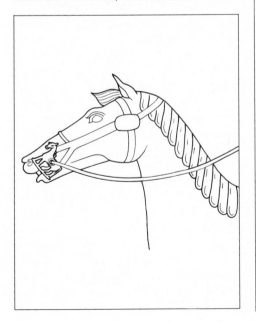

This decorative bit for a horse, with its horse-shaped bronze cheekpieces, was made about 900 BC by tribespeople living in a Zagros mountain region called Luristan, part of what later became Iran. Expert at raising horses and at casting bronze, the inhabitants of Luristan provided mounts for the Assyrians and others living in the Mesopotamian plain west of the Zagros; they also created some of the era's most imaginative equine hardware. The drawing below shows how the reins and other gear were attached to the bit's loops so that a rider or chariot driver could easily control the animal.

bound together by treaties, usually inscribed on tablets of gold, silver, or iron, whose legal force was strengthened by the religious beliefs of this intensely religious people. A treaty, for instance, typically called down an awful curse upon the signatory who failed to meet its provisions. One such agreement — with a neighboring king named Duppi-Teshub — said that if he did not live up to its terms, "may these divine oaths destroy Duppi-Teshub, his wife, his son, his grandson, his house, his city, his land, and everything that belongs to him." As witnesses, the names of no fewer than eighty gods and goddesses were inscribed.

The Hittite chariots were always ready to roll against states that declined to accede to the empire's diplomatic demands. The usual excuse for an attack was that a nation was harboring Hittite fugitives. In that vein, Mursili II wrote to the king of nearby Arzawa, in Anatolia: "My subjects who went over to you, when I demanded them back from you, you did not restore them to me and you called me a child and made light of me. Up then! Let us fight, and let the storm god, my lord, decide our case." Arzawa paid dearly for its recalcitrance. Its king was slain and, as Mursili II wrote, "The total of civilian captives that I, My Majesty, brought back to the royal palace was altogether 66,000." When Mursili II died in 1306 BC, he left to his son Muwatalli an empire strong at its core and buffered by vassal states whose rulers were obligated to answer a Hittite call to arms. Only one cloud loomed on the horizon: To the south, resurgent Egyptian forces were preparing to challenge Hittite control of Syria.

The Hittite frontier in Syria lay on the Orontes River at Kadesh, which Muwatalli's grandfather, Suppiluliuma, had seized almost as an afterthought to his campaign against the Mitanni. And it was toward Kadesh that Ramses II, Egypt's aggressive young pharaoh, marched the four divisions of his 20,000-man army in the spring of 1285 BC. But Muwatalli had warning and more than enough time to mobilize. An Egyptian chronicler of the engagement related that Muwatalli "gathered together all coun-

A huge winged bull with the head of an ornately bearded man guarded a gate of the great palace built about 710 BC by Assyria's King Sargon II. Almost thirteen feet tall and weighing close to sixteen tons, the stone figure revealed the skill of Assyrian sculptors — who gave it five legs so that it would appear balanced, whether viewed full face or in profile. Such mythical creatures, thought to give magical protection against evil spirits, stood at the main portals of all Assyrian palaces.

tries from the ends of the sea to the land of Hatti'' and started out with an army estimated at nearly 17,000 men — including no fewer than 2,500 chariots with their three-man crews.

A guileful commander, Muwatalli concealed his soldiers just beyond the city of Kadesh, then sent into the Egyptian camp two spies who, pretending to be deserters, told the pharaoh that the Hittite army was still lingering far to the north, in Aleppo. The spies must have been convincing, because Ramses accepted the tale. With most of his army strung far out behind him, he advanced on Kadesh at the head of a single division, and Muwatalli, who had wheeled his chariots to a position south of the city, forded the Orontes River and savagely attacked the Egyptian division, which broke and fled (pages 90-91). Ramses was rescued from defeat by the timely arrival of a regiment of allies, the Canaanites, who held the field until other divisions of the Egyptian army came up. The Hittites finally withdrew behind the fortifications of Kadesh. Although both sides later claimed victory, it was the Egyptians who shortly headed for home, leaving Muwatalli and his Hittites in possession of Kadesh — and Syria.

For about fifteen years, the Hittites and the Egyptians were content to glower at each other from within their respective imperial boundaries, the Hittites holding general hegemony over Syria while Egypt exercised power in Palestine. If anything, the Hittites were more disturbed by the rising power of the Assyrians, their troublesome neighbors in upper Mesopotamia, than by the Egyptians. At one point, Assyria's ruler had the temerity to write to a Hittite monarch named Hattusili, calling himself the Great King and addressing the Hittite as ''brother.'' Hattusili quickly put the upstart in his place. ''Were you and I perhaps born of the same mother?'' he haughtily replied. ''Do not write about brotherhood and Great Kingship to me.''

As it happened, Egypt was also fretful about Assyrian ambitions. And it was almost certainly in their mutual perception of the threat that the two old foes decided to put their differences aside. In the year 1269 BC, Ramses II and Hattusili concluded a treaty binding their two nations to refrain from warring against each other and to fight as allies should they be subjected to aggression by another people. Both powers would faithfully observe the agreement; two years after it was made, Ramses II took a Hittite princess as his bride.

Yet the era of the Hittites was waning. After Hattusili came a number of nondescript kings, and near the end of the thirteenth century BC monarchical authority was rapidly decaying. Observed a scribe of that period: ''His Majesty, my lord, found the inhabitants of Hatti to be in revolt.'' Thus weakened, the empire was helpless before the onslaught of a new wave of invaders, seafarers who appeared in the eastern Mediterranean in the late thirteenth century. Their origins are not certain; they would be known by the name the Egyptians gave them — the Sea Peoples. They apparently were an alliance of several groups,

possibly including Phrygians, Indo-Europeans from the west coast of the Black Sea who would occupy Anatolia after the Hittites disappeared.

Whoever they were and wherever they came from, the attackers obliterated the Hittite world, reducing Hattusa to ashes, smashing stone sculptures, slaughtering much of the population, and driving the rest into exile. And so, in 1200 BC, the Hittite empire vanished, creating a power vacuum in the Middle East that was destined to be filled by the Hittites' rivals and neighbors, the Assyrians.

At the time of the Hittite downfall, Assyria was already an old, scarred wolf that had known fat times and lean. Its people were the descendants of Semites who had settled along the middle Tigris and had eventually looked for political leadership to Assur, a city so called for the god Ashur, who became the national deity and also gave his name to the Assyrians. The fertile soil of the Assyrian plains produced fine crops of barley and sesame and good pasturage for cattle and horses. And much of the country was blessed by rainfall sufficient to render irrigation unnecessary in normal times.

Assyria was therefore an object of envy to the predatory peoples of the grim mountains and the barren steppes to the north and east. Moreover, it was only natural that the established powers of the Middle East should seek to control a territory that, by accident of geography, lay athwart the major trade routes between Babylonia and Anatolia and from the Mediterranean east to beyond the Zagros mountains.

For survival's sake, Assyria's sturdy farmers became fierce warriors who fought at first in defense of their homeland, then to maintain their security by establishing around them a ring of buffer states, and finally, in a progression that was perhaps inevitable, to expand into an empire that in military might would stand second to none. In so doing, they wrote a bloody chapter in the story of humankind — one that was all the uglier because it featured deliberate terror and atrocity as instruments of foreign policy. In an early example of the frightfulness that would later become an Assyrian hallmark, a king named Shalmaneser I, who reigned from 1274 to 1245 BC, carried 14,000 defeated enemy soldiers off to Assyria as slaves — after securing their docility by blinding them.

By then the Assyrians had sloughed off their onetime overlords, the Mitanni, and had secured a realm of some 12,000 square miles that stretched from the foothills of the Zagros west to the Euphrates. Shalmaneser's son, Tukulti-Ninurta I, whose reign began in 1244 BC, significantly expanded that territory. For many years, the northeastern Assyrian frontier had been raided by Hurrian tribes who dwelled in the Zagros, a region known to the Assyrians as the Nairi lands. Determined to stop the incursions and to acquire for himself the metals, cattle, and horses with which the northern clans were amply endowed, Tukulti-Ninurta marched into the mountains and defeated, by his count, no fewer than forty kings from Nairi, whom he enslaved and transported to Assur with heavy copper chains around their bowed necks. (In time, they were allowed to return home as vassals.)

While Tukulti-Ninurta was busy with the Nairi lands, trouble arose on a more important front. For longer than a century, Babylonia and Assyria had been at odds over claims to the territory that lay between them. Now Babylonia's King Kashtiliash saw what he thought was an opportunity to settle matters by attacking his preoccupied neighbor. It was a monumental mistake. Tukulti-Ninurta rushed back with his warriors from the north,

Small, delicate ivory carvings from Assyria portray tribute bearers bringing live animals as offerings to a religious ceremony. The animals include *(from top)* a lion and an ibex; a gazelle and an ostrich; and a monkey and an oryx. The ivories, which date from about 700 BC, may have come from Egypt or Phoenicia, or they may have been carved by Assyrian artisans who had learned the craft from the Phoenicians, specialists in such work.

overwhelmed the Babylonian armies, captured the brash Kashtiliash, and in the Assyrian's own words, "trod with my feet upon his royal neck as though it were a footstool." Babylon was looted, and Tukulti-Ninurta declared himself king of Babylonia. The huge statue of Marduk, Babylon's greatest deity, was hauled away to Assur.

The results of victory over Babylonia were not all beneficial. A nation of rude peasants and warriors, Assyria was now exposed to Babylonia's strong, sophisticated, and pervasive culture. Factions sympathetic to Babylon found firm foothold in the Assyrian homeland. The stolen Marduk rose to prominence among Assyrian deities, and some Assyrians came to believe that the looting of his shrine had been a sacrilege. Accordingly, when Babylonia later rose in successful revolt, it was taken in high Assyrian circles that the plundered gods were demonstrating their anger over Tukulti-Ninurta's misdeeds. And so, according to a chronicle, it happened that Tukulti-Ninurta, who "had brought his hand for evil upon Babylon," came to a sorry end: "His son, and the nobles of Assyria, rebelled against him and tore him from his throne. They shut him up and slew him with the sword."

After Tukulti-Ninurta's death in 1208, less than a decade before the Hittite empire was crushed by the rampaging Sea Peoples, Assyria suffered an extended period of internal confusion and economic disarray. During this time, too, the fires of conflict heating the ever-turbulent crucible of the Middle East burned particularly hot as aggressive peoples such as the Philistines, the Aramaeans, the Hebrews, and the Canaanites pushed and shoved one another for position. In these wildly unsettled conditions, almost a century would pass before the Assyrians were prepared to step into the void that the Hittites had left in the Middle Eastern power structure.

At last, under Tiglath-Pileser I, who assumed the throne in 1115 BC, the country's agricultural economy was made to flourish. With prosperity came political stability, and the king could concentrate on the military matters so important to Assyrian rulers. Changes were being made in the Assyrian army. Although charioteers remained the elite, a new form of warfare was evolving: crushing attacks by a massed weight of infantry drawn from the peasantry, wielding bronze weapons, and protected by bronze helmets, corselets, and shields. Tiglath-Pileser soon put the new tactics to a test.

The same year in which Tiglath-Pileser became king, Assyria was threatened by tribespeople known as the Mushki, who had crossed the Taurus Mountains in Anatolia and were moving down the Tigris toward Nineveh. Tiglath-Pileser eagerly advanced to meet them, and before long the severed heads of the Mushki chieftains were decorating Nineveh's gates. Next, he launched an attack on the hillfolk of the Nairi lands, who had risen up against their Assyrian masters. Traversing sixteen mountains, he triumphed over an alliance of twenty-three Nairi chiefs while driving sixty others and their people northward. From the tribes they had subjugated, the victorious Assyrians exacted an enormous annual tribute consisting of 12,000 horses and 2,000 cattle.

Armored in a long jacket of iron mail and carrying a spear and a colorfully painted shield, an infantryman of the Assyrian army strides behind the wheel of a chariot. This fresco was painted for the eighth-century monarch Tiglath-Pileser II; similar works adorned the walls of Assyria's royal palaces, along with superb stone bas-reliefs such as the one shown opposite.

Assyrian archers put a contingent of camel-riding Arabs to flight in a stone panel that decorated the ornate palace of King Ashurbanipal in Nineveh. Bands of Arabs, eager for booty, nipped at the southern flanks of the Assyrian empire during the seventh century BC, forcing Ashurbanipal to mount several punitive expeditions.

More menacing than either the Mushki or the Nairi were the Aramaeans. These Semitic people had moved east from the Syrian desert and had settled along the entire length of the Euphrates, from the Babylonian border northward. Standing as a barrier to trade between Assyria and the Syrian coast, they constantly raided Assyrian territory. To remedy that situation, Tiglath-Pileser took his army across the Euphrates on rafts of inflated goatskin, scattered the Aramaeans, and penetrated to the shores of the Mediterranean, where he won trade agreements from the Phoenician city-states and, in recognition of his imperial status, was honored by the gift of a crocodile from none other than the Egyptian pharaoh himself. While visiting Egypt, Tiglath-Pileser also disported himself on a boat ride by using a harpoon to slay, as he recounted, ''a *nahiru*, which they call a 'sea horse' '' — probably a dolphin or some species of whale.

During his long reign, Tiglath-Pileser launched twenty-seven more campaigns against the vexatious Aramaeans, yet never completely subdued them. After his death in 1077 BC, the routes to the Mediterranean were severed, and Assyrian expansion was checked by steady pressure from the Aramaean tribes. Nearly another century and a half passed before Assyria resumed the march to empire that would win supremacy over the Middle East. By then, the pattern of Assyrian life was fully formed.

Assyria was mainly a nation of serfs who were attached to the land that they farmed; they could be sold along with the real estate. They owed allegiance to the local village. The village, in turn, was tied to a city by the obligation to pay taxes, participate in religious festivals, and obey administrative mandates. The cities — chief among them Assur, Nineveh, Erbil, and Nimrud — were under the authority of the king.

In theory, the Assyrian king possessed absolute power in all aspects of government — economic, diplomatic, political, military, and religious. Although acknowledged as human, he was thought to be the earthly delegate of the gods, especially of Ashur, the principal deity, who was represented by a winged disk. Because of that status, the monarch was aloof from other mortals: Only the superintendent of the palace had regular access to his presence; even the crown prince was allowed an audience only when omens were deemed auspicious, and outsiders were blindfolded when they appeared in court before their ruler. For the king, satisfying the gods was no easy task. He was constantly subjected to such arduous rituals as fasting or retreating for a week at a time in a crude reed hut. Sometimes, the omens indicated that the gods were direly displeased. The most evil sign was an eclipse, lunar or solar, which was taken to portend the death of the monarch. In such cases, the king abdicated his throne temporarily in favor of a surrogate who assumed responsibility for whatever had angered the gods. At the end of 100 days the real king returned, and both the substitute and the substitute's wife were executed, presumably to give the gods the death of the king that had been foretold.

The Assyrian kings and their subjects believed that they were surrounded by hordes of demons as well as by gods. Among the most odious and fearsome was the fever demon Lamashtu, a female spirit who specialized in killing infants and women in childbirth. She was seen as a fiend with a lion's head, the teeth of a dog, and the legs of a panther bearing eagle claws. She was believed to roar like a leopard while clutching writhing snakes and suckling a pig and a black dog at her pendulous breasts. Such monsters were able to penetrate the bodies of both virtuous and wicked humans, thereby causing all the woes with which people were afflicted. Fortunately, Assyrian demons were considered on the whole a doltish lot, and with the help of a priestly exorcist known as an *ashipu,* they could frequently be duped into turning their malevolent attentions to a sacrificial animal. A chronicler related how, with an ashipu presiding, a sick man would share his bed with a goat kid overnight. At dawn the demon who had caused the man's illness, mistaking the goat for a human, would leave the man and enter the kid. At that point the kid's throat would be slit, and the man would be cured.

The demands of the gods and the onslaughts of demons put restrictions on royal authority. No Assyrian king would consider making a major decision without consulting a host of priests, oracles, exorcists, diviners, astrologers, and soothsayers who, in effect, became powers behind the throne. These religious functionaries were enthralled by the culture that Babylonia had inherited from ancient Sumer. The Assyrians, whose own heritage was primitive, fervently believed that what was old was good and must be preserved; innovation was dangerous and should be avoided.

A current swirls around dead and dying Elamite soldiers who have been driven into a river by fierce Assyrian charioteers and other troops *(below),* **in a bas-relief carved to celebrate King Ashurbanipal's victory in the crucial Battle of Til-Tuba. The king attacked the Elamites, whose kingdom lay in what came to be southern Iran, because they had been inciting the people of Babylonia to revolt against Assyrian rule. Such carvings contain minute detail. Here the Elamites are shown wearing knotted headbands — which they did.**

Assyrian thought, religious and otherwise, was permeated by that aversion. Of the hundreds of Assyrian gods, most were of Sumerian origin: Ashur, the chief native deity, took on attributes of Sumer's principal god, Enlil, and Babylonia's Marduk, even while those two divinities were revered in their own right. Assyrian law was based largely on the code promulgated in the eighteenth century BC by Babylonia's King Hammurabi. Assyrian astronomy, along with the mathematics required to support it, reflected the Babylonian interest in the heavens. Many Assyrian scribes were trained in Babylonia and remained faithful to the Babylonian model in their literature. Like the Babylonians, Assyrian artists tirelessly depicted the military exploits of their kings, although Assyrian sculptors also developed an original talent for rendering scenes of the hunt — the favorite sport of Assyrian monarchs. (During a single expedition, Tiglath-Pileser I slew four bull elephants, four wild oxen, and an astounding total of 920 lions, or so Assyrian scribes relate.)

The Assyrians' main intellectual pursuit was collating the knowledge already accumulated by the Babylonians and their Sumerian predecessors. A great library the Assyrians built at Nineveh was filled with cuneiform tablets containing compilations of Mesopotamian religious rituals, prayers, omens, incantations, and curses, along with exhaustive lists of gods, heavenly bodies, minerals, trees, foods, household furnishings, and virtually every other subject to which the ancient Mesopotamians had turned their attentions.

Only in the art and science of warfare did the Assyrians display any great interest in new techniques. Their immense armies, sometimes numbering as many as 200,000 troops, eventually were divided into four branches. The light infantry was largely manned by archers with powerful composite bows constructed of glued-together wood, bone, and other materials. Heavy infantry, the shock troops, wielded bronze spears and swords. The chariotry was gradually giving way to the cavalry. As the newest branch, the cavalry underwent several experimental stages. At first, cavalrymen were little more than highly mobile archers, each accompanied by a mounted attendant who held the reins of his master's horse while the archer dismounted to unleash his arrows. Later, the shield-bearing attendant rode alongside and grasped the reins of both horses while the archer fired at a gallop. Finally, as their skills matured, the archers rode and fought alone as true cavalrymen.

An Assyrian army could march thirty miles a day along roads, some of them paved with stone, that had been constructed throughout the empire by military engineers. The roads also provided an invaluable communications network: Couriers on relays of horses could carry messages to any part of the empire and bring back answers within a

SARGON'S MAGNIFICENT FOLLY

Designed to impress the world with its size and splendor, the fortress-city built by Assyria's King Sargon II at Khorsabad covered an entire square mile with palaces, temples, armories, and dwellings for the nobles and civil servants who helped the monarch rule his empire.

The huge main palace *(top center)*, erected on an elevated platform of sun-dried brick, covered twenty-five acres and contained more than 200 rooms. Just west of it was a religious complex with three temples and a painted ziggurat. The principal buildings were faced with stone that had been incised with larger-than-life-size figures; each gateway was guarded by large stone statues and decorated with multicolored glazed bricks laid in intricate designs. The walls were twenty feet thick, strengthened by scores of defensive towers and punctuated by seven monumental gateways.

For all its strength and grandeur, the great city proved a waste of the immense resources — material and human — that went into its construction. Begun in 717 BC, it was hardly completed before Sargon was killed in 705. Never used, the city was soon abandoned and fell into ruins.

week. Even where there were no roads, the tough Assyrian soldiers advanced relentlessly. One prideful monarch said of his pursuit of an enemy through the mountains: "I led the way like a fierce wild bull with my picked bodyguards and merciless battle troops. I traversed wadis, torrents, ravines, and dangerous slopes in my sedan chair. Where it was too hard going for my sedan chair, I took to my feet and went on in pursuit to the high peaks, like a gazelle." Once in battle, the Assyrians asked for and gave no quarter, and they rejoiced in the butchery. "I cut their throats like sheep," recorded a king. "My prancing steeds plunged into their welling blood as into a river; the wheels of my battle chariot were bespattered with blood and filth."

Military aggression was confirmed by the Assyrian religion: Conquest was the divine mission of kings. Claimed one monarch: "Ashur, father of the gods, empowered me to make broad the boundary of the land of Assyria." All the kings harked to the militant mandate. By the start of the ninth century BC and the reign of Ashurnasirpal II, the Assyrians were again marching to the west. While carrying Assyrian arms to the Mediterranean for the first time in 200 years, Ashurnasirpal waged a campaign that would eclipse the dread deeds of his forebears.

"I caused great slaughter," he boasted. "I destroyed, I demolished, I burned. I took their warriors prisoner and impaled them on stakes before their cities." After sacking one city, Ashurnasirpal stacked the corpses of the dead like firewood outside the gate, then "flayed the nobles, as many as had rebelled, and spread their skins out on the piles." After another battle in which he killed 3,000 soldiers and took many prisoners, he reported: "Many of the captives I burned in a fire. Many I took alive; from some I cut off their hands to the wrist, from others I cut off their noses, ears and fingers; I put out the eyes of many of the soldiers. I burnt their young men and women to death."

This was something new. To be sure, the Middle East was inured to horror, and the Assyrians had indulged in atrocity before. Now and henceforth, however, the region was confronted by a succession of Assyrian kings who, by deliberate design, practiced and proclaimed mutilations, flayings, impalements, and other atrocities for the purpose of spreading terror and thereby encouraging submission. By savage irony, that policy was from first to last a dismal failure. Time after time, hardly had the main Assyrian army withdrawn from a vanquished nation, leaving behind a mangled citizenry, than revolt flared.

To dilute and disperse the potentially rebellious populations, the Assyrians hit upon a debilitating expedient: They shuffled conquered peoples around the Assyrian empire on a massive scale both to obtain forced labor and security. Some civilians were taken to the Assyrian homeland, where they were put to work as artisans or as laborers on farms and public projects; others were transported to lands that, like their own, had been depopulated by Assyrian deportations. In a renowned instance of the relocation policy at work, the Bible laments that after the Assyrians conquered Samaria, a province of Israel, they "carried the Israelites to Assyria and the king of Assyria brought people from Babylon, Cutha, Avva, Hameth and Sepherva'im, and placed them in Samaria instead of the people of Israel."

In time, the Assyrians came to depend on the conquered populations. To support their military ventures, they dragooned entire enemy units into their armies. After King Sargon II built a new capital, Khorsabad, in 713 BC, he wrote that he settled it with "peoples of the four quarters, of strange tongues and different speech, dwelling in mountains and plains." As many as four million people may thus have been

TREK TO A PROMISED LAND

The probable route taken by the Semitic people called the Israelites when they made their exodus from Egypt about 1230 BC is shown by the line on this map. Escaping servile labor in the Nile Delta, they crossed an area of shallow lakes where the Suez Canal was later built. Then, leaving the coastal route, which was dotted with Egyptian outposts, they struck off down the shore of the Gulf of Suez. Finally they marched into the barren, rock-strewn Sinai peninsula, the biblical Wilderness.

In that desert, according to the Bible, they came upon a prominence they called Mount Sinai; there God gave their leader, Moses, the Ten Commandments. In any case, the Israelites' long stay in the Wilderness, probably at the oasis of Kadesh-barnea, together with their law code fused them into a distinct, homogeneous people.

About 1200 BC, the Israelites crossed the Jordan River into Canaan, the Promised Land. Within 200 years they made the region theirs, subduing the Canaanites and other local peoples, and defeating the Philistines. This realm, extending almost 200 miles along the Mediterranean, later was split into the northern kingdom of Israel, with Samaria as its capital, and the southern kingdom of Judah, centered on Jerusalem.

The Royal Sportsmen

Nothing stirred the sporting blood of an Assyrian monarch so much as combat with a lion. The hunting scenes carved into the walls of Assyrian palaces were so prevalent that they vied in importance with reliefs celebrating victories in war. In the dramatic bas-relief at right, one of a series sculpted for King Ashurbanipal's palace at Nineveh about 640 BC, the king dispatches a lion with a well-aimed spear thrust while another beast — wounded but still ferocious — attacks his spare mount. Assyrian rulers not only enjoyed the hunt; they also considered it a royal responsibility. Just as it was a king's sacred duty, imposed by the great god Ashur, to defeat Assyria's enemies in battle, so it was his duty to protect his people from the ravages of wild animals. Lions roamed the Middle East as late as Ashurbanipal's reign and, although of a subspecies smaller than the lions of Africa, they posed a very real danger to farmers and travelers. Large herds of other animals such as wild asses and gazelles also roamed the land, devouring crops. The huge slaughters of which the Assyrian kings boasted were viewed by the royal establishment and the people as both important rituals and civic improvements. Moreover, they proved that the monarch was properly caring for his subjects.

shifted about the Assyrian empire during the last three centuries of its existence. And so with coiffured beards and bloodied hands, Assyrian kings marched in grisly procession across the Middle Eastern stage. In 745 BC, a king named Tiglath-Pileser III captured Aramaean Damascus after a brutal campaign. That ended the military threat of the Aramaeans, who thereafter, to the benefit of themselves, the Assyrians, and the Middle East as a whole, turned their energies almost exclusively to trade. So ubiquitous were their traveling traders that Aramaean became a kind of lingua franca of the ancient Near East, understood and spoken by people throughout the region. A few years later, in 721, the Assyrian king Sargon II put an end to a major annoyance from the bothersome kingdom of Urartu, which had been formed by consolidation of the old Nairi tribes and for nearly a century had been pressing in on Assyria from the north.

Assyrian morale suffered severely during the hard campaign into Urartu's mountains. Wrote Sargon: "The harassed army of Ashur, who had come a long way, very weary and slow to respond, who had crossed and recrossed sheer mountains innumerable, of great trouble for ascent and descent, their morale turned mutinous. I could give no ease for their weariness." Unable to rely on his main body of troops, he met the Urartians in a narrow defile with only his personal household cavalry. Standing in his

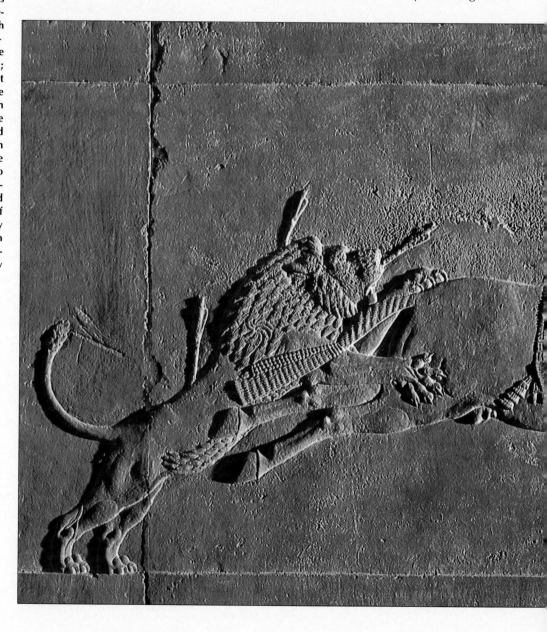

battle chariot, he led a headlong charge. The stunned Urartians retreated, at which the main Assyrian army took heart and fell furiously on the enemy, forcing them into a rout in which great numbers died of exposure in the mountain cold.

Sargon II's successor, Sennacherib, lavished loving attentions on the city of Nineveh, which he took as his capital and beautified with a splendid park. He described it as being "like Mount Amanus, wherein were set all kinds of plants and fruit trees such as grown in the mountains and in Chaldea." Yet for all his esthetic sensitivities, Sennacherib was a true Assyrian ruler, achieving a remarkable reputation for cruelty that contributed to his downfall. He sacked a resurgent Babylon in such utterly ruthless fashion that he incurred the bitter enmity of the durable pro-Babylonian faction within his own country, which had him assassinated by two of his own sons. Another son, Esarhaddon, then avenged his father by shattering the regicides' army and seizing the throne for himself. "I am Esarhaddon," he proclaimed, "king of the world." But he was careful to atone for the sacrilege of his father: He rebuilt Babylon, symbolically molding a brick with his own royal hands.

In the west, where Egypt and the Assyrian empire were separated only by the Sinai desert, the rulers of the Nile had long incited revolt among Assyria's Palestinian and

Syrian dependencies. Determined to put an end to such provocations, Esarhaddon in the year 671 marched fifteen days across the Sinai — which was, he said, infested by two-headed snakes — and captured the Egyptian capital of Memphis. No sooner had he withdrawn, however, than the Egyptians rebelled. He set out to recapture Memphis in 669 but died on the way.

The empire was divided between two sons: Shamash-shumi-ukin, who reigned over Babylonia, and Ashurbanipal, who ruled all the rest. For a time the arrangement worked. Ashurbanipal reconquered Memphis and extended Assyria's Egyptian domain as far south as Thebes. But jealousy festered within Shamash-shumi-ukin, and in 652, his troops attacked a garrison near Babylon under the command of Ashurbanipal. Soon civil war raged across the land. It ended only after a three-year siege of Babylon. In the final days, the dead were piled high in the city's streets, and chroniclers recounted that survivors "ate the flesh of their sons and daughters for their starvation." At the last, Shamash-shumi-ukin flung himself into the flames of his blazing palace. After giving his brother a burial that befitted his royal blood, Ashurbanipal exacted an appalling revenge against the other rebels. "I fed their corpses, cut into small pieces, to the dogs, pigs, vultures, eagles, the birds of the sky, and to the fish of the ocean," he boasted. Curiously, Ashurbanipal would be remembered not as the brute of Babylon but as a scholarly ruler who boasted of his own literacy, who created the great library at Nineveh and, by bringing calm to the Middle East, earned a contemporary paean: *Throughout all lands a peace prevailed, / Like finest oil were the world's four quarters.*

When the studious old warrior's fifty-four-year reign ended with his death in 626 BC, the Assyrian empire seemed at the summit of its power and prestige. In fact, it was on the brink of extinction. The end came so swiftly and was so complete that few details are known. Clearly, Assyria had spread itself thin by its maintenance of a vast empire. Just as clearly, its longtime policies had at last brought their calamitous re-

A shaggy-maned male lion lies dead, pierced by three arrows, in another of the bas-reliefs commemorating King Ashurbanipal's skill and bravery in the hunt. Lion hunting was so symbolic to the Assyrians of their monarch's power and god-given authority that only kings were ever shown actually killing the beasts.

ward: Assyria's atrocious behavior had made it the object of seething hatreds. Its huge army was shot through and through with discontented units incorporated from defeated foes. And thanks to its infamous deportation programs, its great cities may well have housed more inhabitants of foreign extraction than native Assyrians.

Scarcely had Ashurbanipal been placed in his tomb than the Babylonian throne was seized by Nabopolassar. He was a sheikh of the Chaldean tribes, Semitic people who had settled in the swamps and marshland of southern Mesopotamia. Within a few years, the Chaldeans formed an aggressive alliance with the Indo-European Medes, who had migrated to western Iran, and with fierce Scythians, who had swept southward from their homeland in central Asia.

In 612 BC, the allies marched against Assyria, whose King Sinsharishkun, embroiled in factional fighting at home, unsuccessfully battled them at Kablini and Arrapha, then took refuge behind the walls of Nineveh. The heavily fortified Assyrian capital fell within three months. And although the tattered remnants of the Assyrian army fought a running battle for another few years, they were finally eradicated in an engagement at Carchemish. The Assyrian empire was no more, and the rest of the Middle East celebrated its downfall. Declared the biblical prophet Nahum: "All who hear the news of you clap their hands over you. For upon whom has not come your unceasing evil?"

The victors of Carchemish had surprisingly little dispute about dividing the spoils. The Medes assumed power in eastern Assyria and in the former Assyrian provinces north and east of the Tigris. Almost unnoticed — but soon to be of momentous consequence — was the relegation of the Persians, a group of Indo-European tribes who had settled in ancient Elam, to vassalage under the Medes. As for the Babylonians, Nabopolassar died within a year of his triumph and was succeeded by his son Nebuchadnezzar II, an experienced soldier who swiftly moved to take over the western reaches of the Assyrian empire. He subdued Syria and extended his realm to the border of Egypt, which had by then regained its independence.

The little kingdom of Judah remained a trouble spot. There, despite calamitous warnings from the prophet Jeremiah, a King Jehoiakim ignored his promise to pay tribute to Babylonia. No man to trifle with, Nebuchadnezzar laid successful siege to Jerusalem and, although sparing the city, took more than 10,000 leading Jewish citizens back to Babylon as hostages for future good behavior. Yet only a decade later Judah's King Zedekiah, who had been installed as a Babylonian vassal, conspired with Egypt and Phoenicia to oust the Chaldean overlord. Nebuchadnezzar marched again, and this time he meant to obliterate the annoyance. Jerusalem was utterly destroyed, and its remaining inhabitants, except for the very poorest, were taken to Babylon.

At home, Nebuchadnezzar was an enlightened monarch who dedicated himself to restoring Babylon to its ancient grandeur. Among many other projects, he erected a magnificent temple for Marduk and, because his Medean wife still yearned for her native mountains, built a new palace high on a hill that was terraced and profusely planted — the Hanging Gardens of Babylon, which would come to be counted as one of the Seven Wonders of the Ancient World.

But in the Middle East all empires were temporal, and so it was with Chaldean Babylonia. The empire would not long survive Nebuchadnezzar, who died in 562 BC. In Persia, a young prince had cast off the yoke of the Medes and would soon embark on a military campaign that would overwhelm Babylonia. He would become known as Cyrus the Great and would create an empire surpassing any the world had ever seen.

EGYPT'S GOLDEN AGE

In the year 1573 BC, Kamose, a young prince of Thebes, set his sights on revenge and glory in the cause of freedom for his Egypt, a land that had been held in thrall for about 100 years. Assembling around him the noblemen of southern Egypt, he told them of his plans for dealing with the Hyksos, the Asian oppressors who occupied the Nile Delta to the north: "I intend to fall upon him and slit his belly. It is my desire to save Egypt and to smite the Asiatic."

The nobles murmured protests. They were enjoying abundant crops and robust prosperity. The Hyksos even allowed them to graze their cattle around the papyrus marshes of the Delta region. But the Theban prince was resolute. "I am determined to battle the Asiatics," he said, "and the entire land will speak of me in Thebes as 'Kamose, the Protector of Egypt.' " Kamose prevailed, and the armed forces of Upper Egypt sailed down the Nile against the enemy.

The Hyksos were a motley collection of Semitic tribes that had emerged out of the desert around 1700 BC and, in the words of a later Egyptian priest, had "savagely burned the cities, razed the temples of the gods to the ground, and treated the whole native population with the utmost cruelty."

Perhaps the Hyksos had indeed dealt savagely with the Egyptians. Yet these barbarians were also beguiled by the civilization they had conquered. After overrunning Memphis, the Egyptian capital near the head of the Delta, the Hyksos established their own center of power at Avaris on the Delta's eastern frontier. From there, they exercised direct rule over the northern part of Egypt while exacting tribute from the outlying rulers, including the restless princes of Thebes in their sunbathed city some 600 miles south of the Nile's mouth. At the same time, the Hyksos took on Egyptian ways: They employed Egyptian administrators and tax collectors, they wrote in hieroglyphs, they worshiped Egyptian gods along with their own, and their rulers called themselves pharaohs. And the conquerors even contributed to the proud culture that had existed for millennia along the banks of the Nile. They introduced an upright loom that improved Egyptian weaving techniques, and they bequeathed to Egypt such musical instruments as the long-necked lute, the lyre, the oboe, and the tambourine.

Of far more interest to the Theban princes, however, were the weapons and other accouterments of war that the Hyksos had wielded in their conquest — chain armor; battle axes; long-range and high-velocity composite bows made of wood, animal tendons, and horn; and above all the light, horse-drawn chariots that were the scourge of the era's battlefields. By the time that Kamose of Thebes moved against the Hyksos and their king, Apophis of Avaris, the Egyptians themselves had copied the deadly armory that had once wrought their downfall.

"I sailed downstream in might to repel the Asiatics," Kamose later exulted, "my valiant army before me like a fiery flame." A Hyksos vassal commanding a force confronted the prince at the town of Nefrusi, 160 miles north of Thebes. "At break of day," Kamose continued, "I was upon him like a hawk. By breakfast time I had driven him back, destroyed them all, and slain his people. My soldiers were like lions at their prey, carrying off their slaves, cattle, oils, and honey, and partitioning their property with joyful hearts." On that triumphant note, Kamose's account of the campaign ended: He died, perhaps in battle, sometime before the fall of the heavily fortified Hyksos capital at Avaris. His young successor, Ahmose, concluded the long siege and eventually sent the Hyksos scurrying back into Palestine and Syria, their reign in Egypt over. Ahmose pursued, and the progress of his army as it plodded across the burning sands of the Sinai constituted for Egypt the dawn of a new and magnificent age.

Bursting out of the geographic cocoon that had always confined it, Egypt in little more than a century would build an empire that stretched some 2,000 miles in length. Through their control of crucial trade routes, and from the tribute exacted of the lands they had conquered, the Egyptians would achieve an opulence previously unknown to human civilization. Egypt would prosper under a woman who usurped the pharaonic crown and would survive the ruinous effects of a religious and cultural upheaval led by a strange, seemingly misshapen ruler. Under a succession of soldier-kings who resurrected its imperial glory, Egypt would stand resplendent upon a summit of wealth and power — until at last decay set in, and a long, slow decline began.

Ahmose's incursion was but a first, tentative step along the road to empire. For three years the Egyptian king laid siege to Sharuhen, a town in southern Palestine where the Hyksos leaders had taken refuge, and when it finally fell he withdrew from Asia. Ahmose died in 1546 BC and was succeeded by Amenhotep I and then by Tuthmosis I. Although each in his turn renewed the campaigns in Asia, their expeditions were hesitant at best: The two successors were content to wrest whatever tribute they could from the small city-states along the route of march, and to hold at bay the rising pretensions of the Mitanni, who had installed themselves in the watershed of the Euphrates River.

After taking his place on the throne, Tuthmosis I proceeded to march through Syria to the upper Euphrates, where the Egyptians marveled at the peculiar behavior of a river that, unlike their own Nile, flowed from north to south instead of from south to north. To Tuthmosis and his army, this phenomenon was "inverted water which flows downstream when really flowing upstream." When confronted by forces leagued with the Mitanni, Tuthmosis defeated them soundly, and "countless were the captives whom the king carried off in his victory." Yet despite the pharaoh's scribes proclaiming that "the whole earth is under his two feet," the foray was, in truth, little more than a hit-and-run raid. Tuthmosis made no attempt to establish a permanent military or colonial presence in Asia, and hardly had his soldiers left the region than the Syrian princes stopped paying the tribute they had pledged.

Under the warlike pharaoh Tuthmosis III the Egyptian empire reached its greatest extent about 1450 BC, stretching from the Nubian Desert in the south to the middle Euphrates in the north — a distance of more than 1,000 miles. Only the Nile Valley was under the direct rule of Egypt's monarchs; elsewhere they governed through alliances with friendly local princes whose authority was buttressed by Egyptian military outposts.

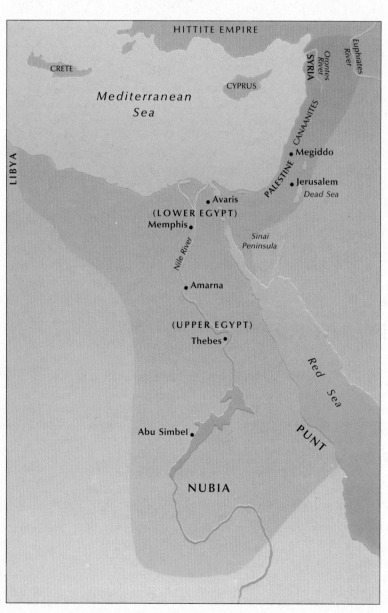

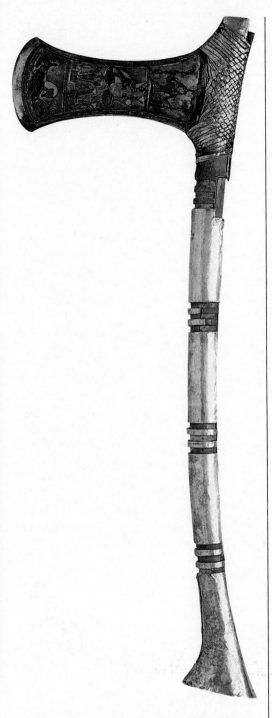

An inscription on this wood, copper, and gold ax indicates that it probably commemorated the pharaoh Ahmose's victory over the Hyksos; his triumph launched Egypt into the prosperous New Kingdom period, during which Tuthmosis III and other pharaohs built Egypt's empire. A god, flowers, and a griffin adorn the blade — which never drew blood. Egyptian soldiers used swords and daggers in battle; axes were ceremonial weapons.

Nubia, to Egypt's south, was a more pressing matter. Known to the Egyptians as the land of Kush, it yielded enormous amounts of gold from its mines. Moreover, Nubia linked Egypt with the Sudanese regions that were the source of treasured African exotics such as ivory, ebony, leopard skins, ostrich eggs and plumes, along with more practical commodities, including cattle and slaves.

The pharaohs had controlled Nubia until the Hyksos invaded Egypt. The Nubians had then seized the opportunity to break away from Egyptian domination. Under Tuthmosis I, Egypt managed to subdue all Nubian resistance and regain hegemony, making Nubia its southernmost province. The land was placed in the charge of a viceroy embellished with the title of "Prince of Kush and Overseer of the Southern Lands." Answerable only to the pharaoh, this governor was responsible for ensuring that Thebes received a steady traffic of "the ships laden with ivory, ebony, and every other beautiful product of the land in addition to the yield of the harvest." Within his own realm, the viceroy commanded the armed forces, administered justice, and built temples, fortifications, and canals. In addition, he indoctrinated the tribespeople so thoroughly with Egyptian ideas and institutions that, in the distant future, Nubia would remain faithful to the Egyptian model long after Egypt itself had fallen to foreigners.

At home, Amenhotep I sought a return to the traditions that had prevailed before the takeover by the Hyksos — particularly pyramid building to house the royal remains. His successor, Tuthmosis I, however, started a new tradition. Instead of constructing a pyramid as his final resting place, he decreed that his mummified remains should be hidden in a tomb hewn out of the limestone cliffs of an isolated valley that lay beyond the mountains of western Thebes. Clearly undertaken to thwart the thieves who were already pillaging the graves of the wealthy, the tomb-building project was, according to a nobleman who supervised the excavation work, carried out in great secrecy with "no one seeing and no one hearing."

Subsequent pharaohs followed the precedent set by Tuthmosis I until the brooding, 1,000-foot-high cliffs of the so-called Valley of the Kings were honeycombed by passageways leading to the sepulchers of no fewer than forty monarchs. For Egypt, the shift in royal burial policy had unforeseen consequences. Previously, the pharaonic mortuary chapels — where last rites were held — had been situated close to the pyramidal tombs, making it easy for the pharaohs' spirits to journey back and forth to them. Now, however, the cramped valley offered no space for the chapels, which were built instead beyond the western mountain barrier.

Perhaps to compensate for the inconvenience thereby caused to the kings' traveling spirits — and certainly to show off the mortuary chapels as tangible evidence of royal affluence — the pharaohs lavished Egypt's wealth on the chapels, which gradually grew in size and grandeur. Thus, in the fifth generation after Tuthmosis I, the chapel complex of Amenhotep III, with its golden doors and silver pavements, was designed as "an everlasting fortress, a possessor of eternity."

The mortuary establishments of the pharaohs, as well as the temples dedicated to the gods they revered, required enormous staffs to conduct religious ceremonies and to maintain the premises. Amenhotep II would claim that he had assigned a staggering total of 89,600 Asiatic slaves to work on temple properties, while Amenhotep III would boast that his own mortuary estate was "filled with male and female slaves, the children of the chiefs of all the foreign lands."

With Tuthmosis I ensconced in his lonely tomb, there occurred an extraordinary interruption in the succession of military-minded kings who had set Egypt on the

This reconstruction of a 1200 BC tomb painting portrays a gathering in the home of a notable Egyptian sculptor of that era named Ipy *(second from left)*. He and his wife receive gifts of bread, waterfowl, and other foods from their son and daughter. The son wears a leopard skin draped over one shoulder, a sign that he is a priest. Both women are attired in long, elaborate wigs and the voluminous robes that came into vogue during the New Kingdom. All four have cones of aromatic fat atop their heads, which not only perfumed the wearer as they melted but provided emollients to protect the skin against the fierce Egyptian sun. Even the family cats are included in this domestic scene: One sports a silver earring and lurks under an ebony-and-rattan chair, while another, a kitten, claws playfully at Ipy's mantle.

course of empire. The dead king's son and successor, Tuthmosis II, was scarcely twenty years old, physically feeble, mentally flaccid, and badly henpecked by his wife, Hatshepsut, who also happened to be his half-sister. Such incestuous arrangements were by no means uncommon in dynastic Egypt. As might be expected, these unions led to some wildly tangled relationships. When Hatshepsut, as the "Great Royal Wife," failed to produce a male heir to the throne, a son of Tuthmosis II by a harem girl was designated to succeed. At the same time, the boy, a mere child, was declared married to one of Hatshepsut's daughters by Tuthmosis II. Thus, when Tuthmosis II died and Tuthmosis III inherited the crown at the age of six, the regent named to control affairs during the new king's childhood was none other than Hatshepsut — who was at once his aunt, stepmother, and mother-in-law.

As a princess, Hatshepsut by her own description had been "exceedingly good to look upon . . . a beautiful maiden, fresh, serene of nature." She was also extremely ambitious, even unscrupulous, and after biding her time as controlling regent for perhaps a couple of years she declared herself to be Egypt's pharaoh, ignoring Tuthmosis III's right of succession. Her qualifications were dubious. As a woman she technically could not rule as pharaoh. To endow her assumption with divine approval, she had reliefs made showing the god Amun-Re wooing her mother on the occasion of Hatshepsut's conception. To gloss over her gender, Hatshepsut was depicted as flat-chested, in king's clothing, and wearing the false beard that customarily adorned the faces of male pharaohs. Indeed, she took for herself all the usual pharaonic titles save one — that of Mighty Bull. Her sovereignty caused endless confusion among Egyptian scribes, who alternately called their royal master "she" and "he."

Despite her treachery, Hatshepsut proved an able ruler. "Egypt was in submission," wrote a scribe, ". . . for she was a dictator excellent of plans." Generally eschewing the military adventures of her predecessors, she focused on restoring Egypt to its former prosperity by renewing the foreign commerce that had lapsed during the Hyksos occupation. In the ninth year of her reign, for example, she dispatched a trading expedition to the fabulous land of Punt on Africa's Somalian coast. Sailing the length of the Red Sea, five great cargo ships made safe landfall at Punt, where the seamen were personally greeted by the local prince and his wife. Egyptians treated the chief and his spouse to a banquet of "bread, beer, wine, meat, fruits, and all the good things of

Egypt." With the feasting done, the trading began, and in exchange for such trinkets as rings and beads the visitors loaded the holds of their ships with "all kinds of beautiful plants . . . heaps of myrrh, live myrrh trees, ebony, genuine ivory, gold, costly woods, incense, eye cosmetics, apes, monkeys, greyhounds, leopard skins, and slaves together with their children." The return of the fleet was an occasion for the pharaoh Hatshepsut to briefly cast aside her masculine pretensions and make "her limbs fragrant as the dew of the gods with ointments and myrrh."

Throughout Hatshepsut's reign, the helpless Tuthmosis III seethed and plotted. He was clearly a stronger man than his hapless father, yet not until he was in his late twenties did he muster enough power to oust the usurper, who apparently died in the process. The manner of Hatshepsut's overthrow is unknown. So is the cause of her death, which under the circumstances may very well have been violent. At any rate, no sooner had he grasped the crown that was properly his than Tuthmosis III, in a burst of released frustration, set out to erase his stepmother's name from Egyptian memory. Following his orders, squads of men spread the length and breadth of the land, hacking Hatshepsut's name from her monuments and from the walls of her temples. Tuthmosis also let it be known that he meant to reverse the hated Hatshepsut's peaceable policies: On the day he assumed power, the new ruler proclaimed a general mobilization of Egypt's armed forces.

He was well prepared for the role of conqueror. During the long and restless years he had spent waiting to become pharaoh, Tuthmosis, in the established tradition of the sporting king, had schooled himself in martial arts and avocations. Although small of stature, he was immensely strong, and his scribes were tireless in describing his physical feats. "He used to shoot at a copper target," wrote one. "It was an ingot of beaten copper, three fingers thick, with his arrow stuck in it, having passed through and protruding on the other side by three handbreadths . . . . I speak accurately of what he did. . . . After all, it was in the presence of his entire army."

In the spring of 1483 BC, Tuthmosis set forth with his army toward Syria, where the bonds forged by the early pharaohs of the Eighteenth Dynasty had been cast off while Hatshepsut reigned. With the lapse of Egyptian influence, the Mitanni had moved into northern Syria and had set up a group of vassal states in northern and central Palestine as a buffer against future Egyptian incursions. And so it was that Tuthmosis III found himself confronted with a coalition of 330 Canaanite princes loyal to the Mitanni and commanded by the king of Kadesh.

After leaving Gaza on the Mediterranean coast, the Egyptian army took a caravan route that led inland to the town of Yehem, at the foot of the Carmel Ridge. There,

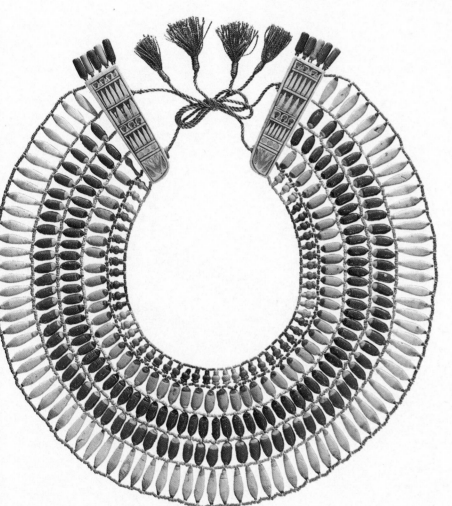

Powering small drills with stringed bows, the Egyptian artisans in the painting at left make beads by boring holes through semiprecious stones such as carnelian, lapis lazuli, and hematite. Celebrated for their skill, Egyptian beadmakers were also masters at fabricating richly colored beads of glass and of the glazed ceramic called faience, used in the ornate collarlike necklace above. To make such gemlike bits of faience, artisans shaped a ceramic compound of quartz and silicon into beads, applied colored glazes, then baked them.

Tuthmosis ascertained through spies that the enemy had taken a defensive position in the neighborhood of Megiddo, a fortified town that lay beyond the ridge on the Plain of Esdraelon.

Of the three routes that the Egyptians might take to attack their assembled foes, the shortest and most direct was through the mountain defile of Aruna. But, as the army's cautious commanders pointed out at a war council, it was also by far the most dangerous: The pass was so narrow that the army would have to march "horse after horse and man after man," thereby offering the enemy superb opportunities for ambush. Alternatively, the Canaanites could choose to wait until the Egyptian divisions began to emerge from the pass, then attack and defeat them piecemeal. Tuthmosis himself made the decision. "I will march on this road to Aruna," he declared. As related by Egyptian chronicles, the choice was based mostly on considerations of prestige. "They will say, these enemies whom Re abominates: 'Has His Majesty set out on another road because he has become afraid of us?' — so they will speak." Yet given the military acuity Tuthmosis III would demonstrate throughout his career, it seems likely that the pharaoh also calculated that the perilous Aruna pass would be the last route the Canaanites would expect him to take. Whatever motivated the pharaoh's decision, it proved a good one in the end. The Canaanites failed to seize the advantage, and the Egyptians made their way through the pass without incident, camping on the edge of the Plain of Esdraelon.

On the eve of battle, the proclamations sounded in the Egyptian camp: "Prepare ye! Make your weapons ready, since [the pharaoh] will engage in combat with that wretched enemy in the morning." At dawn, the Egyptians debouched on the plain, led by Tuthmosis III. The pharaoh subsequently

Female musicians play — and graceful dancers twirl — in these details from wall paintings that capture the joyous mood pervading the banquets of the Egyptian well-to-do. The instruments being played are, from left to right, a harp, a lute, a double oboe, and a lyre.

related that he rode in a "golden chariot, arrayed in his panoply of war like Horus mighty of arm." As one Egyptian told it, the Canaanites were waiting to meet them — "millions of men, and hundreds of thousands, of the chiefest of all lands, standing in their chariots." This was an exaggeration. The enemy army, which barred the direct approach to Megiddo, probably was relatively weak, and larger forces guarded routes to the north and south — just as Tuthmosis may have foreseen.

At any rate, the famed Battle of Megiddo was in fact a rout. Only eighty-three Canaanites were killed and 340 taken prisoner. The rest fled to the fortifications of Megiddo, to find the gates already shut against the Egyptians. Many Canaanite warriors — including the king of Kadesh — were forced to knot their own clothing into ropes and haul themselves over the town's walls. Still the Egyptian troops failed to press their assault, and as a result Tuthmosis was required to undertake a siege.

Seven months passed before the Canaanite leaders, starved at last into submission, emerged from the town and fell at the pharaoh's feet, as Tuthmosis himself put it, to "beg breath for their nostrils." Tuthmosis showed mercy in that instance. He reported that he allowed his enemies to leave. "And they went, all of them, on donkeys," the king said. "For I had taken their horses, and I carried off all their citizens to Egypt and their property likewise." The Egyptian booty included 924 chariots, 2,232 horses, 3,929 cattle, and 20,500 other animals, along with eighty-seven children of the Canaanite rulers and 1,796 persons of lesser rank. Far more important, the fall of Megiddo was to Tuthmosis as significant as "the capture of a thousand cities" — it brought nearly all of northern Palestine and southern Syria under Egyptian control. The pharaoh's martial ambitions were by no means satisfied, however: He envisioned an Egyptian empire that would extend throughout Syria to the banks of the middle Euphrates and the ranges of the Taurus Mountains.

To achieve that aim, Tuthmosis III was constantly on the march. Spring after spring, in the course of at least fourteen campaigns, he led his legions into battle. Capturing the ports of Phoenicia, he thereafter transported his troops by water and used the newly won cities as bases of supply and communication for his inland incursions. Finally, making his major move against the Mitanni, he constructed a fleet of boats from the cedars of the Lebanese mountains near Byblos and carted the vessels on ox-drawn wagons across bleak and hostile terrain. Arriving at the Euphrates, the army was ferried across the great stream and fell upon the Mitannian homeland. Wrote Tuthmosis: "My Majesty devastated it and it was turned into red dust on which no foliage will ever grow again." Having made his point, Tuthmosis withdrew, recrossing the river and erecting a monument to himself beside the one commemorating the brief incursion of his grandfather Tuthmosis I. This time, however, the Egyptians were there to stay, and even the expansion-minded Mitanni came to recognize the Euphrates as the boundary beyond which they dared not pass. Indeed, so willing were the old enemies to accept the status quo that they eventually entered into a treaty of alliance and, to cement the relationship later, an Egyptian pharaoh took a pair of Mitannian princesses as brides.

In their administration of the Syrian and Palestinian territories, Tuthmosis III and most of his successors showed a lenient touch that they failed to display elsewhere. In Nubia, for example, where Egyptian holdings by now extended as far as the Nile's Fourth Cataract, the Egyptian overlords forbade local chiefs to exercise power. But the petty rulers of Palestine and Syria were generally permitted to keep their seats and to enjoy a certain independence — so long as they behaved themselves as good vassals and kept paying tribute into Egyptian coffers. Above all, they had to

Tools of Beauty

Lips and cheeks rouged, eyes shadowed and bejeweled wig meticulously arranged, the stylish Egyptian queen Nefertari in the wall painting at right would have used all of the implements shown on these pages and the next when making her intricate toilette. Fittingly, the tools that helped to make an Egyptian woman a breathing artwork were themselves small works of art.

One of her essential implements was a set of tongs for curling her wig. Another was a razor, since fashion demanded the removal of body hair. The graceful, horse-shaped curling tongs displayed here include a sharp edge — the shell-like device comprising the animal's back feet — and so performed both jobs.

An Egyptian woman would also have had an ornate ointment spoon in which she kept her rouge and lipstick, concoctions of red ocher mixed with fat or gum resin. For her supply of eye shadow — a powdered sulfide of lead called kohl — she would have employed a special pot; these were often made in the form of the deity Bes, the familiar domestic god of good luck. A lady also required a comb for the wig and a suitably ornamented mirror of polished bronze or silver. The handle of the mirror at right shows the face of Hathor, goddess of beauty and fertility.

Glass-and-gold kohl pot

guarantee to the Egyptians unimpeded use of the historic trade routes that opened the way north to Asia Minor, east to Babylon and Assyria, and west to Crete, Cyprus, the islands of the Aegean, and even the Greek mainland.

In a sort of insurance policy against revolt, the sons of the vassal monarchs were often taken as hostages to Egypt, where they were treated royally, housed in a splendid palace, and schooled as Egyptians. That practice also paid a long-term premium: On the deaths of their fathers, the thoroughly Egyptianized princes were often installed upon their native thrones, where they ruled in fond and faithful recollection of the time when they "had been taken to Egypt as children to serve the king as their lord and to stand at the door of the king."

Yet the Asians yearned to chart their own destiny, and uprisings were inevitable. Such transgressions were of course rudely punished. As one pharaoh warned a vassal king: "If for any reason you harbor any thought of enmity or hatred in your heart, then you and all your family are condemned to death." On the other hand, the rewards of loyalty, which included the pledge of protection against all foreign and domestic enemies, could be considerable. Wrote a pharaoh: "If you show yourself submissive, what is there that the king cannot do for you?"

To keep the subjugated domains under control, an Egyptian military presence was deemed necessary. Garrisons of archers and charioteers, charged with keeping the peace, were stationed throughout Syria and Palestine; they were supplied by the vassal states, which were required to provide Egyptian soldiers "with food and drink, with cattle, sheep, honey, and oil."

The Egyptian army reached the peak of professionalism under Tuthmosis III. It was organized in four divisions, each numbering about 5,000 men and marching under the standard of a god after whom it was named, as in the "Division of Amun" or the "Division of the Beauty of Re." Like all armies, it was heavily endowed with staff officers, among them a "master of the horse," who supervised the mounts and chariots that carried Egypt's warriors into battle; a "keeper of the army registers," who was in charge of conscription; and a "keeper of hostages," who was responsible for tending and controlling prisoners of war. In addition, the pharaoh was supported by his own retinue, which included the "king's charioteer," the "king's bow-carrier," the "king's armor-bearer," and even the "king's barber." It would appear, however, that such positions were no rear-echelon sinecures: The Eighteenth-Dynasty pharaohs often led their troops into battle, and where they went so did their personal retainers. Thus, as rewards for valor, one barber was given as a slave a prisoner whom he had personally captured, while a king's butler received seven head of cattle.

Silver hand mirror

Horse-shaped curling tongs

As always, the life of the lowly infantryman was hard. "Let me tell you the woes of the soldier," went one lament of the sort that has been heard ever since humans first bore arms. "He may not rest. His march is uphill through mountains. He drinks water every third day. His body is ravaged by illness. The enemy comes, surrounds him with missiles. He is told: 'Quick, forward, valiant soldier!'"

Yet such a life was hardly more arduous than one spent by the peasant laboring in the fields or on the pharaoh's construction gangs, and there were compensations in the form of food, clothing, shelter, and medical aid. Moreover, although the rank-and-file soldier probably did not receive regular wages for his service, he was often allowed to share in the spoils of war. And an even greater incentive was the chance for a man to rise above his station in the army's lowest rank to a proud position as a standard-bearer and perhaps to end his career as a battalion commander.

For those born of means, an army career offered opportunity almost without limit. Many high-ranking officers had been companions of the pharaoh since childhood, when they had been selected on the basis of their aristocratic status and potential merit to attend the royal nursery and to matriculate in the king's court. They formed an unofficial yet highly exclusive club whose members combined the characteristics of the courtier and the soldier. As army officers, both they and others who proved their worth on the battlefield could expect to receive from a grateful pharaoh splendid gifts in the form of ceremonial weapons, valuable gold necklaces known as the "gold of valor," and grants of tax-free land on which they could build their estates.

Army officers might also take on duties that had little if anything to do with their military service. One talented general, for example, was given appointments as "overseer of the buildings of Amun," "overseer of fields," and "overseer of the priests in Upper and Lower Egypt." In that manner, the military gradually insinuated itself into the civil branch of a nation that had since its earliest times depended heavily upon a pervasive bureaucracy. The day would come when no position in the Egyptian realm would appear to be beyond the reach of an ambitious general — not even the awesome office of pharaoh.

This army unparalleled in the ancient world, and the mighty empire it helped create, was Tuthmosis's legacy. When he died in 1425 after a reign of nearly fifty-five years, his mummified remains were placed in a shaft reaching deep into the cliffside at the Valley of the Kings, not far from the spot where his old stepmother and enemy Hatshepsut was entombed. Such was the power of his armed legions that during the forty years between his death and the accession of his great-grandson Amenhotep III, no major foe arose to challenge Egyptian supremacy. That must have been satisfactory to

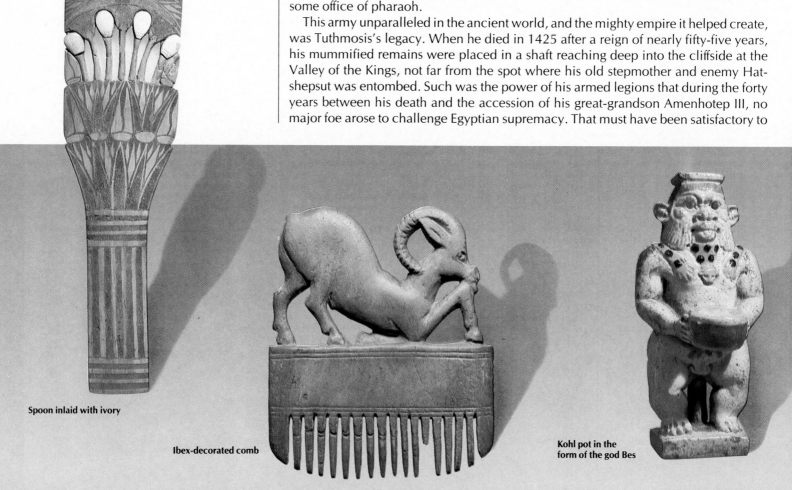

Spoon inlaid with ivory

Ibex-decorated comb

Kohl pot in the
form of the god Bes

Amenhotep III, who took easily to the ways of the voluptuary while his nation, flourishing upon the wealth of the entire Middle East, followed him into a golden age largely devoted to the pursuit of pleasure.

In an Egyptian tomb of Amenhotep's time there appears a poetic inscription that aptly characterizes both that pharaoh and his people: "Spend the day merrily! Put ointment and fine oil to your nostrils and lotus flowers on the body of your beloved. . . ." From the outset of his reign, it was apparent that Amenhotep III was of softer fiber than his tough Theban forebears. For example, although Tuthmosis III had been a mighty huntsman who had once come perilously close to being impaled on the tusks of an angry elephant, Amenhotep III, in attempting to establish his own image as a hero-king, chose a safer route. He ordered that wild bulls be penned up within an enclosure. "Then," says the chronicle, "did His Majesty proceed against all these wild bulls. Tally thereof: 170 wild bulls."

Amenhotep apparently married for love, taking as his principal wife a commoner by the name of Tiy, who was the politically astute daughter of a lieutenant general. For her enjoyment, the king created a beautiful, large lake, which measured some 6,400 feet long and 1,200 feet wide, on the grounds of his palace at Thebes. Despite the immensity of the project it was completed in a mere fourteen days, and many were the happy hours that Amenhotep and Tiy thereafter idled away on the lake, drifting along in their royal boat.

Yet Tiy was far from being the only woman in the life of Amenhotep III. During his long regime he married additional Egyptian women, as well as foreigners: two princesses from the kingdom of Mittani, one of whom arrived in Egypt with 317 ladies-in-waiting; two from Syria; two from Babylon; and one from the kingdom of Arzawa in Anatolia. The pharaoh also maintained an extensive harem and tirelessly nagged his provincial governors about populating it. "Send beautiful women," he urged one such official, "but none with shrill voices. Then the king your lord will say to you, 'That is good.' "

Given the example presented by the pharaoh, it was only natural that other Egyptians indulged in luxuries. For the highborn, home was likely to be a whitewashed villa of as many as thirty rooms, with a suite set aside for the master of the house. (Although others might have had to be satisfied with cruder facilities, the nobleman's accommodations customarily included a toilet consisting of a portable pot underneath a seat that was supported by bricks.) Bathed by the shafts of sunlight that flooded the interior through clerestory windows, the walls were decorated with paintings of birds and flowers in vivid hues of blue and green and orange, while columns gleamed with golden trim.

In the cool of an Egyptian evening, the lord and his wife often lolled beside a pool in a walled garden fragrant with blooming flowers. There, surrounded by children playing with dolls or frolicking at a game of leapfrog, they could amuse themselves with a board game called *senet* or relax to the soft, sweet strains of a harp. Almost certainly curled in a corner was a descendant of the African wildcat. First domesticated in Egypt, the cat was called by the phonetically fitting name of *miu*. It was the most pampered of pets, and even the formidable Queen Tiy, who was not accustomed to spreading her affections around, permitted her tabby to lie beneath her chair at the dinner table.

Usually the noble's villa was only part of a self-supporting complex that included a stable, a dairy, a bakery, a slaughterhouse, and perhaps a carpenter's workshop. On the outskirts stood vineyards, hives that provided honey, and ponds for the geese that provided eggs. Beyond stretched pastures for grazing herds of cattle and fields that yielded grain for bread and beer.

Among Egyptians of this era, clothing was a sure sign of status. While peasants went naked or wore loincloths and artisans, who comprised the nation's middle class, wore simple cloth wraps, more affluent men and women draped themselves in long, carefully pleated skirts and fancied such heavy adornments as gold bracelets and broad gold necklaces festooned with beads of lapis lazuli, carnelian, and turquoise. Both sexes favored wigs made of human hair, saturated with beeswax and, on festive occasions, topped with small cones of perfumed fat.

Egyptian women used a wide range of cosmetics and beauty aids. There were green malachite and gray galena for shadowing the eyes and protecting the flesh from the glare of the sun; red ocher for rouge and henna for dyeing the hair, the fingernails and toenails, the palms of the hands, and the soles of the feet; ointments from the fat of hippopotamuses, snakes, crocodiles, and lions to make the hair luxuriant, along with razors and tweezers to remove unsightly patches; scents for the breath; and myrrh or oil of lily to perfume the body. Aphrodisiacs were available to arouse flagging passions, and magical formulas could presumably turn rivals into withered crones.

Women occupied a respected place in Egyptian households. A sage urged fair treatment of wives with some advice for husbands: "Do not supervise your wife in her house if you know she is doing a good job. . . . Do not say to her, 'Where is it? Get it for me!' when she has put it in the proper place." Wives were even accorded certain legal rights: Not only could they own and dispose of property, but in the event of divorce they were entitled to one-third of the couple's possessions.

In their outdoor pastimes, the Egyptians took full advantage of their riverine habitat. The crocodiles that slithered from the banks of the Nile and the hippopotamuses that wallowed in the mud of its shallows were cudgeled to death in what amounted to combat at close quarters. The most popular sport was hunting waterfowl. In family outings in the Delta marshes, light skiffs were poled through the papyrus islands; the women on board languidly plucked water lilies and the children gazed in awe at their skillful fathers, who used an ivory throwing stick that operated on the principle of a boomerang to bring down waterfowl. The family cat, specially trained for hunting, retrieved the fallen birds.

With the fall of night, Egyptian society came to life in all its sybaritic excess, dedicating itself to Bes, a leonine deity who was the god of merriment, virility, and childbirth. The Egyptians enjoyed parties. They adored the delights of alabaster tables groaning beneath haunches of beef, legs of lamb, tangy cuts of wild antelope and gazelle, sweet clusters of grapes, and sticky heaps of figs. They appreciated the wine that flooded from jars into goblets decorated with golden rims and the delicate forms of lotus petals — always served by nearly naked maids, who also stood ready to wipe the lips of a guest with a napkin. They longed to hear the clash of the cymbals, the throb of the drums, the shrill of the pipes, and the strains of the stringed instruments. And they loved the sight of the slender, supple dancing girls — slaves who had been imported from the conquered Asian or African lands — moving to the beat of the music.

This Egypt, the land of Amenhotep III, was destined to experience a radical upheaval. The old king — thoroughly debauched, sagging in his obesity, and tortured by the pain of his abscessed teeth — died around 1365 and passed the throne to his son, Amenhotep IV. The young pharaoh would soon launch a religious revolution that would shake the very foundations of the land.

The name Amenhotep means "Amun is pleased," a sentiment that honored the leading deity of the era. Amun had been the obscure local god of the Thebans. When they gained the throne in the Eighteenth Dynasty, they sponsored the god's rise to unrivaled preeminence in the Egyptian pantheon. Amun won even more status when he was merged with the sun god, Re, to become Amun-Re. The truth was, however, that Amun-Re lacked definition and seemed colorless when compared to such earthy personalities among the ancient deities as Osiris, Horus, and for that matter, the goddess Isis. Amun-Re was the "hidden one" who, in his ubiquity, "transforms himself into an infinity of forms — every god is in him." Notwithstanding his enigmatic character, however, Amun-Re's special relationship with the Theban monarchs had brought measureless wealth and power beyond calculation to the estates of his priesthood.

Inevitably, both Amun-Re and his cult were the objects of bitter envy on the part of the priestly followers of gods who had been eclipsed. The young prince Amenhotep was prominent among those who developed a virulent hatred of Amun-Re. Just why this happened is not known; perhaps he was influenced by his priest-teachers of the temple at Heliopolis, which was the center of the sun cult. At any rate, scarcely had the crown been placed upon his head than he launched an obsessive campaign to outlaw not only Amun-Re but all the other deities and to replace them with the one and only Aten — the sun disk.

The chief promoter of the Aten was a most peculiar king. Amenhotep IV was grotesque in appearance. He had a huge gourd-shaped head that perched on a neck so long and slender it seemed hardly capable of bearing its burden; slanted eyes, pulpy lips, and a knobby chin; a potbelly remindful of a woman in early pregnancy; gigantic thighs and matchstick shins. His lineaments were strangely effeminate, and it was speculated he suffered a glandular disorder that resulted in eunuchism, deformed his body, and unbalanced his emotions.

Such theories were, however, seriously undermined by the fact that Amenhotep indisputably sired six daughters and, less certainly, one or two sons, by his wife, Queen Nefertiti, who was an aggressive partner in championing the cause of the sun-disk god. (Her name meant "the Beautiful One is come" — and she more than lived up to the epithet.)

The new pharaoh espoused a god devoid of human characteristics. In the Egyptian language, aten was a noun meaning "disk of the sun" — no more and no less. To the mind of the young Amenhotep IV, however, the Aten was no mere disk: He was the sublime "living sun disk — there is none other than he." At first, the king made a concession to tradition by allowing his god to be personified in the form of a man with a falcon's head. But that soon ceased, and thereafter the Aten was represented by the hieroglyphic symbol of a disk radiating rays that terminated in hands, which held the ankh, or symbol of life. Thus, the deity that Egyptians were now under obligation to worship was one completely removed from human appearance, with neither the substance of statuary nor the fabric of legend to lend him credibility.

During the early years, the pharaoh permitted the conventional gods to co-exist with the Aten, although with greatly reduced status. In the fifth or sixth year of his reign, however, the pharaoh further displayed his dissatisfaction with the old gods by changing his own name: No longer would the king be called Amenhotep, a word that honored Amun with its first two syllables. Instead the pharaoh's name would reflect the glory of the new deity. And so, *Amen*hotep IV became Akhen*aten,* or "the spirit of the Aten."

At about the same time, Akhenaten began looking for a suitable place to build a new capital that he could dedicate to the Aten. The site he chose, on the east bank of the Nile about 200 miles north of Thebes, was a grim, sandy plain, cloistered by frowning

cliffs, where no gods had ever been worshiped, no one had ever lived, and no one but Akhenaten would ever wish to. In the full flood of his enthusiasm, he himself laid out the building plans for five temples of the Aten and a sumptuous palace where the pharaoh and his family would dwell; he even drew up the city's street plan. Although it has since become known as Amarna, Akhenaten called his new capital Akhetaten — "the horizon of the Aten."

Work proceeded in frenzied haste, but so eager was Akhenaten to live in his new city that he had a huge tent erected for himself and his court. After four years of construction, the buildings were ready for occupancy. Yet before he departed from Thebes for his new home, Akhenaten fired a blast that shook the empire to its foundations: Henceforth, he decreed, all Egyptians — and all Syrians and Nubians in Egypt's thrall — would worship only the Aten, whose light bathed humanity in each of its affairs. What was more, only Akhenaten, as the "beautiful child of the Disk," could engage in dialogue with the Aten; the pharaoh alone was privy to his god's designs for the universe, and he alone could interpret the divine will by which humanity must exist. And Akhenaten enforced his mandate with a fanatic's fury. He was especially ruthless in his treatment of Amun-Re, the god brought to prominence by his own Theban forebears. All citizens were required to follow the pharaoh's example by changing their names if they honored the offending deity. Squads of workers, chisels in hand, were sent out to expunge the name of Amun-Re on monuments, walls, or temples; indeed, even Akhenaten's former name, along with that of his father, Amenhotep III, was obliterated. Statues of Amun-Re were smashed, his temples closed, the revenues of his vast estates confiscated. Some citizens resisted clandestinely. They quietly continued to worship their favorite deities — even at Amarna, where amulets to the god Bes were still being used during the time of Akhenaten's reign. But their secret opposition made little difference.

Because the priestly cults of the traditional gods were deeply embedded not only in Egypt's religious behavior but in its society, its economy, its administration, and its politics, the results of Akhenaten's campaign proved devastating. Obsessed with his god, the pharaoh paid little attention to his government and allowed corruption to creep into the Egyptian bureaucracy. At every level of his administration, offi-

The blade-thin face of Akhenaten *(right)* seems to reveal the character of the man. He was a religious fanatic who for a time overturned his nation's structure of beliefs, and the prime mover in a comparable artistic revolution. Ordering the palace sculptors to abandon Egypt's long tradition of idealizing portraiture, he insisted that he and his family be shown in candid domestic scenes. The relief at left pictures Akhenaten kissing one of his daughters while two others play with their mother, Queen Nefertiti. Over the scene hovers the sun disk, the Aten, which the pharaoh tried to make the sole object of Egyptian worship.

cials bribed and stole while the king pressed his religious crusade. In the confused state of affairs, public works deteriorated and trade dwindled.

Yet by no means were all of Akhenaten's influences malign. Into the visual art of the Egyptians, for example, he breathed a new and vibrant life. Early in his reign, the pharaoh assembled about him the royal sculptors, led by a man named Bek, and issued instructions: No longer would pharaohs be depicted in the style that had been conventional for millennia and had rendered them as stiff as obelisks, as expressionless as mummies, as alike as the papyrus reeds of the Delta marshes. Akhenaten was singular, he was unique, he was the son of the Aten, and he must be portrayed in all his individuality. The sculptors took him at his word — and then some, possibly exaggerating his physical grotesqueries.

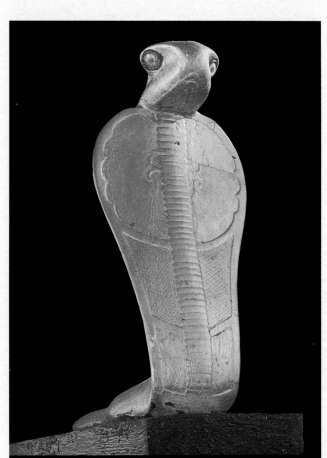

A new naturalism swept the spectrum of Egyptian art, from statuary to reliefs to painting. For the first time, Egyptians were allowed glimpses of their pharaoh in the intimate surrounding of home and family. A charming scene carved in stone showed Akhenaten kissing one little princess while another sat on Nefertiti's lap and a third played with a toy that just happened to be the crown of imperial Egypt. Similarly, in long, curved lines, man and beast came alive, the elderly showed their age, married couples were portrayed with warmth, children looked like children instead of stunted adults, and birds seemed to fly rather than appearing lifeless and frozen as they had in earlier eras.

The art thus promoted by Akhenaten would by far outlive both the heretical pharaoh himself and the god that he championed. For while the Egyptian king was pursuing his obsessions, his empire was menaced. In Syria, vassal kings called for help from the Egyptian army, but the pharaoh was too preoccupied to listen. Bearing down on them from Asia Minor were Hittite warriors under the mighty King Suppiluliuma, who had defeated the Mitanni once and for all, and was moving to challenge Egyptian hegemony in the Syro-Palestinean littoral. The salvation of the empire would be left to Akhenaten's successors. He died in the seventeenth year of his reign and, to all intents and purposes, his sun-disk god died with him.

The death of the heretical king brought a baffling interlude. Late in Akhenaten's reign, a willowy youth named Smenkhare had been his constant companion and, clearly, his heir apparent. At about the same time, Nefertiti had evidently vanished from public view. Although the riddle of Smenkhare's identity remains unsolved, it has been speculated that he was Akhenaten's homosexual favorite; or that he was either the pharaoh's nephew or a son by another wife; or even that he was a legitimate son of Akhenaten and Nefertiti who had, for some reason, been kept out of sight during his childhood. Whoever he was, he died either before he had a chance to accept the crown or a very short while thereafter. His place was taken by the boy-king Tutankhaten, whose familial origins are also obscure. (He was possibly Smenkhare's younger brother — or even a much younger brother of Akhenaten.) Tutankhaten set about restoring the traditional

Made of gilded wood, with eyes of translucent quartz, this rearing cobra *(left)* served as a guardian spirit in King Tutankhamen's tomb. Such serpents helped guide the dead through the underworld to their rebirth in a paradisiacal afterlife — just as they helped the sun through the night's darkness to its daily reappearance. Cobras also were symbols of the pharaoh's rule over Lower Egypt. (Upper Egypt was represented by the vulture.)

religion. Changing his name to Tutankhamen and thereby substituting Amun's compound for the Aten's, he abandoned Akhenaten's desert city and moved his court back to Thebes. Yet he was helpless to remedy the ills that had beset his empire, and by the time of his early death, conditions had reached such a state that his widowed queen was obliged to offer her hand in marriage to a Hittite prince. After long and querulous negotiations, a young Hittite noble did arrive in Egypt — only to be put to death as he crossed the border. His murder was generally attributed to a courtier who had somehow assumed the pharaoh's office in the meantime.

Long a shadowy figure in the Egyptian court under Akhenaten, the courtier, Ai, a former priest and "master of the horse," reigned only four years and then died. But he had made arrangements for a successor, reaching into his military past and designating as the future pharaoh one Horemhab, who was the commander in chief of the Egyptian army. And so began a line of professional soldiers on the throne of Egypt.

Despite his warlike calling, Horemhab was an energetic and dedicated ruler who devoted the three decades of his reign to peaceable affairs. As a first order of business, he launched an implacable campaign to erase from Egyptian minds all memory of the sun-disk Aten and his sponsor, Akhenaten. The heretic's desert city of Akhetaten was torn down pillar and post, its masonry transported for use in reconstructing the temples of Amun-Re, who was now being restored to godly supremacy. As for the late pharaoh Akhenaten, his statues were demolished and his name removed wherever it had previously appeared. When he was mentioned at all, it was as "that criminal."

A wall panel from the tomb of Sannedjem, a nobleman of the Nineteenth Dynasty, portrays the god of mummification — a part-man and part-jackal called Anubis — at work preparing Sannedjem for his journey to the afterlife. Part of the panel appears to be a cutaway drawing showing the internal structure of an Egyptian coffin.

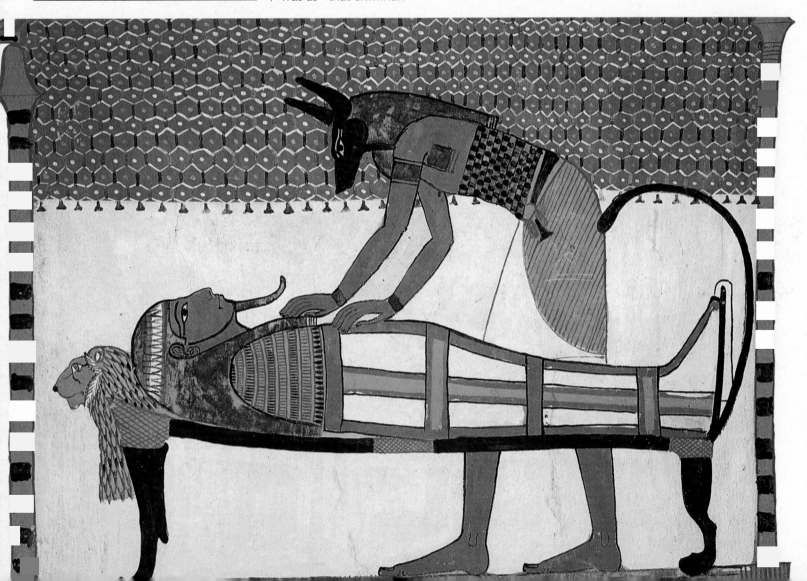

Horemhab also moved to stamp out the governmental corruption that had persisted since Akhenaten's fateful tenure. He issued a sweeping edict of reform that resulted in substantial numbers of venal officials, especially tax collectors, being exiled to the Sinai wasteland with their noses cut from their faces. Horemhab governed Egypt for twenty-nine years and, as death became imminent, selected yet another general to follow him. The officer he chose, who became Ramses I, presently died, leaving little mark. In contrast, both his son, Sethi I, and grandson, Ramses II, were military commanders of the first rank. During four campaigns into Asia, Sethi I reasserted Egyptian control over most of Palestine, although his efforts to regain Syria were frustrated by the Hittites. Ramses II fought the Hittites to a standoff at the great Battle of Kadesh and subsequently signed the treaty that recognized Egyptian hegemony over Palestine and southern Syria.

Ramses II ruled for sixty-seven years, and by the time of his death his son and successor, Merneptah, was already quite old. As the thirteenth son, Merneptah had probably never expected that he would rule. But eleven of his brothers had died, the other entertained no pharaonic ambitions, and Merneptah found himself king. Almost immediately, he was assailed by a threat that would have taxed the energies of a man much younger than he. Pushing out of the west in 1220 BC came a hostile confederation of Libyans and mysterious Asiatic allies. Merneptah met the challenge head on, administering a sound defeat to the enemy forces in a battle lasting six hours. In commemoration of Merneptah's victory, a monument was erected near Thebes: "Men come and go with singing, and there is no cry of men in trouble." But the problematic invasions persisted, and in 1186, during the rule of Ramses III, the so-called Sea Peoples descended on the Nile kingdom, sweeping southward by land and by sea. While a fleet of their warships sailed down the Mediterranean coastline, a host of warriors marched through Syria and into Palestine, accompanied by their women and children in clumsy oxcarts. In what would be the last great display of Egypt's imperial might, Ramses led his army to confront the invaders on his own northeastern border. He succeeded in trapping their ships as they attempted to land troops at the mouth of the Nile and destroyed the fleet. Then the Egyptian force shattered the army of the enemy in a bloody land battle. As an uneasy peace prevailed, Ramses III returned to Thebes to devote most of his long reign to domestic affairs—and indulged his penchant for monumental building.

All of the so-called Ramesside kings were builders on a grand scale. Ramses I had begun construction on an enormous colonnaded hall in the Karnak section of Thebes. Sethi I had continued work on the project. When it was completed by Ramses II it covered 6,000 square yards—and was probably the largest Egyptian temple ever built. Ramses II also assured himself of a place in history by introducing at Abu Simbel, 100 miles south of Thebes, a colossal new temple hewn out of the solid rock of a cliff. From the temple façade, which comprised four immense statues of the seated pharaoh, to the sanctuary deep in the virgin rock of the cliff, was a distance of some 200 feet.

Ramses III continued the building program with colossal structures of his own.

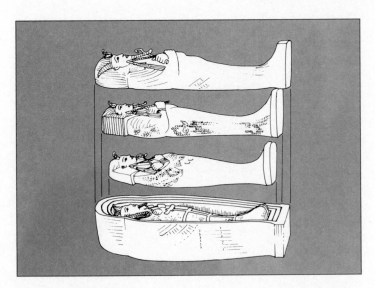

The mummified body of King Tutankhamen was protected by no fewer than three elaborate coffins, one inside the other. The assembly of coffins in turn was encased in a carved stone sarcophagus *(above)*. As shown at left, the outermost coffin was made of gilded wood and, as did the others, bore a likeness of the deceased pharaoh. The second coffin was also made of wood decorated with inlays of precious stones and other materials. The innermost coffin was of solid twenty-two-karat gold and weighed almost 250 pounds. Within it was a magnificent mask — made of gold inlaid with lapis lazuli, quartz, and obsidian — that covered the mummy's face.

The huge temple at Abu Simbel, built about 1260 BC to honor the pharaoh Ramses II, was cut from the solid rock of a cliff overlooking the Upper Nile. The inner great hall, pictured here, housed eight massive statues of Ramses, each thirty feet tall. The entire temple, from its main portal *(inset right)* through its two halls to the inner sanctuary, measured 180 feet long.

In addition to the statues inside the temple, the ebullient Ramses ordered his sculptors to make four colossal images of himself flanking the main portal, two on each side. Between the legs of the four colossi are smaller statues depicting Ramses' mother; his wife, Queen Nefertari; and several of the monarch's 100 children.

The temple was precisely situated so that on two days of the year, the sun streamed through the entrance and down the halls, flooding with light the sanctuary and two of its four statues: Ramses wearing a crown and the god Amun, Egypt's chief deity. The dates, one in mid-October and the other in mid-February, may have celebrated Ramses' most brilliant military victories.

RAMSES' INCREDIBLE TEMPLE

Such undertakings were, of course, astronomically expensive. So was the cost of maintaining the Egyptian army, which was at this point peopled largely by mercenaries from foreign lands. Additional siphons on the royal treasury were the priesthoods, particularly that of the resurrected Amun-Re. During the thirty-one years he ruled as pharaoh, Ramses III gave various places of worship tremendous quantities of gold, silver, and precious stones, together with a total of 169 towns, 113,433 slaves, 493,386 head of cattle, 1,071,780 plots of ground, and eighty-eight barks and galleys.

Inevitably, as the priestly cults and the mercenary soldiers grew rich, the royal treasury was severely depleted — and so was royal authority. Ramses III narrowly survived an assassination attempt by disgruntled members of his court. By the time of his death in 1162, events outside the kingdom had conspired to send Egypt into precipitous decline. The Sea Peoples had turned the Middle East upside down. The Hittite empire, Egypt's onetime ally, had disappeared. Flexing its newfound muscle, Assyria had seized Egypt's possessions in Syria and Palestine and was filling its coffers with goods that once had supported the Egyptians' extravagant lifestyle. With its trade routes constricted or severed, Egypt no longer had a source of income from abroad, and the hapless kingdom faced a drawn-out and melancholy descent into corruption, usurpation, and near-anarchy. Some of Egypt's tomb-building artisans actually went on strike. So widespread was the problem of tomb robbing that officials eventually removed many pharaonic mummies from the Valley of the Kings and placed them in a common tomb, in order to guard them better; Egyptian ambassadors were insulted in Syrian city-states that had once groveled at mention of the imperial name.

Egypt suffered an ignominious succession of rulers: Priest-pharaohs gave way to encroaching Libyans, who were in turn forced from power by Nubians. At one point, even an Ethiopian sat for a brief period on the Egyptian throne. The Nubians succumbed to the Assyrians, who were replaced by the Chaldeans of Babylonia.

During the seventh century BC the beleaguered country enjoyed a brief resurgence of national unity and power, but this flickering flame was soon to be snuffed out. As the sixth century neared its end, the Persian tide that had washed over Babylonia rolled on toward Egypt, that ancient and honored civilization whose days as an independent nation were now numbered.

THE UBIQUITOUS GODS

The Hebrew prophet Jeremiah scoffed that statues of gods gave no more protection against the perils of life "than a scarecrow in a plot of cucumbers." Indeed, he and his fellow prophets, who created a religion with a single, all-powerful deity, scorned all representations of gods as "graven images."

But the Hebrew religion was the exception. Most ancient peoples worshiped a multitude of deities, each in charge of its own special realm, and fervently believed in the potency of sacred images such as the ones shown on the following pages. Not surprisingly, since the travails and terrors of life were much the same everywhere, the pantheons worshiped by these societies resembled each other strongly. Dwellers in all climes feared the vagaries of the weather, so the Aryans of India, the Hittites, the Etruscans, the Assyrians, and many others prayed to similar storm gods. Humans in all latitudes wondered at the sparkling galaxies and saw deities in the skies. In many cultures the great giver of warmth and life, the sun, was itself a supremely powerful god.

Gods and goddesses of fertility were ubiquitous. People as different and distant as the Mycenaeans of Greece and Indians of Mexico believed that, if properly placated with gifts and ritual, such deities would ensure bountiful harvests. Other gods removed some of the terror and mystery from death, overseeing life beyond the grave whether in some shadowy Hades or in an Elysium of otherworldly delights.

Animals were worshiped, too, notably those with attributes that made them seem marvelous and mysterious. Bulls and goats were revered for their virility by a number of Middle Eastern peoples. Cats — from domestic felines to lions, tigers, and jaguars — became cult objects in China, the Near East, Egypt, and the Americas. The epitome of sleek swiftness on the hunt, cats exhibited an almost godlike self-possession in repose.

The depth of many people's devotion to their various gods is shown in their portrayals of themselves in postures of supplication. Intended for temples or other sacred places, or for the family hearth, these images expressed their makers' fundamental dependence on the divine. By propitiating the gods in this manner, men and women felt that they had some protection against the hazards and cruelties of their existence, and a direct connection with the enigmatic world of the unseen.

With his arms spread in
the traditional Egyptian
posture of prayer, a
small bronze figure of a
priest invokes the gods
of the pharaohs.

An Assyrian king kneels
in prayer in a bas-relief
from the palace of
Tukulti-Ninurta I.

POSTURES OF FAITH

With a ceremonial sa-
lute, a bronze Mycenae-
an figurine expresses
recognition of the
presence of the divine.

An Olmec jade figurine
portrays a priest holding a
divine child, probably
intended to be the offspring
of a jaguar god and a
human female.

The pharaoh Akhenaten presents offerings to the sun disk, which he established as Egypt's only god.

HOMAGE TO THE SUN

The three bull-like creatures above help one another support the winged disk of the sun god in a Syrian bas-relief.

A golden disk haloes the head of the Hittite sun goddess called Arinna, known as "Queen of Heaven and Earth."

The ram-headed Egyptian creature below represents the god Harsaphes, linked with fertility and virility. The part-human, pregnant hippopotamus is the Egyptian symbol of the goddess Taweret, the divine midwife.

The goddess on the ivory box lid above, probably a Canaanite deity, symbolizes fertility.

Carved on a large gold ring, three Mycenean women *(left)* celebrate nature's spring rebirth by carrying flowers to an altar. The two-headed female figure below was sacred to an ancient Mexican fertility cult.

THE PROMISE OF FERTILITY

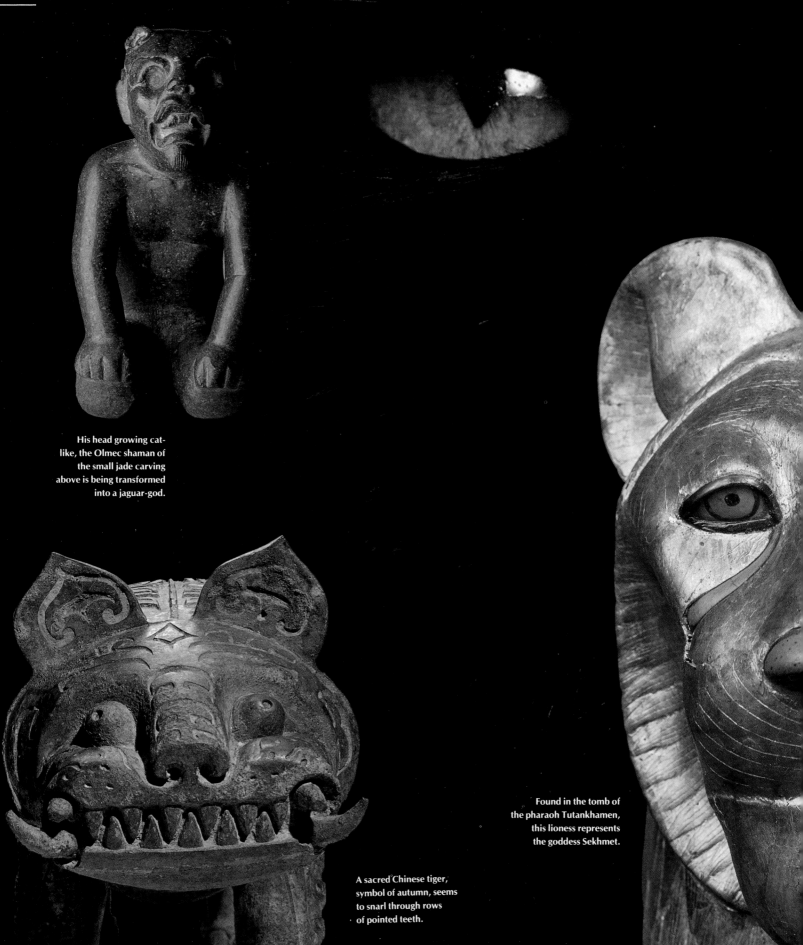

His head growing cat-
like, the Olmec shaman of
the small jade carving
above is being transformed
into a jaguar-god.

Found in the tomb of
the pharaoh Tutankhamen,
this lioness represents
the goddess Sekhmet.

A sacred Chinese tiger,
symbol of autumn, seems
to snarl through rows
of pointed teeth.

THE LURE OF THE CAT

A thirteenth-century
Syrian bronze shows the
god Baal poised, per-
haps, to hurl a thunderbolt.

The lance of lightning
held by the storm god at
left is topped by a
growing plant, symbol of
rain's life-giving power.

Equipped with a thunder hammer and a handful of jagged lightning bolts, a Hittite weather god *(left)* strides across a ninth-century relief.

This grim-visaged, winged Assyrian demon named Pazuzu represents the malign spirit of the dry desert winds that brought drought.

THE WRATHFUL STORM GODS

Escorted by a pair of guides, an Etruscan matron sets off for her life in the next world in a vivid tomb painting.

Images of a devoted Hittite man and wife were carved on their own coffin lid to give their spirits a human form in the hereafter.

PASSAGE TO THE AFTERLIFE

THE GREEK CRUCIBLE

They came out of the north — hordes from the plains of the Black Sea and of northwest Asia Minor. For almost a millennium, between 2800 and 2000 BC, the human tide swept around the Aegean Sea and poured into the nearby peninsula, making its way across mountains and fields until it had covered most of what would one day be called Greece.

These alien, Indo-European invaders were horsemen, skilled in the handling of their war chariots and apparently invincible. They first conquered, and then over the centuries settled among, the original inhabitants of the Greek peninsula. By 1600 BC, this union of invaders and natives had evolved into a distinctive culture that had spread throughout mainland Greece.

The people who would become the Greeks had in common a language — the ancestor of classical Ionic Greek — and a strikingly bellicose nature. A few of their warriors, who were rich enough to own chariots and who had a knack for administration and a penchant for power, set themselves up as the aristocratic rulers of a number of fiefs. Eventually they formed a loose economic and political alliance that led them to erect well-protected citadels on carefully chosen high ground, from which they controlled most of southern and central Greece. The largest and strongest of these fortresses exercised a precarious hegemony over the others, and from that settlement at the center of the peninsula the new civilization took its name: Mycenae.

Something similar had been happening in the Middle East. There, too, for a thousand years barbaric invaders had been overrunning indigenous populations, and the intermingling spawned a succession of war-loving, migratory tribes — the Mitanni, the Kassites, the Hyksos. Their social structures and political systems, all based on a chariot aristocracy, bore a marked resemblance to those of the Mycenaeans. And just as the Middle Eastern conquerors borrowed and adapted the culture of such civilized peoples as the Babylonians and the Egyptians, so too the lords of Mycenae turned to the oldest, best-established civilization close at hand — that of the Minoans, on the island of Crete.

The Minoans were at their zenith when the Greeks first made contact sometime around 1600 BC. The Minoans not only controlled Crete, a large island situated some sixty miles south of the mainland, but had established colonies on islands in the Aegean. Wherever the Mycenaeans sailed on the Aegean Sea, it seemed, they found a Minoan settlement.

The Minoan culture dazzled the newcomers, and they adapted much of it for their own. From the Minoans, the Greeks learned to combine copper and tin to make the alloy called bronze. Skilled Minoan workers and their Mycenaean pupils shaped gold, silver, ivory, rock crystal, and other materials into handsome luxuries for the lords of their palaces and citadels. Mycenaean pottery makers closely mimicked the works produced by Minoan masters. Because the Mycenaeans had no written language of their own, they adapted the linear script that Minoan scribes had been using to keep accounts.

The Mycenaeans had special need for a good system of writing. Their royal citadels at Mycenae — and at other places such as Sparta and Pylos — had become centers of trade as well as of defense, and like the Minoans, the Greeks now employed an army of officials to govern and direct production and to keep accounts.

The various Mycenaean states gradually expanded their fleets and thereby multiplied their wealth. This seafaring tradition distinguished them from the powers of the Middle East. The Hittites, the Kassites, and the Mitanni were land-bound, while the aristocrats of Greece commanded ships with which to ply the seas.

Prosper though they did through trade, the Mycenaeans still retained their warlike

Soon after 1200 BC, waves of Dorians swept down from the north into Greece and smashed the great citadels of the Mycenaeans, who for more than two centuries had dominated the region. Surging across the mainland, then seizing Crete, Rhodes, and smaller islands, the invaders killed or drove out the local populations. Some refugees fled to the mountains; others sailed off to resettle on the coast of Asia Minor. These migrations plunged Greece into an era of poverty and backwardness lasting several centuries. But by 750 BC, powerful city-states such as Athens, Sparta, and Corinth had emerged and were starting to colonize throughout the Mediterranean.

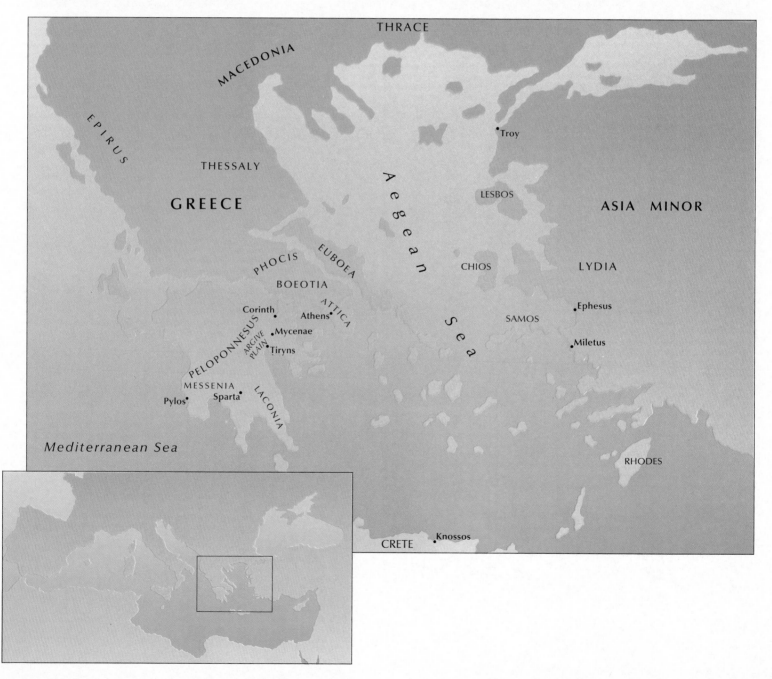

ways, fixed upon weapons and hunting and the glory of battle. They had an appetite for conquest. And the rich Minoan kingdom to the south was there to satisfy it. Around 1450 BC, a volcanic eruption on the island of Thera produced a tidal wave that destroyed most of Crete's ports and irreparably damaged much of its fleet. Suddenly the Minoans had become vulnerable; within the space of 100 years the Minoan empire was reduced to a vassal state. The Mycenaeans became the unquestioned leaders in the Aegean.

At that time, Egypt was emerging as the dominant power of the civilized world. The Egyptians held sway over Palestine and Syria, and their army controlled key overland trade routes that radiated southward into the kingdom of Kush and northward into the Fertile Crescent. Egyptian goods were known from the Baltic Sea to the lowlands of Mesopotamia.

In the fifteenth-century marketplace metal reigned supreme, and Egypt was rich in Nubian gold. The pharaohs exported it to places such as Babylonia, while importing silver from Asia Minor. The interchange of metals and weapons among Europe, Africa, and Asia had made Crete, too, rich in gold — and in silver and copper. The Mycenaeans on the mainland were the eventual inheritors of that wealth.

In this detail from a Greek earthenware vase, plume-helmeted Trojans accept the gift of a giant wooden horse proffered by the Greeks — and thus seal the fate of besieged Troy. Greek soldiers hidden inside the horse are portrayed peering through windows at their unsuspecting enemies. Made during the seventh century BC, the vase with the Trojan horse celebrates victory in a legendary campaign, waged hundreds of years earlier and described in Homer's epic poem the *Iliad*.

The essential metal in the everyday life of the Mycenaeans, however, was bronze, which the Minoans had taught them to make. Mycenaean builders needed bronze tools — axes, adzes, saws, chisels, and hammers — just as the farmers required bronze hoes, plowshares, and sickles. Weapons and armor also required bronze — for swords, daggers, and spearheads, protective leg greaves, even whole suits of body armor. Carvers of ivory and wood demanded fine bronze tools, as did the engravers of signets from semiprecious stones, which the Mycenaeans used to create official seals for their stores of wine, oil, and other valuables. There were some 400 bronzesmiths in the two dozen or so towns governed by the king of Pylos alone.

Yet metal and metal goods were only a portion of the enormous trade enjoyed by the Mycenaeans. Their artisans excelled in making pottery and developed a style that combined the earlier Minoan flair for decoration with a Mycenaean predilection for formal design. In addition, the Mycenaeans exported hides, timber, wine, and olive oil in exchange for precious metals, tin, copper, ivory, linen, papyrus, and rope. Trade with other Mediterranean lands expanded gratifyingly, and the Mycenaeans grew more prosperous by the year. Still, they were pirates at heart. As long as the Egyptians vigorously maintained their military might and the control of major commercial routes, Mycenaean fleets were content to engage in peaceful trade along the Levantine coast. But after 1400 BC, as the Egyptian empire entered its decline, the distinction between trade and piracy became blurred for the lords of Mycenae. Large-scale sea raids became increasingly frequent.

As the Mycenaeans grew aggressive at sea, they also consolidated their power on the mainland. Late in the fifteenth century, a new dynasty evidently assumed the throne in the city of Mycenae, set high on a hill overlooking the fertile plain of Argos to the south and the Aegean beyond. There a succession of ambitious rulers

FORTRESS MYCENAE

The citadel at Mycenae, seat of the most powerful of the early Greek kingdoms, stood on a forbidding eminence overlooking the farmland of the Argive plain in the Peloponnesus. Isolated by a pair of precipitous ravines and surrounded by a wall up to forty feet high and as much as twenty feet thick, the citadel was all but impregnable.

Just inside the narrow western gate, a circular wall of large stones *(lower left)* enclosed the cemetery where several early kings of Mycenae lay buried along with a fabulous trove of gold. A broad ramp and staircase led to the lavish halls and royal apartments crowning the summit of the acropolis *(center)*. In a separate enclave *(foreground),* dozens of humbler structures provided workshops for artisans as well as housing for the king's priests and retainers.

Late in the twelfth century BC, as military pressure on Mycenae grew, its rulers extended the northeastern citadel walls *(upper right)* to enclose a vital cistern and storerooms. For easier access to this area they added a north gate, ensuring that it could be blocked up quickly in case of siege.

enlarged the citadel, turning it into a palace of stepped terraces with sumptuous apartments, halls, and courts, and they erected an immense wall around the entire hill. Huge lions, carved in stone, guarded the gate, and the individual blocks of the wall were so massive that legend would attribute the work to giants. Under the new rulers, such walls became standard features for far-flung Mycenaean fiefdoms, which by the fourteenth century controlled most of mainland Greece. So powerful was this royal house that its princes would come to be known as the Pelopids, or descendants of the hero Pelops, who had fought from a winged war chariot. The name was also given to the peninsula on which Mycenae was situated, the Peloponnesus.

Under the rule of the Pelopids the Mycenaean world enjoyed a remarkable material uniformity. A traveler or wandering bard would encounter the same architecture wherever he might chance to roam. The men would all carry similar weapons, and the women would wear the same kind of jewelry; his hosts everywhere served him food spiced with cardamom, coriander, fennel, sesame, celery, or mint, and thick, syrupy wine that was blended with water for drinking. The plates on which he ate and the goblets from which he drank would all look like pottery he had seen everywhere else.

At the heart of each kingdom lay the palace, home and fortress of the local king. It was a distinctive feature of Mycenaean culture. A visitor could enter this looming mountain of masonry only via an outside ramp that led through the monolithic gates. From there the visitor passed down a long corridor, eventually to arrive at yet another gate, with decorative columns rising on either side. Through the columns lay an open courtyard perhaps thirty feet wide. On the far side of the court was a vestibule that led to the palace's great hall, called the megaron. In the center of the megaron was a large circular hearth, and to the right, facing the hearth, stood the king's throne. Here the Mycenaean ruler would hold court and preside over the ceremonies of state. The megaron's floor was of painted stucco, bordered with a row of gypsum slabs. Its walls were decorated with frescoes dear to a Greek king's heart: chariots in battle, horses with their grooms, beautiful women, and magnificent palaces.

The domestic quarters lay off the courtyard in an upper story. And highest of all was the northernmost corner of the palace, which held several shrine rooms containing cylindrical altars of painted stucco. There, the king might worship Potnia, the Mycenaean earth goddess.

From his citadel, the local ruler controlled every aspect of Mycenaean society. Individuals could own private residences, some of which were substantial and luxurious, with cellars full of wine and oil and stores of painted pottery. The palace, however, served as the main channel of economic distribution, the kingdom's armory, and the public archives.

Although the various kings may have paid allegiance to the ruling dynasty at Mycenae, each was autonomous and regarded his kingdom as something of a personal estate. In each king's administration, a group of aristocrats, often royal relatives, filled the senior offices. They owned slaves and chariots, lived in splendid houses, and were richly appareled. In each fiefdom, members of the landed gentry served as governors in the subordinate towns. The region of Pylos, for example, was divided into sixteen administrative precincts, each of them controlled by a governor and a deputy.

The kings of Mycenae conducted their official business around a circular fireplace in the palace megaron, or great hall. Four wooden columns supported a clerestory that let in light and functioned as a chimney for the smoke that arose from the hearth. Brightly painted frescoes and geometric designs on the megaron walls, floor, and ceiling served to remind foreign emissaries of the great affluence and power of the city's rulers.

Some lands were farmed directly in a king's name, but the majority of landowners simply paid the monarch his tribute out of their annual yields. The Mycenaeans grew wheat and barley and produced olive oil, wine, and figs. They raised bees, some oxen, a few horses, and large numbers of sheep, whose wool was exported. Numerous specialized artisans were employed in the kingdoms — carpenters, masons, shipwrights, bronzesmiths, potters, goldsmiths, weavers, spinners, perfume makers, physicians, and heralds. Women toiled in both domestic and industrial trades — and accounted for most of the slaves. There was no merchant class. The king controlled trade; his official scribes kept track of production, exchange, and shipping.

As the treatment of the dead illustrated, the gulf between the king and his subjects was wide. Ordinary Mycenaeans buried their dead in family chamber-tombs that had been cut into rocky hillsides; they furnished the deceased with a supply of ornaments, weapons, and utensils; they offered a farewell toast, then

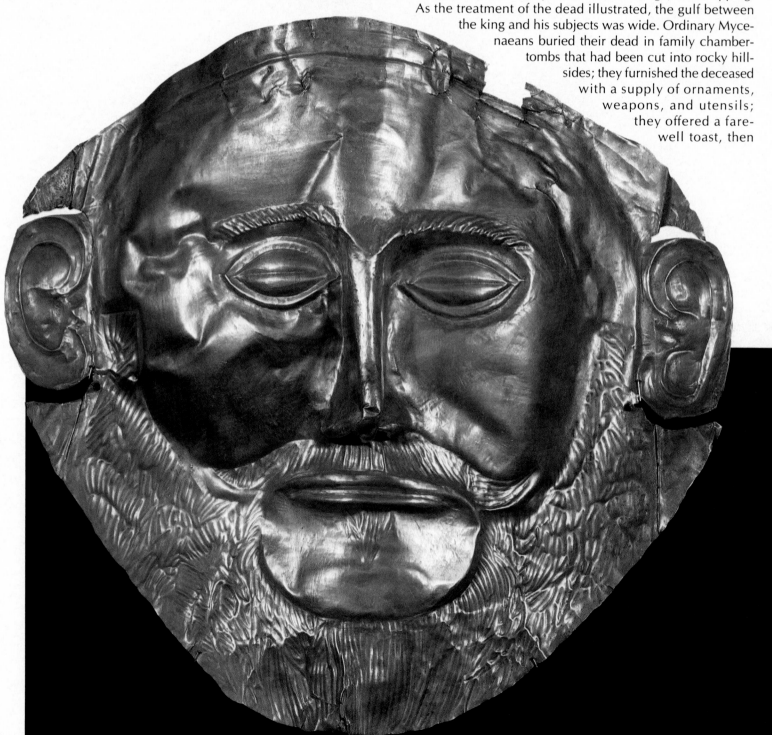

smashed the goblet. When it came time to bury someone else in the vault, they reopened it and pushed the old bones aside to make way for the newly deceased.

Not so the king. His final resting place was an awe-inspiring, earth-covered mound with a cavernous stone interior, shaped like a rounded cone reminiscent of a gigantic beehive. Leading to these mounds were walkways edged by massive stone walls that ascended to an entrance as high as sixteen feet. Immense bronze doorways pivoted on the tomb's threshold, and the entrances were flanked and surmounted by carved stone columns and reliefs, above which rested lintels that could weigh as much as 100 tons. The vast conical chamber itself could be as wide as fifty feet and equally tall; the walls and ceilings were adorned with ornaments of bronze. The king was buried in a pit in the chamber floor. Such was the splendor of the grave goods, which included death masks of gold, that the tombs were known as "treasuries" to those who later robbed them. In addition to the precious objects laid out in the pit with the royal corpse, the Mycenaeans heaped riches on a pyre inside the tomb chamber and burned them. They might then sacrifice lambs, dogs, or horses — and occasionally a human victim.

Foreign gold and other valuables were the lifeblood of the Mycenaean kingdoms, for only by commerce could each king reward his allies and followers, pay his armed forces, and maintain his power and dignity. When trade with Egypt fell off abruptly after 1300 BC, the Mycenaean domains suffered an economic decline that emphasized how dependent they were on older, richer civilizations. The disorder within Egypt, and concurrent trouble within the Hittite kingdom, so quickly reduced Mycenaean wealth that the kings were impelled to take by force what they could no longer acquire by peaceful means. Around 1200 BC, the Mycenaeans launched a fierce and devastating attack on Troy, a prosperous and powerful city situated on mainland Asia Minor at the Hellespont, the narrow gateway between Europe and Asia. According to the *Iliad,* an epic account of the struggle composed around 850 BC, the war dragged on a full decade. "Nine years of mighty Zeus have gone by," the fabled Mycenaean king Agamemnon laments at one point in the saga, "and the timbers of our ships have rotted away and the cables are broken and far away our own

Gold from Royal Tombs

The immense wealth of Mycenae's warrior-kings followed them into the grave. The deceased monarchs were interred with gold masks, breastplates, signet rings, crowns, necklaces, earrings, drinking cups, and engraved disks. Such was the array of riches that the shaft graves cut into the rock of the acropolis at Mycenae became treasure troves of exquisitely crafted gold objects.

Although the Mycenaeans had no gold mines of their own, they acquired large quantities of the precious metal through trade and conquest, or as payment for serving as mercenaries in foreign wars. Their hard-fighting soldiers may have earned Egyptian gold by helping the pharaohs to drive the Hyksos out of the Nile Delta.

Mycenaean goldsmiths were strongly influenced by Crete's sophisticated Minoan artisans. Indeed, some of the goldsmiths who made the beautiful objects on these and succeeding pages were probably Cretans hired or enslaved by their warlike neighbors on the Greek mainland.

Perhaps hoping to preserve the stern features of their dead king for eternity, artisans hammered his likeness into the sheet of gold at left. This death mask — one of several found at Mycenae — was once believed to be that of Agamemnon, legendary leader of the Greek invasion force at Troy in the twelfth century BC. It is more likely that the mask was made for a much earlier Mycenaean ruler, who reigned in the sixteenth century BC. The diadem on the right was buried with a princess at Mycenae and also dates from the 1500s.

wives and our young children are sitting within our halls and wait for us, while still our work here stays forever unfinished as it is.'' But in due course, Agamemnon prevailed, overwhelming the Trojans with the help of the legendary warriors Achilles and Odysseus.

Around the time of the Trojan War, the entire Mediterranean world seethed with war, piracy, and revolution. Several peoples, perhaps including the Phrygians from Thrace, in the Balkans, joined together to destroy the Hittites and occupy their land. A new dynasty, later named the Heraclidae, overthrew Lydia, in southwest Asia Minor. The Philistines conquered the coast of Palestine, ending Egyptian domination of the region.

The Mycenaeans suffered reversals along with the others. Every town that their pirates sacked meant less wealth in the long run to support their institutions. The general disorder cut off trade routes and disrupted commerce. And even as their wealth dwindled and their power disintegrated, the kings of Mycenae saw ominous signs of a growing threat to the north: Tribes were on the move, heading toward their land. The lords prepared for siege. At Tiryns the walls were strengthened; at Mycenae and Pylos cisterns were built inside the walls in case attackers cut off the water sources to the citadels.

But in the end, it was all for nothing. Around 1140 BC, barbarians from central Macedonia swept down into Epirus and Thessaly, driving out the indigenous tribes. These displaced peoples, known collectively as the Dorians, then flooded south and besieged the Mycenaean lords in their citadels; the Dorians' strict tribal organization — and the internal weaknesses of the Mycenaeans — made for easy conquest. One by one the citadels fell. The palaces were looted and destroyed, the rulers put to death, the peoples enslaved or driven away. The Dorian invaders were poor, illiterate nomads, singularly ill suited to their role as inheritors of the Mycenaean world. The Mycenaean settlements offered good pasturage and farmland, and the Mycenaean booty was even better, but the conquerers rejected Mycenaean society and its seafaring traditions. At first, they continued the

These golden masterpieces were buried with Mycenaean royalty. The lion's-head rhyton at left once held libations used in sacred rituals. The ring seals above, used to make marks of ownership, portray battle and hunting scenes. The engraved disks, necklace, and earrings on the facing page were too flimsy to survive frequent handling and probably never adorned the living. Artisans cut them from thin sheets of gold for use as grave offerings.

life-style they had been accustomed to living in the north, roaming from place to place, camping in tents and huts, using wooden utensils, and worshiping small wooden idols. Being shepherds and hunters, they initially favored familiar inland locations and followed their flocks from winter pastures on the plains to summer pastures in the hills.

The invaders were organized into tribes and subdivided into clans, or family groups. Eventually each family received a more-or-less equal allotment of land, and possession conferred membership in the free community. But it was a violent community. The Dorians' rude sense of justice called for the victim of a crime or relatives to seek revenge and retribution, and the resulting feuds were long and bloody. Personal security was at a premium as village fought village; men went about their business armed and ready, and the vendetta reigned supreme.

Bound together by kinship loyalties, the various clans occupied the hilltop ruins of the old Mycenaean citadels or created new settlements on high ground nearby. These fortified sites offered the peoples of the surrounding villages an asylum to which they might flee in time of danger, bringing with them their flocks and belongings. In time of peace, the hilltops were convenient spots for local clans to make sacrifices to the gods and to barter among themselves for local goods.

In their homeland, the nomads had been commanded by tribal kings who earned their status through military accomplishments. These warrior-kings consulted the clan chieftains before taking action. Yet each king made final decisions alone and announced his orders to his troops. When the tribes ceased their wanderings and the various clans settled onto their allotments of land, the monarchies became hereditary. Kings continued to consult an advisory council and summon an assembly of citizens to hear decisions. From their headquarters in the old Mycenaean citadels, they rendered judgments on the squabbles among the surrounding clans. At best, it was a crude political system.

By 1000 BC, the Dorians had overrun the entire Greek mainland, except for a few enclaves. In the wilds of Arcadia, the mountainous region of the central Peloponnesus, bands of strong-willed Myce-

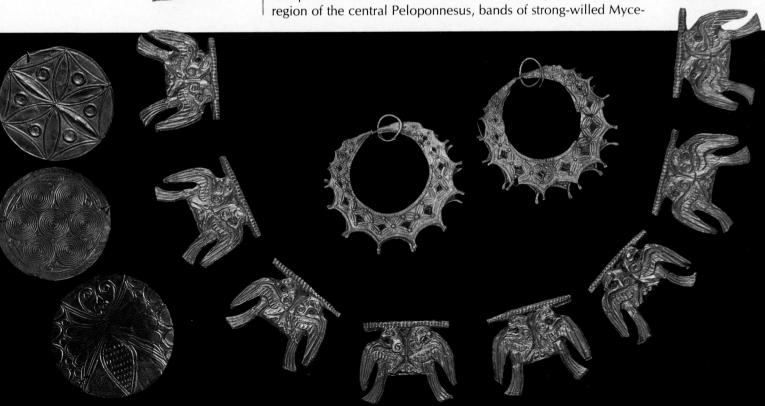

naeans clung to their ways. And across the isthmus from the Peloponnesus, on the peninsula of Attica — an area that had been bypassed by the Dorians as they surged southward — the rising city of Athens had become a haven for refugees.

The importance of Athens extended far beyond the shores of Attica. Its people were tied by language and custom to the thousands of Greeks who had fled the Dorians by sea, voyaging eastward across the Aegean to establish new coastal settlements. Most of those fugitives, like the Athenians themselves, spoke a dialect called Ionic, and they came to be known collectively as the Ionians. With the port of Athens as their base, the sea-wise Ionians began to expand their domain. By 900 BC, they could claim ten thriving settlements on the coast of Asia Minor — including Miletus, Ephesus, and Colophon — and four more on the Aegean islands of Tenedos, Lesbos, Chios, and Samos. Together with Athens, these centers would develop a sophisticated new culture that one day would blossom into the splendid Hellenic civilization of classical Greece.

In song and verse the Ionians preserved the memory of a glorious past. Their bards pointed to the Bronze Age Mycenaean ruins that lay everywhere; these could only be the work of heroes, gods, or giants, and in their epics, the poets challenged their people to emulate the magnificence of the ancient kings. It was a ninth-century Ionian poet, Homer, who composed the sagas that defined the spirit of the new culture: the *Iliad* and the *Odyssey*.

The effect of these two poems was profound. With its affirmation of vigorous action along with heroic sacrifice, the *Iliad* became basic to the Greek concept of life. And the feats of the wandering Odysseus, who ''learned the minds of many distant men, and weathered many bitter nights and days in his deep heart at sea,'' led Greeks everywhere to look back to the glorious accomplishments of their ancestors. The poems formed an essential component of all Greek education, and their canon of aristocratic ideals and of religious belief grew to be a unifying force among the diverse Greeks. Indeed, such was the power of the poems that they played a significant role in the ultimate emergence of Ionian as the universal tongue of the Greek world.

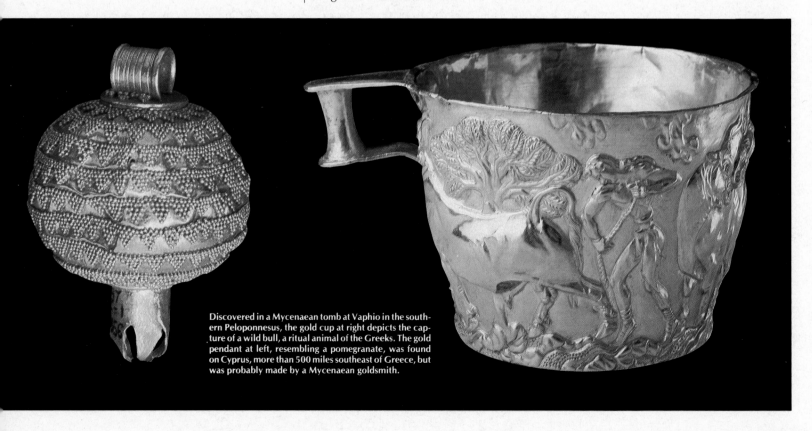

Discovered in a Mycenaean tomb at Vaphio in the southern Peloponnesus, the gold cup at right depicts the capture of a wild bull, a ritual animal of the Greeks. The gold pendant at left, resembling a pomegranate, was found on Cyprus, more than 500 miles southeast of Greece, but was probably made by a Mycenaean goldsmith.

Aside from Athens and the Ionian settlements, a number of other states in the Near East had managed in the upheaval of migration to preserve the legacy of Bronze Age civilization. Egypt, though stripped of its empire, remained a cosmopolitan center. The independent Philistine kingdom in Palestine reached its apex in the eleventh century, and Israel, under King David and King Solomon, achieved its pinnacle a century later. The Syrian states of Hama and Damascus prospered, and to the north of them a neo-Hittite culture rose up. During this period Phoenicia, always a commercial power, sent its mariners throughout the eastern Mediterranean and into waters to the west.

In this oasis of culture, the Phoenicians developed an alphabet from the old hieroglyphs and the syllabaries of Bronze Age linear scripts. And as trade gradually resumed around the Aegean, the Greeks gained this great gift, immediately adapting it to their own language. The alphabet reached Attica about 750 BC, and the Greeks quickly found that it could serve other uses than commerce. They started to write down the oral compositions of their bards, recording Homer's epics and later the works of Hesiod, an eighth-century Boeotian poet. Hesiod's *Theogony* helped to complete the development of a Greek religion that Homer's less systematic theology had begun. Under their tutelage, the Greek people generated an exuberant blend of beliefs centering on the immortals of Mount Olympus. This towering, cloud-shrouded peak in northern Greece had the attributes of a paradise: "There the happy gods spend their delightful days," Homer averred, "shaken by no wind, drenched by no showers, and invaded by no snows." Just as the human community was ruled by kings and aristocrats, so the heavenly world was ruled by a family consisting of nine principal gods: Zeus made his palace on the summit of Olympus, and the other gods dwelled beneath him.

As the great migrations were coming to an end, a new political world was beginning to emerge from the shadows of the dark age. The young Greek settlements in Asia Minor led the way. Surrounded by an alien and potentially hostile world, forced to start their lives afresh, the Ionians contrived a system of government that fostered cooperation and mutual support. So doing, they laid the cornerstone for what would become the central institution of Greek civilization: the polis, the self-governing city-state.

Isolated one from another, the Ionian settlements had to be strongly defensible merely to survive. As in Mycenaean days, the colonists built their cities on hills and clustered their farms and pastures around the bases. Because they were unable at first to make contact with their sister settlements, they became self-contained communities of citizens who focused their social and political energies on the good of their comrades. Instead of accepting autocratic rule, representative councils of elected citizens met formally and regularly to assist the leaders in arriving at decisions. Composed of immigrants from different districts and regions, the settlements became culturally tolerant as well.

On the largely Dorian-dominated mainland, the polis was also developing. Once the Dorians abandoned their wanderings, tribal leaders tended to transform themselves into landed aristocrats. As time went on, a hereditary king found it difficult to reign over this aristocracy. Such was their power that he had no real choice but to abdicate a good portion of his power to a council composed of the more influential nobles. Once acting in a merely advisory capacity, the council began to take on real authority.

In a detail from a terra-cotta vase made about 600 BC, opposing Greek infantrymen, or hoplites, battle at close quarters as a fallen warrior lies bleeding from a leg wound. The shield carried by the man on the left shows the arm brace and handgrip that enabled him to wield this all-important defensive weapon. When arrayed in a tight formation called a phalanx, Greek soldiers fought from behind a protective rampart of overlapping shields.

By the seventh century BC, the aristocratic landowners of mainland Greece had acquired governing power in most of the better-developed regions of the country. Commerce and culture both experienced a revival, and more and more noble families deemed it advantageous to organize their individual holdings into groups of adjacent villages. Such a cluster gradually assumed the characteristics of a budding polis.

In the early polis, citizenship was hereditary, reflecting the nobility's strong sense of kin. The Dorian city of Sparta, for example, grew from the union of four neighboring villages: Pitana, Mesoa, Limnae, and Conooura. Only people descended from one of the old local tribes — Hylleis, Pamphyloi, and Dymanatae — could claim citizenship in Sparta.

The aristocratic origin of early town life put an enduring stamp on Greek urban society everywhere. In Ionian Athens as well, citizenship was a matter of birth. The right to acquire an estate in Attica continued to be the exclusive privilege of the citizen. The flourishing city attracted sizable numbers of metics — free people, both Greek and non-Greek, who resided in Athens or in surrounding Attica. They were permitted — and even encouraged — to engage in commerce or to ply a trade. But they were not eligible for citizenship and could not own land. Noncitizens were required to register as metics within a month or so of their arrival; they had to find an Athenian citizen who would be willing to sponsor them; and they had to pay taxes and fees for the right to live in Athens and trade in the city's marketplace. Metics who failed to abide by the rules risked being sold into slavery. Even those in good standing possessed no political rights. But sweeping changes were in the wind, and the very power of the Greek aristocracy would lead to its decline. A swelling population had begun to pose serious problems in many regions of Greece. The land of a city-state could no longer provide the resources necessary to support the increasing numbers of people. Farms of modest allotment had been subdivided by inheritance, and farm families were unable to grow sufficient crops to support themselves, let alone the burgeoning peasantry. People began to eat the seed that would have been planted for crops, and farmers found themselves forced to borrow seed or food from the wealthy nobles. In return, they pledged their land or their liberty, and an increasing number of them had to forfeit both when they failed to repay the loans. As a result, bitter class conflict broke out in many districts — and spread to the cities. Soon an outcry for redistribution of land echoed throughout Greece.

Revolution was averted in some states by a change in military tactics that tended to give the small landowners a stake in the political future of the polis. Heretofore, cavalry had dominated the armies maintained by the city-states. Because grass was scarce in Greece and horses had to be fed grain most of the year, only wealthy landowners could afford to keep the animals. Thus, making war was an aristocratic endeavor. By the year 700 BC, however, the hoplite, a heavily armed and well-armored infantryman, had replaced the horseman as the key to victory on the battlefield.

Although the foot soldier was as familiar as war itself, the hoplite carried a new kind of shield that made possible the introduction of the phalanx — a densely massed formation of foot soldiers who were trained to run and charge in unison. The phalanx was really no more than a block of men, usually eight ranks deep, arranged so that when one man fell, his place could be taken by the man behind him. In open order, the men in the ranks were spaced at intervals of a yard and a half, but in close order that space was cut in half. And it was in close order that the new shield played its key role.

In earlier times, the Mycenaeans had used a figure-eight shield as high as a man's body, which the warrior carried in front of him like some great moving tower. But these were awkward, heavy, and not ideally suited to close formation. Then, probably in the eighth century, a much lighter, round shield with an armband in the center and a handgrip nearer the rim came into the armory. When held across the chest in the left arm, the new shield covered the left side of a warrior from chin to knees, and if he was in close order, his shield was wide enough to protect the unguarded right side of the man on his left. Massed together, keeping pace by the rhythmic shouts of a war song known as a paean, protected by their shields, foot soldiers in phalanx proved capable of sweeping cavalry or loosely organized infantry from the field.

The ability of one phalanx to overpower or outflank another in battle depended to a large extent on its size. In order to swell the ranks, the aristocrats turned to the yeoman farmers — small landowners who were able to produce enough of a surplus crop to purchase their own weapons and armor. Within the ranks, all men were considered to be equal, and all were equally dependent on one another. What was more, they provided defense for the state, so that each man could feel he had a stake in the future of his polis.

Of all the city-states, Sparta put the phalanx to greatest use. The militant Dorians

Probably intended as gifts for the gods, the bronze figurines pictured here offer glimpses of the ancient Greeks at work and play. Above, a craftsman wearing the skullcap characteristic of ancient artisans hammers away at a new helmet for a Corinthian hoplite. Below, a soldier, who likely once marched on the rim of a vase, strides off to war. On the facing page, a shepherd carries a ram on his shoulders, a youth runs — probably as a contestant in a race — and a rider sits straight-backed on his horse. The figure represents one of the brothers of Helen of Troy and was made as an offering to Zeus.

of Sparta possessed the tactical skills and discipline to expand their influence throughout the Peloponnesus. Sometime after 800 BC, Sparta succeeded in annexing the entire region of Laconia, and those who resisted were reduced to the level of serfs. Around 740 BC, the Spartans waged war against neighboring Messenia, pounding its settlements into dust. They transformed free Messenians into serfs who toiled, according to the Spartan poet Tyrtaeus, "like asses under great burden, rendering half of the plowlands' produce to their masters under bitter constraint." Sparta now had the potential to be the wealthiest, most powerful state in all of Greece. To the rest of the Hellenic world, the message was abundantly clear: The larger the phalanx, the stronger the city.

Sparta stiffened its military resolve in the middle of the seventh century BC, as a response to a rebellion by the conquered Messenians. Such was the danger that the city initiated a succession of political reforms — attributed to a lawmaker named Lycurgus — directed solely at making the phalanx invincible and its hoplites as numerous as possible.

The Lycurgan constitution diminished the franchise of Sparta's two hereditary kings and placed power in the hands of its assembly. This group was composed of every arms-bearing citizen of Sparta — in other words, the hoplites, who were also known as "equals." The kings still commanded the army in war and performed religious duties, but otherwise they sat as regular members of a council of elders who advised the assembly. The councillors were elected in the assembly, and only citizens aged sixty or older were eligible for seats on the council. At regular meetings of the assembly, the council could conduct business and introduce motions, but the final voice belonged to the hoplites.

As part of the reforms, the Spartans also instituted the *ephorate,* a board consisting of five ephors — or overseers –– who were elected every year by the assembly from among the equals. These men supervised the social system and the education of Spartan youths.

The Spartan training was the foundation of the society. Only males were eligible for citizenship or for schooling. A father presented his infant son to the ephors at birth for their inspection. If they found the child in any way defective, they condemned him to death by exposure. If he was healthy, the child was handed into their keeping when he reached the age of seven; they saw to his education at state expense. Living in barracks, the youth mainly engaged in physical sport; after the age of twelve, he was schooled in music and in poetry. At eighteen, the young Spartan started rigorous military training, practicing the hoplite drills and participating in the *krypteria,* a sort of state secret police. When he was nineteen, he was permitted to marry; and at twenty, his training complete, he left his wife — except for conjugal visits — to spend the next ten years of his life in barracks, where he kept himself ever ready for battle. At the age of thirty, his active military service having ended, he faced another trial that would determine his future. Only if he was elected unanimously to one of the men's clubs, or messes,

that were integral to Spartan society could he become a full citizen. With even one dissenting vote, he was relegated to the status of an ''inferior,'' a noncitizen who had no vote in politics. If he was elected, the citizen sat in the assembly and campaigned and dined with the fifteen members of his club until he had attained the age of sixty, at which point he could be elected to the council.

Every equal was assigned an estate of fixed size on state-owned property. The estate was farmed not by the citizen, who devoted his energies to military and public affairs, but by state-owned serfs, known as helots. To maintain his citizenship, the equal was obligated to donate a portion of his annual yield to his club. Thus, through the Lycurgan reforms, the single-minded Spartans became the finest hoplites of their age — one Spartan foot soldier was equal to about a dozen from any other state.

But the cost was enormous. Forbidden by law to engage in economic activity of any kind, the Spartan citizen was dependent for all his needs on helots and on a group of noncitizens called ''the dwellers around,'' a vast underclass whom he held in contempt. The Spartan's life was organized by the state, which he blindly followed. An insidious fear of corruption through contact with the outside world pervaded Spartan life, and this obsession was made even worse by the fear of revolt from within: The function of the *krypteria*, in which citizens in training served, was to spy on and terrorize the helots. By 600 BC, Sparta had become completely introverted — yet fiercely aggressive toward any neighbors that might appear to be threatening its preservation.

Athens was suffering in the seventh century BC from the same problems that afflicted most other regions of Greece: a growing population, a shortage of food, and a resulting indebtedness that forced many citizens into slavery. Powerful aristocratic clans controlled the city, grew ever richer from the misfortunes of their smaller neighbors, and engaged in bitter disputes among themselves. Wealthy landowners gobbled up the small farms that had belonged to their fellow citizens and reduced the poorer among them to penury. By the turn of the century, Athens had arrived at the brink of civil war. So the Athenians appointed in 594 BC a citizen-poet by the

name of Solon to be its Lycurgus — its lawgiver — and granted him extraordinary power to revise the laws.

Solon forgave all outstanding debts and forbade further debt slavery for Athenians. He returned the small landowners to their farms and to the status of free citizens, and he abolished the hereditary requirement for holding public office. Aristocrats were not disenfranchised. But now, because a man could hold government position by virtue of the wealth he possessed, the elite were joined in power by the commoners.

Other Greek city-states were being swept by the tide of reform. In Thebes, Locri, Catana, and Chalcidice, lawgivers were relaxing the laws of heredity, extending the franchise, and attempting to regularize the administration of justice by the councils. But along with the reformers, a tough new breed of ruler had emerged to impose order — the tyrant.

When a man gained power by force, the Greeks called his regime a *monarchia,* or "sole rule," and the man himself a *tyrannus,* after a Lydian word for *king* or *ruler* that had come into general use. Naturally, wealth — or at least the promise of wealth — was a prerequisite of tyranny; there was no profit for a tyrant in an impoverished and struggling village. "In general," explained the historian Thucydides, "tyrannies were established in the city-states as revenues were increasing, when Greece was becoming more powerful and progressing in the acquisition of capital wealth."

Indeed, it was the Lydian tyrant Gyges who first made money out of electrum, a natural alloy of gold and silver that could be found throughout Asia Minor. Gyges began minting coins sometime between 687 and 652 BC. Soon after, the nearby states of Miletus and Ephesus began issuing electrum currency imprinted with their state emblems — a lion's head, and a bee or a stag. Other states followed their example, some even issuing coins of pure silver. Before long, coinage reached the mainland, where it contributed to a continuing epidemic of tyrannies in the seventh and sixth centuries.

Some states that had, like Sparta, already equalized property distribution proved immune to the threat of tyranny. But other, more commercially minded states fell victim. In Sicyon, Corinth, and Megara, all centers of commercial expansion, a rapid influx of wealth exacerbated the problems that so many city-states had been struggling to overcome.

In Corinth, around 650 BC, the tyrant Cypselus overthrew the aristocratic clan called the Bacchiadae. Cypselus's own mother was a Bacchiad who had married into another noble Corinthian house; her son joined the citizen army, became its commander, killed the Bacchiadae ruler, and exiled the rest of the clan, redistributing their land among his hoplite supporters. He ruled Corinth for thirty years and was succeeded by his son Periander, who was so disliked that he felt the need of a bodyguard whenever he was abroad in the city.

Nevertheless, Corinth attained a pinnacle of its wealth and prosperity under Periander. He laid a roadway, called the *diolklos,* for hauling ships across the Corinthian isthmus, connecting central Greece to the Peloponnesus. He made plans to construct a canal across the isthmus. He passed laws that discouraged the movement of population from the countryside into Corinth, put controls on expenditures, and attempted to reduce extravagance, immorality, and the purchase of slaves. But Periander also displayed the tyrant's vices. He murdered his wife and banished his son

Lycophron, only to call him back after many years. The citizens of the town in which Lycophron had lived out his exile murdered him before he was able to make the return trip to Corinth.

These tyrants, and others like them, were able men. In a number of cities such as Corinth, they provided a measure of relatively stable government throughout a century marked by economic expansion. Small-scale manufacturing was taking hold in parts of Greece. In Asia Minor, where the land was conducive to raising sheep, a textile industry was thriving: Miletus garnered renown for its fine woven wool, its embroidered hats and robes. Aegina, together with Euboean Chalcis, became famous for bronze work. On the mainland, Corinth took advantage of its two harbors, one in the Saronic, the other in the Corinthian Gulf, to become a flourishing marketplace and center of industry. Megara, whose stony soil compelled its people to resort to manufacturing, produced coarse woolens and heavy potteries. Attica, still essentially an agricultural region, had started to export olive oil, wine, and beautifully decorated vases.

But the tyrant did little to distribute that growing wealth; he did not fundamentally alter the social conditions that produced him. In the end, under the rule of tyrants, the rich grew richer, land remained in the hands of the few, and the explosive overpopulation of the city-state became worse still.

With wealth and poverty sitting uneasily side by side, with rich nobles, slaves, laborers, and the new merchants all vying for a say in how their lives should be run, city governors sought some means to relieve the pressure. The remedy, for many of them, was a time-tested one: migration. Since the middle of the eighth century, waves of Greek colonists had been spreading across the Aegean, seeking new lands in which to satisfy their yearnings.

The settlers took with them sacred fire from the hearths of their cities, but a Greek colony was an *apoikia,* or "settlement far from home." Once the colony was established, the connection between it and the founding city was severed. With only a few exceptions, founding cities exercised no political rights over the colonies, and in fact took measures to ensure that the emigrants remained where they were. Colonists were not allowed to return home and enjoy the privileges of citizenship unless their colony disintegrated, and some cities refused to accept failed settlers even then.

The colonists ventured in all directions: north toward the Black Sea; southwest to North Africa; and west to Sicily, Italy, southern France, and Spain. Colonists from Chalcis were the first to land on the Italian boot, where they settled Pithecusae in the Bay of Naples around 750 BC, and then Cumae and Neapolis. Tribespeople known as the Graii were among the Chalcidian colonists, and from them the indigenous Romans derived the word *Greek,* which they used to describe the newcomers. The Greeks in turn referred to themselves as Hellenes after the Homeric name for their land.

Sparta, satisfied by the land it took from the conquered Messenia, uninterested in trade, and fearful of social pollution, founded only one colony—Tarentum, on the instep of Italy. Corinth founded the greatest colonies. It seized the island of Corfu, then moved on to Sicily, and in 734 BC established on the nearby island of Ortygia the city of Syracuse, which came to rival the power and prestige of the most important city-states in Greece itself.

To the northeast, the Greeks colonized the Hellespont, the Propontis, and the Black Sea region. From these colonies the Macedonians, a backward Greek-speaking people, slowly acquired the civilization of their southern kin; one day they would conquer Greece itself under their King Philip II and then much of the world under his son, Alexander the Great. And on the strategic Bosporus Sea, Megara first established Byzantium, destined a thousand years later, as Constantinople, to become the capital of the Roman Empire.

The colonies conducted a lively trade. Cumae manufactured vases and metalware to exchange with the Latins. Colonies surrounding the Black Sea in an almost unbroken chain sent back to Greece a broad range of products: fish, timber, dyes, wheat, metals, cattle, and slaves.

In the middle of the seventh century, the Egyptians permitted a group of Ionian traders to establish a port at Naucratis, on a branch of the Nile. The trade center soon became well known for importing papyrus and other goods in exchange for olive oil and wine. But Naucratis's greatest imports were intellectual. Babylonian and Egyptian scholarship, as well as the elementary facts of geometry and astronomy, reached the Greeks through Naucratis, helping to stimulate the birth of Greek science and philosophy.

The impact of these wide and diverse cultures on Greek thought was enormous. Even more important, the colonial expansion of trade greatly enhanced the prosperity of the polis. The merchant fleet — and the workshops, warehouses, and markets that the colonies engendered — contributed substantially to the maintenance of the city-state.

By 550 BC, the polis was as central to Greek life as the palace had been to the Mycenaeans. Within its shelter, the Greeks would pursue their politics, their art, their literature, their religion, and their livelihoods. But the polis, the city-state, was not merely a physical site; it was an idea as well, an idea that would tap tremendous energies in the centuries to come, an idea that in time would command almost total dedication on the part of its citizens. When the polis became firmly established, with its notion of good citizenship and its open market, Greece was transformed into the first truly western civilization, the classic model for Rome and the modern nation-state.

THE MACHINES OF WAR

In the tumultuous epoch launched by the barbarian migrations, warfare came to be the rule among nations rather than the exception. The first civilizations had all endured periods of strife, but most of their energies had gone into building cities rather than sacking them. Once the tribes bordering the civilized world brought their combative genius to bear early in the second millennium, however, no power dared neglect the study of war. Henceforth, rulers would be quick to abandon the comforts of court for the rigors of the field. And the inventions of greatest consequence would be new modes of destruction.

The first breakthrough in the machinery of warfare — the two-wheeled chariot introduced by Asiatic tribes — reached the height of its glory in 1285 BC at the Battle of Kadesh *(pages 90-91),* where the Egyptians and Hittites deployed thousands of the highly maneuverable vehicles. The men, horses, and equipment that made up these huge forces were expensive to maintain, however, and such clashes sapped the resources of the two powers. Soon they concluded a peace treaty and relaxed their guard, creating an opening along the Mediterranean coast for the migratory bands known as the Sea Peoples. With their advent, the galley came to rival the chariot as an instrument of aggression.

The Sea Peoples were not the first to rely on fighting ships, of course. The Egyptians in particular took pride in their fleet, and around 1185 they bested the Sea Peoples in one of the first recorded naval battles *(pages 92-93).* Yet the defeated forces proved resilient. Among their number were the Philistines, who settled in Palestine, where they ended Egyptian domination of the region and entered into an epic struggle with the Israelites and Judeans.

Several centuries later, the rival powers of Palestine were overwhelmed by the Assyrians — among the first and most formidable exponents of total war. Following the example of his predecessors, Assyria's King Sennacherib waged campaigns in Palestine directed mainly against population centers. Equipped with a mighty siege machine, his forces took the fortified Judean city of Lachish in 701 *(pages 94-95),* reducing to submission the defiant King Hezekiah.

For all its grim efficiency, the Assyrian army had a flaw: It relied heavily on foreign conscripts of sometimes-questionable loyalty. It remained to the Greek city-states to develop dedicated, strictly disciplined citizen armies. Nowhere was that goal pursued more rigorously than in Sparta, where boys trained together from the age of seven. Such regimentation made the Spartans masters of the phalanx, the close formation in which the men themselves functioned as a machine *(pages 96-97).* The militancy of Sparta transcended family ties, inspiring the tale of the mother who commanded her son as he left for battle to return clasping his shield — or lying upon it.

In 701 BC, the Assyrian king Sennacherib, intent on subjugating the land of Judah, brought his army to bear against its proud ruler, Hezekiah. While Hezekiah held out at Jerusalem, Sennacherib targeted the other Judean strongholds — chief among them the walled city of Lachish. Set high on a bluff, Lachish was vulnerable only at its southwest corner, where a saddle of land linked the bluff to a nearby hill. Atop that rise the Assyrians made their camp.

The first task of the assault force was to build stone ramps for moving heavy siege machines up the slope to the foot of the city walls. Once the ground was prepared, the Assyrians held the upper hand. In the final drive, they wheeled several armored battering rams up the inclines. Each machine had two levels: Soldiers crouching on the lower level pounded the battlements with a metal-tipped ram, while those on the platform above took aim at the Judeans or doused the vehicle's wooden frame with water to counter the torches hurled by the foe. At one point, the Judeans set some chariots afire and pushed them over the ledge; but the rams withstood the punishment. At last the wall was breached and the city razed.

Isolated now at Jerusalem, Hezekiah yielded. "He himself I shut up like a caged bird," Sennacherib boasted. Besides rich tributes, the battle yielded Judean captives, who were deported to Nineveh, where some were put to work on Sennacherib's new palace. There they could witness again the fall of Lachish, chiseled in alabaster on the palace walls.

In the eighth century BC, the Greek city-state of Sparta developed a citizen army of prodigious strength. By century's end, the red-cloaked Spartan troops had pushed westward from their homeland of Laconia into the plain of Messenia, where they were locked in a bitter struggle with the Messenian phalanxes.

For all its fury, the series of battles was governed by a certain protocol. The phalanx — a mass of soldiers usually eight men deep and up to 200 men wide — could not function on hilly terrain, so contests were waged on fairly level ground. And the lines generally met head on; unless one force possessed vastly superior numbers, it could not envelop the foe without endangering its own flank.

Before battle, the two sides placed their best soldiers up front. Armored in bronze, each of these infantrymen, or hoplites, wore a sword at his belt and carried a spear in his right hand and a shield in the other. Those behind were armed in like fashion and stood ready to step up as the men in front of them fell; until then, their task was to press forward, adding impetus to the mass. As they closed with the enemy, the men sang hymns to strengthen their resolve.

In the end the Spartans prevailed. They had fought with a keen élan, summed up by one of their own, the soldier-poet Tyrtaeus: "This is a common good for the city and all its people, when a man stands in the front line unyielding . . . staking his life and his enduring heart, and standing by the next man, encourages him with his words."

THE MEDITERRANEAN TRADERS

4 Greek writers of the first millennium BC liked to refer to the Phoenicians and Etruscans as "pirates." It was not that mariners from these lands behaved any worse than the general run of ancient sailors, including the early Greeks themselves: Seafarers from every corner of the Mediterranean engaged in nautical larceny when unprotected merchant vessels hove into view. The threat of piracy was one of the risks of doing business by sea.

What annoyed the Greeks was the astounding success of these rival maritime peoples in establishing lucrative trade routes through much of the Mediterranean basin. Beginning about 1000 BC, the Phoenicians boldly ventured forth from their cities, which lay along a narrow strip of the sea's eastern shore — the area that eventually became known as Lebanon — to explore and then establish trading posts and colonies in the farthest reaches of the known world. Phoenician merchants in their deep-hulled ships sailed past Sicily — long the western limit for most navigators — to brave the unknown winds, tides, and currents of the western Mediterranean. And they founded settlements just about everywhere they touched: all along the North African coast, in Spain, and on Malta, Sicily, Sardinia, Corsica, and the Balearic Islands. Then they dared to sail through what the Greeks called the Pillars of Hercules — known much later as the Strait of Gibraltar — and explore the Atlantic coasts of Africa and Europe. The Phoenician navigators may have even circumnavigated the African continent, a bold feat that would not be repeated for 2,000 years. These traders were, in short, the most adventurous and determined of the ancient Mediterranean world.

In about 700 BC they were joined in their maritime ventures by another trading folk, the Etruscans, whose rich city-states lay along the western coast of the Italian peninsula, close to the Tyrrhenian Sea. The civilization of this remarkable people would eventually be absorbed by the growing power of Rome. But for a time the Etruscans shared with the Phoenicians the growing trade in the western Mediterranean, profiting by trade in the metals — copper, lead, tin, and especially iron — that they mined from their own hills. For more than 100 years, the Phoenicians and Etruscans between them outclassed the understandably envious Greeks as naval and mercantile powers in the waters beyond Sicily. And it was they who largely shaped events and set cultural patterns around the rim of the western Mediterranean for centuries to come.

The Phoenicians did not start as seafarers. Their ancestors were part of a large group of Semitic people who, by 3000 BC, had migrated into a region later to be known as Canaan, which encompassed Syria and Palestine as well as the Lebanese coast. For hundreds of years, most of the Canaanites remained land-bound people who gained their living from herding sheep and growing crops in the fertile valleys of their adopted homeland.

But some of the Canaanites who had settled along the craggy shore, in the narrow corridor between the sea and the Lebanese mountains, turned to trade. These ancestors of the Phoenicians had a superb resource: choice lumber from the large stands of cedar, cypress, and pine that forested the slopes of their mountains. The trees afforded a seemingly inexhaustible supply of timber for building the traders' own ships — and for export. In addition, the rocky coast with its promontories and offshore islands provided unusually fine anchorages.

During the first centuries of Canaanite shipping, the port towns along the Mediterranean shore evolved into small city-states, each with its own monarch; their chief trading partner was Egypt, only a few hundred miles down the coast. In that tree-poor land, builders prized the Canaanite lumber, especially that cut from the fabled cedars of Lebanon. Planks hewn from these majestic trees, some of which grew as tall as 135 feet, were used to build hundreds of the ships that plied the Nile. As early as the twenty-seventh century BC, an Egyptian wrote that a huge consignment of Lebanese cedar, forty shiploads' worth, had provided enough timber to make three large vessels — and the doors of the royal palace. The Egyptians also pressed oil from the fragrant wood for soaking the cloths that bound the mummified bodies of their dead kings.

So attractive, in fact, were the small Canaanite kingdoms and their wealth that by the sixteenth century Egypt had them under its own powerful control, not only trading with them but exacting tribute to fill its treasuries. The Egyptian presence was apparent in Byblos, the earliest active port in what would become Phoenicia. In addition to its tributes, Byblos sent forth shiploads of cedar and large jars filled with wine and olive oil, as well as the skilled laborers who built the pharaoh's ships and the mariners who helped to sail them. Byblos in turn became a distribution center for Egyptian goods, in-

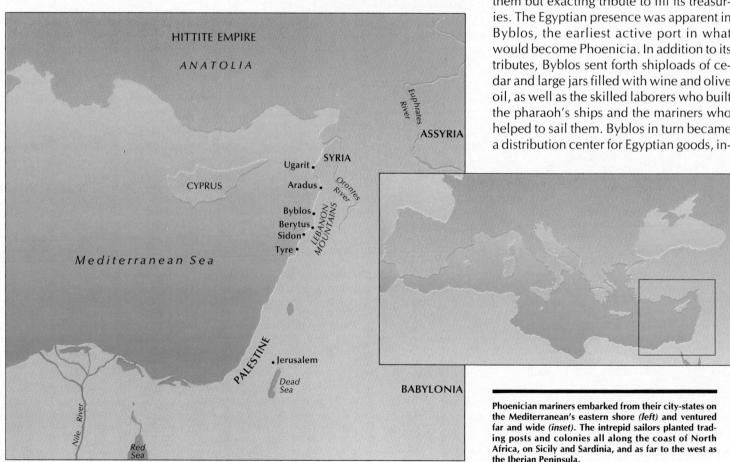

Phoenician mariners embarked from their city-states on the Mediterranean's eastern shore *(left)* and ventured far and wide *(inset)*. The intrepid sailors planted trading posts and colonies all along the coast of North Africa, on Sicily and Sardinia, and as far to the west as the Iberian Peninsula.

cluding papyrus. (This circumstance led the Greeks to adopt the name of the city as their word for *book*. From *byblos* eventually came the English word *Bible*.) And in imitation of their southern masters the people of the city built an Egyptian temple, adopted Egyptian gods, and wore Egyptian dress.

The Egyptian yoke held for four centuries before a series of political convulsions wracked the Near East and set the Phoenician city-states free to expand as maritime powers. The Israelites took control of the hill country of western Palestine. A people called the Aramaeans moved into western and northern Syria. Then the polyglot raiders known to the Egyptians as the Sea Peoples overran western Syria and razed the Phoenician cities of Tyre and Sidon. One group of the Sea Peoples, the warlike Philistines, threatened Egypt shortly after 1200 BC and then occupied a broad swath of the Palestinian coastal plain.

After a century of this violent upheaval, the Phoenician city-states emerged as virtually all that remained of the old Canaanite culture. They no longer had access to the arable lands over the mountains, formerly cultivated by friendly fellow Canaanites. Instead, they faced the distinctly unfriendly Aramaeans inland to the east, while other alien folk hemmed them in to the north and south. The sole avenue that offered growth and prosperity was the sea.

Fortunately for the Phoenicians, the sea was theirs. Their old masters, the Egyptians, were weak from fighting off the Philistines and other sea raiders. The greatest maritime power of the previous era, Mycenaean Greece, had been driven to its knees by Dorian invasions from the north. And in 975 BC, the Israelites under King David — who had united much of Syria and Palestine under his rule — fell upon and defeated the Philistines on the Palestinian coast. Now the Phoenicians saw their chance for maritime supremacy, and they seized it.

The city of Tyre led the way. The Phoenicians rebuilt Tyre after its devastation by the Sea Peoples, then annexed a pair of small, rocky islands a few hundred yards offshore. Workers filled in the gulf between these islets with boulders and rubble, making them one. Seawalls went up on the north and south shores of the new island to form two harbors. In between, tightly packed houses — constructed variously of brick, stone, clay, and timber — towered up to six stories high, presenting a sight so grand that the biblical prophet Isaiah described Tyre as "the crowning city, whose merchants are princes, whose merchants are the honorable of the earth."

Tyre was not the Phoenicians' only island port. A hundred or so miles to the north stood Aradus. Only a mile in circumference, this tiny, rocky bastion was inhabited by a people known for their skills as both sailors and engineers. According to the Greek historian Strabo, the Arvadites made up for their lack of freshwater wells by tapping springs that lay at the bottom of the sea between the mainland and their island. They covered the springs with a lead housing to keep out the salt water and then, through an attached leather enclosure, piped the fresh water up to the surface, where boats collected it.

From Tyre, Aradus, and such other ports as Berytus (Beirut) and Sidon, the Phoenicians launched fleets of merchant vessels. The merchantmen had a rounded, tublike hull shape that increased cargo space. Their warships, on the other hand, tended to be long and slim, built for speed. In time, these war galleys bore at the prow a new and revolutionary weapon, a ram that could puncture the hull of an enemy vessel.

A Canaanite, richly robed and with elaborately plaited hair, appears in a mosaic that decorated a temple built by the Egyptian pharaoh Ramses III in the twelfth century BC. The man was probably held in Egypt as an aristocratic prisoner of war.

For propulsion, both types of ship carried a mast and a single square sail. But on windless days — common during the Mediterranean summer — the crews could lower the sail, unstep the masts, and take up the oars. Originally the oarsmen were all seated on the same level inside the ship. But as warships grew in size, a new rowing alignment was developed to add power and conserve space. In this arrangement, the oarsmen sat on two different levels, their seats staggered above and below. Ships with this double configuration were called biremes. In later centuries a further refinement, the trireme, was perfected, with rowers on three levels.

At first, most of the Phoenicians' ships remained in the familiar waters of the eastern Mediterranean. Their vessels sailed to Cyprus, less than 150 miles away, to trade for the island's plentiful copper. West of Cyprus, at the Greek island of Rhodes, their traders bartered for wool that had been brought from the nearby Anatolian

Artistry in Glass

The Phoenicians excelled in making objects of glass. Learning their techniques from the Egyptians, Phoenician artisans came to rival and even to surpass their teachers in skill.

The method that they used was later called core-forming. In the first step, the artisans shaped a core of clay on a metal rod; then they wound "trails" of viscous, semimolten glass around the core, as illustrated below. They continued to add glass, often in contrasting colors, until the finished object had been built up. To create decorative patterns, they scored the still-soft glass with a pointed implement. The last step was to scrape the core of clay from inside the finished piece.

Using this incremental technique, the artisans made astonishingly varied glass objects. The Egyptians and subsequently the Phoenicians were famous for their necklaces of glass beads, which were made in great numbers and sold throughout the Mediterranean world. But they were capable of making more imaginative and even whimsical creations, including the expressive face at right, which formed the pendant of a necklace, and the colorful fish-shaped vessel, intended for an Egyptian lady's cosmetics, that is shown on page 104.

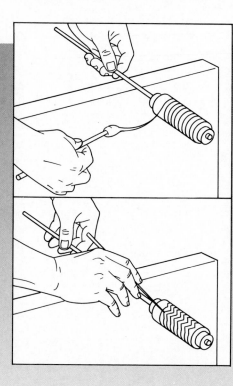

Pendant from Carthage

mainland. Sailing southwest from home to the Egyptian port of Memphis, the Phoenicians continued to barter for papyrus, linen, and ivory.

Gradually the navigators grew more venturous, striking out westward along the Egyptian coast, thus exploring the shores of what came to be called Libya and Tunisia. Eventually they jumped across open stretches of the Mediterranean to the islands of Malta, Sicily, and Sardinia. The more daring open sea voyages forced the sailors to refine their navigational skills. It is said that they were the first to undertake regular trips beyond the sight of land and to travel at night, steering by the stars. More often, however, they proceeded cautiously, sailing only when they had light, staying close to the shore, and covering no more than twenty-five miles a day.

For the purposes of safety and practicality, the sailors established a network of anchorages. Most of these places were simply suitable beaches or coves, but others were more elaborate, constructed for ships caught far from home by the winter storms that usually limited the sailing season to half the year. These anchorages were ports, where ships could be brought up onto dry land in order to be reconditioned and crews could be quartered and fed. The ports required permanent staffs to handle administration and at least small groups of armed men to provide defense. During the late tenth century BC, as they voyaged ever farther westward, the Phoenicians founded more than a dozen permanent posts along the North African coast that in time became bustling towns. Cyrene was one of the first, then Lepcis and Oea, later known as Tripoli. Then came Utica and Hippo, and finally Carthage.

By the eighth century these merchant sailors had managed to make themselves at home in large sections of the western Mediterranean, a realm explored before only fitfully by a few Mycenaean navigators. Then, sailing through the Strait of Gibraltar, 2,500

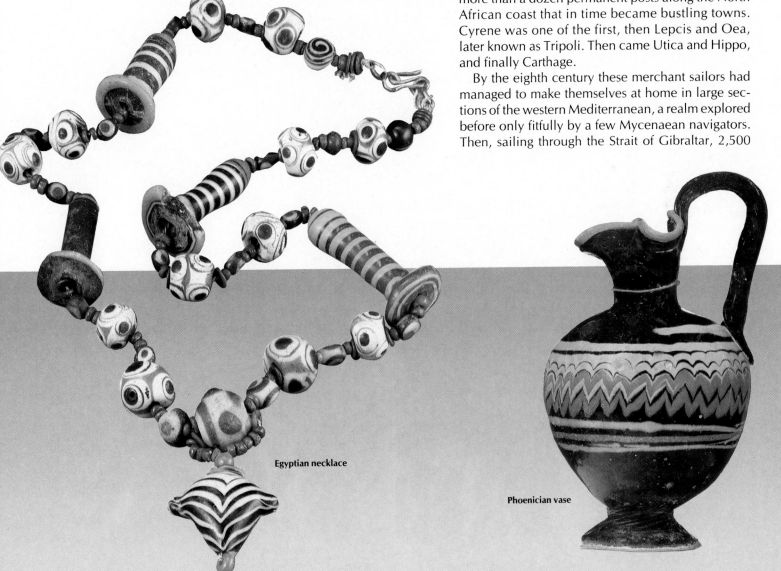

Egyptian necklace

Phoenician vase

miles from their home ports on the Lebanese coast, they turned south and began to trade with the people of the Moroccan coast. Here, according to the Greek historian Herodotus, bargaining tended to follow certain rituals. The Phoenicians would spread their wares on a beach, then return to their ships and start a smoky fire to signal their presence. The local people would go down to the beach, inspect the goods, put down what they felt was an appropriate amount of gold, and then withdraw. The Phoenicians would return and collect the gold if they deemed it adequate; if not, they would go back to their ships while the buyers added to the pile of payment. Surprised at the efficacy and fairness of this silent bargaining, Herodotus wrote, "Neither side cheats the other, because they [the sellers] did not touch the gold until it seemed to them to have reached the value of the goods, and the others did not touch the goods until the Phoenicians had taken up the money."

Beyond Gibraltar the bold traders also turned north and, sailing less than 100 miles up the coast of the Iberian Peninsula, discovered an island that gave easy access to the rich silver mines of southern Spain. On the northern tip of this slender, thirteen-mile-long island the Phoenicians established a trading post. They called it Gadir, which evidently meant "fort" in their language; later it became better known by its Roman name, Gades, then by its modern name, Cadiz. It is also thought that the Phoenicians founded a second outpost on the Iberian coast, from which they voyaged north to Ireland and England, trading for tin and other metals.

The Phoenicians profited handsomely from these far-ranging mercantile ventures. Trade in the Mediterranean world was increasingly dominated by the demand for metals: gold and silver, of course, but also copper, the tin needed to make copper into more useful bronze, and iron for yet harder tools and weapons. For valuable cargoes of metals, the Phoenicians traded goods of lesser worth. The profit margin was huge and amply repaid the merchant voyagers for their long journeys.

What these merchants had to trade was a range of attractive goods fashioned by artisans in their own coastal cities, who worked with their plentiful raw materials, such as cedar and flax, and with imported metals, ivory, and gems. Their techniques and designs tended to be imported; there seems to have been no pronounced Phoenician style. It was from the Egyptians, for example, that the craftsmen learned to make

Egyptian glass fish

inexpensive beads, bottles, and bowls of glass. Nonetheless, the Phoenician artisans were prolific — and expert. The metallurgists of Sidon and other cities were particularly skilled. They excelled in fashioning ivory into ornaments and gold and silver into elegant jewelry and other objects that excited even the haughty Greeks. In Homer's *Iliad*, for instance, a silver bowl offered as a prize for runners at a warrior's funeral games draws lavish praise: "For its loveliness it surpassed all others on earth by far, since skilled Sidonian craftsmen had wrought it well, and Phoenicians carried it over the misty face of the water."

But the Phoenicians' most famous products were textiles. Out of cloth woven from cotton, flax, and wool they created elaborate garb: close-fitting tunics, long flowing robes, pointed caps. In vivid contrast to the plain garments of the Egyptians and the Greeks, the Phoenician fabrics were dyed in brilliant colors ranging from a soft pink to a lustrous deep violet. The name *Phoenicia*, in fact, probably derives from a Greek word meaning "purple dye," and *Canaan* may come from an older Semitic word with roughly the same import.

The source of the dye that yielded such handsome clothing was a small sea mollusk called the murex. Two closely related species of this spiny-shelled creature, both only a few inches long, were collected from the waters just offshore. Workers smashed the shells, extracted the mollusks, and placed them in vats. As the dead creatures decayed, they secreted a yellowish liquid that, boiled for varying lengths of time, produced dyes of differing hues.

The yield from each murex was minuscule: an average of two drops, or one-tenth of a milligram. The resulting dyes were so highly prized that the secretion was considered worth at least ten times its weight in gold. So valued was cloth dyed the deepest shade of violet that for centuries it was called "royal purple" and in many regions was reserved for kings and others of high rank.

The dye factories were situated on the leeward side of cities such as Tyre and Sidon to spare the citizenry the pungent odor of decaying mollusks. Thousands upon thousands of the animals were needed; enormous mounds of crushed shells piled up next to the dye factories, and eventually the murex became virtually extinct in Mediterranean waters.

In addition to sending abroad textiles, Phoenician cities also exported their considerable expertise in construction. Their people built one of the ancient world's most famous buildings: the great Temple of Solomon in Jerusalem.

Phoenician involvement in the temple stemmed from an earlier exchange with the Israelites. When David was crowned king of Israel in 1000 BC, King Hiram of Tyre, as a gesture of diplomacy, sent a contingent of carpenters and stonemasons to Jerusalem — along with a quantity of cedar — to make the victorious Israelite monarch a sumptuous palace. When King David died and his son Solomon ascended the throne, the new king resolved to have a great temple built. Naturally he turned to Hiram and the skilled workers of Tyre. This time, according to the Bible, it was strictly a business proposition. "I will pay you for your servants such wages as you set," wrote Solomon.

The Bible quotes Hiram's enthusiastic response: "I am ready to do all that you desire in the matter of cedar and cypress timber. My servants shall bring it down to the sea from Lebanon; and I will make it into rafts to go by sea to the place that you direct and I will have them broken up there, and you shall receive it." For his part, Solomon would give Hiram an annual payment of 20,000 "measures of wheat for food to his household, and 20 measures of pure oil."

Constructed by Israelite laborers working under the direction of Phoenician architects and craftsmen, the temple included a lofty central hall made of smoothly shaped stone slabs, side chambers that stood three stories high, and an inner sanctuary paneled with cedar from floor to ceiling. Two elaborate bronze pillars guarded the entrance.

After completion of the temple in about 960 BC, the two kings embarked on another joint enterprise. Hiram, in return for payment not specified in the records, agreed to equip Solomon with a navy. Composed of Tyre-built ships manned by Phoenician sailors, the new Israelite fleet was based near what came to be called Aqaba on the Red Sea. From there it apparently sailed to such exotic and mysterious regions as Ophir, which may have been located on the coast of Africa or Arabia. Wherever it was, it seems to have had a wondrous variety of items for export. According to the Bible, King Solomon's Phoenician fleet returned from Ophir with gold and silver, ivory, and apes and baboons.

As the Phoenicians sailed abroad, they carried to their trading posts and new settlements their traditional religious beliefs and practices. Although the names of the gods in the pantheon varied from city to city, a triad of deities prevailed throughout: a principal god known as El, Baal, or Melqart; an earth-mother goddess sometimes

A lioness mauls a youth in a masterly Phoenician ivory carving dating from the eighth century BC. Such carvings, often decorated with jewels and gold leaf, were used as inlaid panels in the wooden furniture for which Phoenician craftsmen became famous. To execute these ivory works, the artisans of Tyre and other cities imported elephant tusks from their trading posts along the African coast — especially from Carthage, where elephants were raised on farms.

called Ashtart; and a young god, often Ashtart's son and usually called Adonis, whose yearly death and resurrection reflected the annual cycle of the seasons.

Throughout the Mediterranean, Phoenicians worshiped these three deities in great temples, which resembled that designed for Solomon, and in humbler open-air sanctuaries, often situated on hills. According to Greek and Israeli accounts, it was customary in some city temples for respectable women to prostitute themselves in obeisance to the goddess Ashtart. And in Carthage, in an open-air sanctuary called a *topheth* or "place of sacrifice," young children were sometimes killed, evidently by cremation, to satisfy the deities. Thousands of earthenware vases containing the ashes and bones of infants sacrificed in the Carthage topheth were left in underground repositories.

A more benign aspect of the Phoenicians' culture was the efficient writing system that they developed around 1000 BC. By that time, written language had evolved from pictographic systems, demanding hundreds of characters, to various alphabets, in which each symbol represented a spoken sound. By 1500 BC, for example, scribes in the Syrian city of Ugarit had stripped down older Mesopotamian scripts to a far simpler system using only about thirty cuneiform characters. Elsewhere, alphabets were drawn

with linear signs — crosses, circles, slanting lines — that were ideal for busy accountants making hurried notations on papyrus. The Phoenicians inherited and simplified this form of alphabet and passed it on to the peoples with whom they came in contact on their voyages. The Phoenician system thereby became the model for several later alphabets, including the Greek — which in turn became the foundation of all Western scripts. The twenty-two signs of the Phoenician alphabet stood for consonants only — all that was needed for reading Semitic language. Phoenician readers, however, could mentally supply the vowel sounds in the proper places as they scanned a text, just as readers of Arabic script do to this day. (The characters for the five vowel sounds needed for other languages were added to the alphabet by the Greeks.)

The Phoenician alphabet could be adapted to express the sounds of a variety of tongues, and it proved a great boon to humanity. Literacy was no longer limited to professional scribes, who had to study many years to master the complex signs of cuneiform or Egyptian hieroglyphics. The new alphabet gave Phoenicia's seagoing merchants an edge on the competition. It enabled them to keep books on their business with minimal effort. Without using scribes, they could correspond with each other and with overseas trading partners. In the same way, the alphabet helped knit together the Phoenician outposts and colonies established in distant parts of the Mediterranean and beyond.

Masks for the Dead

The people of the first civilizations customarily buried masks with the dead. Several Mediterranean and Near Eastern peoples fabricated these representations of the human face, as did the far-off Chinese and groups in the still more distant Americas, including the Paracas people of Peru and the Olmecs of Mexico. The purpose of the masks seems everywhere to have been the same: to help the deceased pass readily into the afterlife either by warding off evil spirits or by providing them with a human form in which they could make the journey.

The oldest of the masks shown on these and the following pages is the effigy *(far right)* that formed part of the lid of a coffin interred in the Canaanite town of Beth Shean about 3,000 years ago. The people of Canaan doubtless adopted the custom of burying the dead in human-shaped coffins from the Philistines, who in turn had borrowed it from the Egyptians.

The seagoing Canaanites who came to be called Phoenicians fashioned terra-cotta masks that were smaller than life size *(right)*. These masks were not intended to be worn by the living or the dead, but served solely to repel evil spirits from the tomb.

The mask from Peru, on the other hand, was evidently attached to the cloth-wrapped body to give the spirit of the deceased an identity in the next world. The lid of an Etruscan urn that contained a dead man's ashes *(page 110)* presumably had the same purpose; a supplementary bronze mask was affixed to the lid with wires running through the tiny holes in its surface. The Olmec mask had a more ambitious aim: Its covering of jade — a magical stone to the early Mexicans — and its lordly expression were thought to give the departed soul a kingly power beyond the grave.

By the late eighth century BC, a few of the Phoenician colonies had grown into cities as large as those of the homeland. The most important of the new colonies was Carthage, which had been founded by a band of settlers from Tyre. The settlers named their outpost Qart Hadasht, or ''new city,'' words that came to be pronounced ''Carthage.''

A new city it was, built from scratch on a North African hill, and the idea of a fresh start pervades the legends that grew up about its founding. According to one story, the first settlers were highborn refugees from a bloody feud between two branches of Tyre's royal family. The leader of the refugees was Elissa, sister of King Pygmalion, who fled with her followers when the king plotted to murder her husband. The legend goes on to say that Elissa resorted to a ruse worthy of the most devious Phoenician merchant when the time came to purchase the hill on which the city was to be built. She told the natives that she would buy only the amount of land that could be covered by a single

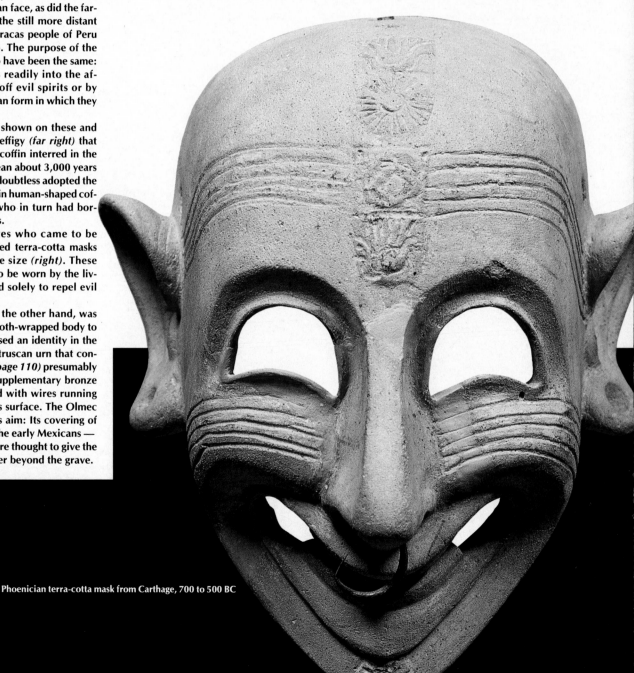

Phoenician terra-cotta mask from Carthage, 700 to 500 BC

ox hide, and she paid them accordingly. Then she cut the hide into narrow strips and with them encircled the base of the hill. That this was a slander cooked up by Greeks seems likely; the Greek name for the place was Byrsa, which in Greek means "hide."

Whatever ghosts of historical fact that legend contains, the people of Tyre had excellent reasons to found a haven overseas. There was profit to be had. And there was danger at home. Shortly after 900 BC, the Assyrian empire had begun to threaten the Phoenician metropolises along the Lebanese coast. The Phoenicians needed a place beyond Assyria's clutches that in time could be the new hub of a Tyrian trading empire.

Carthage grew and prospered, while in the homeland problems mounted. For more than 250 years, Assyria dominated Tyre and other Phoenician cities, exacting tributes of gold, silver, ivory, and cloth. The Assyrians even taxed timber cut in the Lebanese mountains. When Tyre and Sidon joined forces with Egypt and tried to rebel in 672 BC, the Assyrians crushed the revolt. In his triumph, the Assyrian ruler Esarhaddon had himself portrayed in stone, restraining the kings of Tyre and Egypt on leashes, like dogs.

The collapse of the Assyrian empire in 612 BC brought only the briefest respite. Three years later, Egypt seized control of the entire region, to be followed by the Babylonians under King Nebuchadnezzar II. These invaders captured Jerusalem and enslaved the Jews in 587 BC, then besieged the island fortress of Tyre, which fell only after thirteen years of doughty resistance.

Relief from the harsh Babylonian rule came when a new and mighty force, the Persian empire, gained control of much of the Near East in about 540 BC. The Persians tended to rule their conquered lands by guile rather than by terror, and as time went on, the Phoenician

Paracas clay mask from Nazca, Peru, 500 to 400 BC

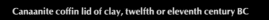

Canaanite coffin lid of clay, twelfth or eleventh century BC

Top of an Etruscan clay funeral urn, seventh century BC

Olmec jade mask from Veracruz, ninth century BC

city-states were happy to lend their still-powerful war fleets to the Persian kings for their campaigns against the Egyptians and later the Greeks.

It was during this period of invasions that a small flotilla of Phoenician cargo ships sailed around Africa, according to Herodotus. He wrote that the Phoenician mariners claimed to have started from the Red Sea, sailing down the coast of the continent. Far to the south, they rounded a cape and, turning northward, found the sun rising on their right hand. If this was so, then the cape they passed would have been the Cape of Good Hope.

Herodotus wrote that the voyage took three years. At intervals, the explorers beached their ships and rested on strange shores, planting and harvesting crops to sustain themselves before sailing on. They returned home at last by way of Gibraltar and the familiar waters of the Mediterranean.

During the long years of Phoenician decline, Carthage was strengthened by a constant stream of refugees, people who fled their troubled home cities and sailed west to the new colony. By 700 BC — roughly a century and a half after its founding — Carthage was sufficiently prosperous and powerful to sever the formal ties it had maintained with Tyre. So firm were the old loyalties, however, that the former colony continued for many years after independence to pay to its beleaguered mother city the tribute that once had been obligatory.

Stronger now than any of the cities at home, Carthage gradually took over leadership of the western outposts and colonies. To protect the trade routes to the silver and tin mines of Spain, Carthage's leaders reinforced existing settlements on Sicily and Sardinia and helped establish additional outposts on those islands and others, including Ibiza in the Balearic Islands, just off the eastern coast of Spain.

The principal motive for much of this activity was Carthage's growing concern over Greek expansion in the western Mediterranean. Mariners from the Greek city-states had started moving westward soon after 800 BC, searching for places to establish their own colonies, outposts that would stimulate trade and also relieve population pressures at home. First, the Greeks founded towns in Sicily and southern Italy. Then the best Greek sailors of the day, the Phocaeans from Asia Minor, pushed farther westward in swift warships known as penteconters, or 'fiftiers,'' for the number of oarsmen they carried. In about 600 BC, the Phocaeans succeeded in establishing a port on the Mediterranean coast of France. This was Massalia, which would someday become Marseilles. From there, they traded actively down the east coast of Spain and even set up an outpost in or near Tartessos, a mining region vital to the Carthaginians.

The Phocaean presence at Massalia ignited the first serious fighting between Carthaginians and Greeks. When Carthaginian ships failed to dislodge the intruders, Carthage's leaders looked about for allies — and settled on the Etruscans, the remarkable people who controlled much of the Italian peninsula. Ambitious maritime traders, the Etruscans were also bent on curbing Greek penetration of the western Mediterranean. In the Greeks these two trading peoples had a common enemy. The alliance was cemented when the determined Phocaeans continued to muscle their way into the region, establishing a settlement at Alalia on the east coast of Corsica, only eighty miles from the heartland of Etruria in what later became Tuscany — and within easy striking distance of the Phoenician bases on Sardinia to the south. The threat was clear. It was time for the allies to act.

The confrontation came in 535 BC. Near Alalia a Phocaean fleet of sixty ships encountered a combined force of Etruscan and Carthaginian war vessels almost twice as large. In the battle that followed, the allies inflicted such severe losses on the Greeks that they were forced to abandon their designs on Corsica and their hopes for further trade with Spain: They would remain customers, not conquerors of the people of the western Mediterranean.

The sea power of the Etruscans, like that of the Phoenicians and their Carthaginian descendants, evolved naturally from geographical circumstance. The jagged coastline and offshore islands of Etruria favored seafaring. Ships launched from Etruscan cities could easily dominate that part of the Mediterranean known as the Tyrrhenian Sea. Specially designed Etruscan merchant ships — fitted with massive spurs set above their bows to fend off warships attempting to ram — traded with the island of Sardinia and traveled as far as the North African coast to carry on commerce with Carthage. Etruscan merchants may even have sailed as far east as the Aegean Sea to trade with the Greeks of the island of Lemnos.

Even so, the Etruscan economy was not based primarily on overseas trade. The Etruscans were blessed with a homeland far more fruitful than those of either the Greeks or the Phoenicians. Stretching from the Arno River in the north to the Tiber in the south, Etruria was a country of fertile plains and valleys, where farmers tilled rich fields of wheat and tended lush olive groves and vineyards. Etruscan farming was among the most prosperous in the ancient world.

But the region's greatest asset lay beneath the landscape in thick veins of iron and copper — and to a lesser extent of lead, tin, and silver. The Etruscans extracted ores from the foothills of the Apennines, the range that formed the spine of the Italian peninsula, and from other mineral-rich regions, such as the nearby island of Elba. They smelted the ores in furnaces fired with timber from their dense forests of oak and beech and fashioned the metals into trading goods or sold them abroad unworked. Elba alone is thought to have produced 10,000 tons of iron annually.

Mining and smelting helped to transform Etruria from a primitive agrarian society into a sophisticated civilization. Before the development of these industries, the region was mostly one of small villages occupied by a mixture of peoples. Some of them were doubtless native to the peninsula. The others, according to Herodotus, had come originally from Lydia in Asia Minor. In any case, they spoke a strange language unlike any other found in the Mediterranean basin.

Whatever their origins, the people took naturally to metalworking and were already casting bronze when the Mycenaeans of Greece came in search of tools and weapons. So eager were these traders to exchange gold for the products of Etruscan mines that in about 775 BC Greeks from Euboea planted a colony on the island of Pithecusae in the Bay of Naples, 100 or so miles down the coast from what was then the Etruscans' southern border. When driven out by volcanic eruptions about twenty-five years later, the Euboeans founded another colony a dozen miles away across the bay at Cumae on the Italian mainland. The proximity of Greek customers quickly stimulated production of metals in Etruria.

The Greek presence had a decisive impact on Etruscan development in other ways. Although many aspects of Etruscan culture were influenced by their Phoenician and Carthaginian allies, Greek ideas predominated on the Italian shore. The merchants of Cumae, together with other Greeks who later established trading enclaves within the Etruscan ports, brought with them a powerful culture — their gods, their art, their ideals. They taught the Etruscans to use the alphabet to write their own language. And they passed on to the Etruscans other essential skills, such as the finer points of seamanship and olive growing. Evidence of Greek influence appears in their tombs, which preserve more Greek vases than have been discovered in Greece itself.

Trade with Greece spurred the evolution of Etruscan cities into a dozen or so prosperous city-states. As in both Greece and Phoenicia, these small kingdoms shared a common language, culture, and religion but never merged to form a larger political union.

Tarquinii was the first and largest of the cities. It was set on a broad hill by a river, a few miles from the Tyrrhenian shore, and was sheltered by protective walls five miles in circumference. Its status and wealth came from the mineral riches of the nearby Tolfa Hills — and from trade with the Greek colony at Cumae.

Tarquinii, however, was in time outpaced by a neighboring city, Caere, situated twenty-five miles to the southeast just on the other side of the Tolfa Hills. Caere possessed similar geographical advantages, and during the seventh century BC it gained control of Tolfa copper and iron ores and usurped Tarquinii's commercial supremacy. By 600 BC, Caere housed about 25,000 people, including a sizable Greek trading community.

The city's growing power was buttressed by its navy, which for a time was the most powerful fleet in Etruria. Caere's merchant ships and war galleys operated from the seaside town of Pyrgi and a couple of other satellite ports because Caere, like most other Etruscan maritime cities, actually stood a few miles inland, on a rocky spur, for protection against sea raiders. The only major city situated on the shoreline was Populonia, a copper- and iron-smelting center opposite the island of Elba, and Populonia was perched safely atop a 700-foot-high cliff.

Three views of an Etruscan rooster-shaped inkwell reveal the twenty-six letters of the alphabet inscribed around the bird's midsection. This alphabet was introduced by the Phoenicians, amended by the Greeks, and then adapted by the Etruscans to express their own language. The cleverly made inkwell — the top of the rooster's head forms the lid — is an example of the black, glossy pottery called bucchero, an Etruscan specialty.

At the southern edge of Etruria was the city of Veii, which earned its fortune in a different way from the other Etruscan states. The principal source of Veii's wealth was the abundant salt beds that it controlled; they lay about fourteen miles away at the mouth of the Tiber River. Thanks to the skills of its hydraulic engineers, Veii also possessed highly productive farmland. Some of the land was irrigated, fed from cisterns that the engineers dug into the rock of Veii's hills. The rest of the fields were reclaimed swamp, drained by an ingenious honeycomb of underground channels nearly two miles in length. Thriving on salt, agriculture, and trade with the Greeks at Cumae, Veii eventually succeeded Caere as Etruria's leading city-state; at least one Greek writer of the period thought it worthy of comparison in size and culture with Athens itself.

Etruscan mastery of the Greek alphabet helped the various city-states carry on their trade. What survives of their writing has a prosaic tone. Most of the 13,000 inscriptions that have been found on the ruins of monuments, on sarcophagi, and on the walls of tombs consist of only a few words. And they characteristically deal with such matters as names of the deceased and family lineage. In the case of the oldest surviving document, which contains nearly 1,200 legible words, the form is as striking as the content. Written on cloth late in Etruria's history, it found its way to Egypt, where it was eventually cut into strips and recycled as mummy wrapping. The document, preserved by Egypt's dry desert air, seems to have been a manual for priests; it prescribes the appropriate liturgies for certain religious holidays.

The liturgy, in fact, was crucial to Etruscan life. As the Roman historian Livy described the Etruscans a few centuries later, they were "a people who above all others were distinguished by their devotion to religious practices." Religion, like language, bound together the disparate city-states. Even though they refused to unite politically or militarily, they sent representatives, beginning in the fifth century BC, to an annual holy festival at a sanctuary near Lake Bolsena in central Etruria. It was an event dedicated to Voltumna, a local divinity whose function remains a mystery.

Part of the Etruscan pantheon resembled that of the Greeks. Several deities were similar and others, such as Artumes and Hercle — the Greeks' Artemis and Hercules — were borrowed outright. But the es-

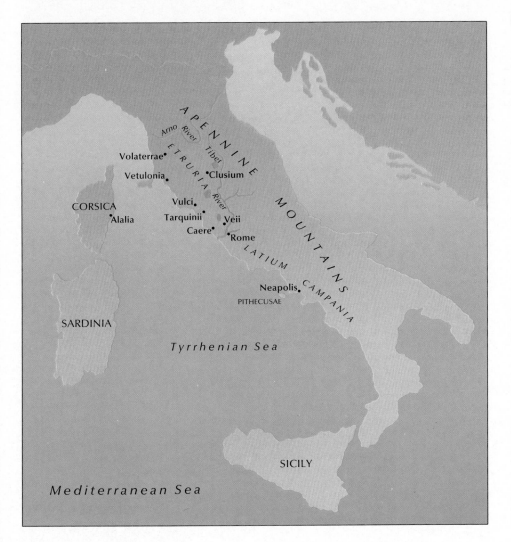

The map below indicates the large sections of the Italian peninsula controlled around 600 BC by the Etruscans and the locations of their most important city-states. Generally, the main centers of Etruscan wealth and power stretched from what became the province of Tuscany, in the north, to the province of Campania, in the south.

sence of Etruscan belief, with its emphasis on the powers of the supernatural, deviated sharply from the increasing rationalism that characterized Greek religion. The Roman writer Seneca later pinpointed the contrast: "The difference between us and the Etruscans is the following: that whereas we believe lightning to be released as a result of the collision of clouds, they believe that clouds collide so as to release lightning: for as they attribute all to the deity, they are led to believe not that things have a meaning insofar as they occur, but rather that they occur because they must have a meaning."

To the Etruscans, fate was all. They believed that their destinies had been predetermined by what they called *saecula,* or phases of history, and to discover the form of destiny, they developed elaborate rituals of divination. Priests were specially trained to study the signs manifested by various aspects of nature. Among these priests were those known in Latin as the *fulguriatores,* who attempted to interpret the divine will by observing the patterns formed by thunderclouds and lightning. Another type, the *haruspex,* studied the entrails of sacrificial animals.

Central to Etruscan religion was the belief that life continues after death. During the culture's earliest days, when cremation was prevalent, Etruscans symbolized their belief in an afterlife by placing ashes and bones in urns shaped like houses or molded to resemble the faces of the dead. When some Etruscans abandoned cremation during the eighth and seventh centuries BC in favor of burying their dead, they placed bodies in large underground tombs that were designed to reproduce as closely as possible aspects of life on earth. Some tombs, cut from the coastal region's soft volcanic stone, recreated the dead person's home down to the most minute details. Carving in the stone simulated woodwork; there were often beds, tables, and stools; candelabra hung from false roof beams of stone. Tools and other implements were placed beside the stone coffins along with food and drink, all to sustain the deceased in the afterlife.

The tombs of the rich were especially sumptuous, lavishly decorated by Etruscan artists and artisans. Terra-cotta sculptures and bronze statuettes often were placed

in the graves. Delicate jewelry made for the afterlife was sometimes buried with well-to-do women, along with the exquisite gold brooches, bracelets, and earrings they had worn during their lifetimes. The beauty and fine workmanship of this jewelry won the Etruscans renown in the ancient world. Employing techniques learned from Phoenician goldsmiths, the artisans mastered the style of hammered relief called repoussé and also the extraordinarily difficult technique known as granulation — soldering onto the surface of an ornament tiny grains of decorative gold.

The masterful jewelry aside, most Etruscan work, from sculpture to vividly painted pottery, reflected Greek influences. Greek artists and crafts-

The brilliant, fluid tomb paintings on these two pages and the next page convey the Etruscan love for music and dancing — and the general vivaciousness of Etruscan life, at least for the well-to-do. The lively figures, discovered in three tombs near the city of Tarquinii, were all painted about 470 BC.

men who came with merchants to the cities of Etruria sometimes set up shops and studios in the trading communities there, and the Etruscans learned from them.

Etruscan artists, however, always added a special twist of their own. Whereas Greek art tended to be cool and formal, Etruscan painting often displayed great energy and exuberance. Etruscan artists adorned the walls of tombs, notably near the city of Tarquinii, with large paintings that demonstrated an uninhibited love of color, depicting in splashes of green, blue, and red the feasting and other pleasures that would enhance the afterlife.

The wall paintings faithfully recreated how Etruscans — or the more fortunate among them — actually lived. The wealthy spent much time enjoying themselves at banquets and other entertainments. Resplendent in the richly colored mantles that were forerunners of Roman togas, and wearing gold-laced sandals or other elaborate footwear for which Etruscan shoemakers were known, men and women danced to the music of seven-string lyre and double flute. So much did the Etruscans love music, in fact, that it was said they did practically everything to its accompaniment — fighting, hunting, cooking, even beating their slaves. They also enjoyed watching circuses, horse races, boxing, wrestling, and a rougher form of hand-to-hand combat that foreshadowed the grisly gladiatorial contests of Rome.

An unusual feature of the Etruscan aristocracy was the freedom women enjoyed. They could legally own property and retain their own names after they married. A sign of their status was that they shared banquet couches with their men, a custom unheard of in Greece, where the only women permitted at parties were hetaerae, or courtesans.

So free living were these people that the more austere Greeks censured them as luxury-loving and lustful. Theopompos, a Greek historian of the fourth century BC, accused the Etruscans of all manner of degeneracy, including the sharing of their women in common. At parties, he recorded with more than a touch of voyeurism, "the servants bring in sometimes courtesans, sometimes handsome boys, sometimes their own wives. They all engage in making love, some watching one another, some isolating themselves with rattan screens set up round the couches, each couple wrapped in one cover."

The Greeks were also eager to criticize the Etruscan social structure, which reflected Greek society at an earlier stage of its evolution. Etruscan society was distinctly feudal. At the top were clans so rich and powerful that they dethroned the kings who had once governed the city-states and set up their own rule. At the bottom were slaves — and most other Etruscans. There was no broad middle group of reasonably well-off citizens, as in many Greek city-states.

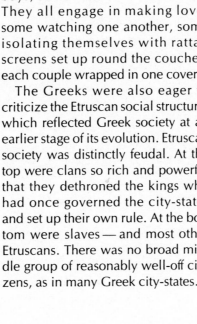

The vast disparity in wealth between the aristocracy and the rest of the people caused tensions and eventually outright strife. For many centuries, however, the Etruscan cities offered a safety valve for social outrage by expanding their domains, thereby providing new places for the frustrated poor to live. The expansion led eventually to Etruscan control of much of the Italian peninsula. Having reached north of the Arno and what would become Florence, they spread eastward through the valley of the Po River to the Adriatic Sea, adding to their domain a number of cities that later became famous as centers of Italian art and culture, among them Bologna, Mantua, Ravenna, and Rimini.

The Etruscans also expanded down the western coast of the peninsula, into Latium and fertile Campania, a movement that would have the greater significance for them. There, at a bend in the Tiber River, a non-Etruscan folk had established a city — Rome — which would in time become the center of a new and supremely powerful civilization.

According to local tradition, Rome had been founded in 753 BC by an indigenous Latin-speaking people. By the end of the sixth century, the budding hill town just south of the Tiber — only a dozen miles from salt-rich Veii — had fallen under Etruscan control, as evidenced by the name of its first foreign ruler, Tarquinius, who probably came from the Etruscan city of Tarquinii. Under Tarquinius and his successors, Rome grew increasingly important as a communications center between the Etruscan homeland and the new colonies in Latium and Campania. The Romans absorbed from their rulers and powerful neighbors much culture and expertise — the alphabet, temple design, military organization — although they retained their own language, along with their sense of being a special people with their own destiny.

In a quest for independence, the Romans rebelled against one of Tarquinius's descendants, an exceptionally vicious and arrogant ruler called Tarquinius Superbus. What was even more surprising, the Romans, assisted by Greek allies, succeeded completely with their insurrection, achieving independence in 509 BC. At that

point, Etruscan expansion came to a halt. Unable to band together even to confront the increasingly dangerous Romans, and beleaguered by internal strife and foreign incursions, the Etruscan cities fell one by one. At last, by the first century BC, what had once been Etruria was becoming little more than a memory — although the Romans, of course, had adopted numerous Etruscan customs. Seldom in human history has such a flourishing and important civilization been so nearly obliterated by a culture succeeding it.

In time, the tremendously powerful Roman empire claimed yet another victim — Phoenicia. Rome came to control the old ports on the Lebanese coast and the majority of the Phoenician overseas colonies as well. But for 1,000 years the Phoenicians, opening markets in every corner of the Mediterranean, had expanded trade and communication throughout the ancient world. In doing so, they had changed that world profoundly.

MAKING THE MARITIME ROUNDS

As the supreme merchants of the Mediterranean, the far-ranging Phoenicians reaped generous profits — and a wealth of abuse. "Your busy trading has filled you with violence and sin," the biblical prophet Ezekiel warned the king of Tyre, foretelling doom for that great Phoenician port. In Greek lore, the Phoenicians were said to entice people aboard their vessels, hold them captive, and sell them into slavery. Homer's hero Odysseus tells of a Phoenician merchant who "took me in a deep-sea ship for Libya, pretending I could help in the cargo trade; he meant, in fact, to trade me off, and get a high price for me."

Such yarns were not entirely without foundation. Like other acquisitive peoples of the time, the Phoenicians dealt in slaves, some of whom they retained to help man their galleys. But they were far too shrewd to rely unduly on the slave trade or any other single item. Precious metals were their most lucrative line, one that lured them west to the mines of Iberia. Yet no commodity that promised profit was overlooked by the Phoenicians, and their trade routes grew to include most of the Mediterranean *(left)*. In fact, they had only one specialty: the business of seafaring itself. As illustrated on the following pages, they made the ocean their thoroughfare, systematically reducing the daunting hazards of sea trade while increasing their profits. Such acumen prompted grudging admiration even from that fierce critic Ezekiel. "Who could compare with haughty Tyre, surrounded by the seas?" he asked. "When you unloaded your goods to satisfy so many peoples, you made the kings of the earth rich with your excess."

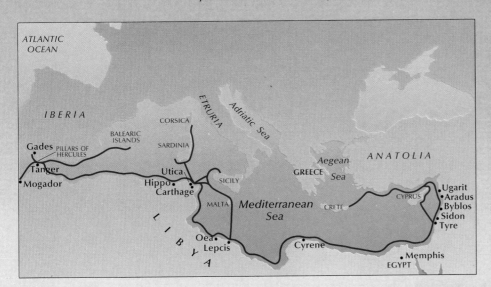

Two Phoenician merchant vessels, their prows arching horses' heads, put out to sea as warships forge ahead to patrol their trade route. The sleek Phoenician fighting ships — equipped with oars for closing with hostile vessels and bronze-tipped rams for piercing their hulls — were roughly three times faster under sail than the bulky traders they protected. Rather than serving as close escorts, the warships ranged the sea lanes, deterring pirates tempted by the rich Phoenician cargoes.

Calling at one of their far-flung trading stations, the crewmen of Phoenician merchant ships unload their wares, including oil, wine, and grain held in amphorae that were packed in sand in the vessel's hold. Ports such as this were home to Phoenicians involved in the trading business. They lived in clusters of houses close to the jetty; at major stations, the sailors themselves might lay over through the stormy winter months before resuming their long expeditions.

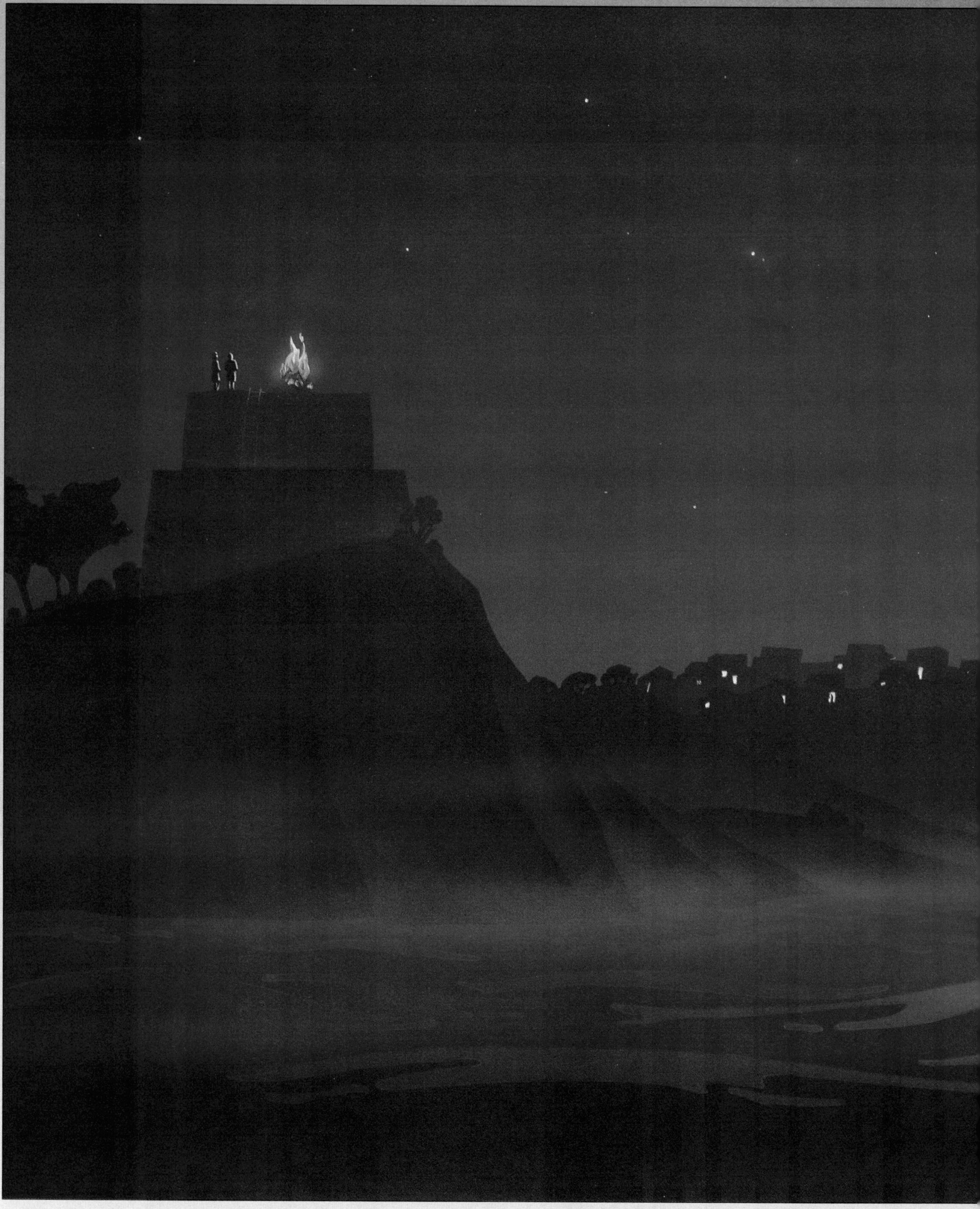

Guided by a flaring beacon, Phoenician traders approach their home port, where the raw materials they have garnered during their journey will be crafted into items for export. Although the Phoenicians could navigate by the stars, they preferred to avoid the uncertainties of night voyages; their watch fires served mainly to signal those who had been delayed beyond sunset by high seas or opposing winds.

ASIAN EVOLUTIONS

5 The Aryan nomads who trekked over the Hindu Kush mountains and settled on the plains of northern India during the second millennium BC were given to musing about the origins of the universe. An ancient hymn of theirs about the creation posed some thoughtful questions: *There was neither nonexistence nor existence then. There was neither the realm of space nor the sky which is beyond. What stirred? Where? . . . There was neither death nor immortality then. There was no distinguishing sign of night nor of day. . . . Darkness was hidden by darkness. . . . Whence was [the universe] produced? Whence is this creation? . . . The one who looks down on it, in the highest heaven, only he knows — or perhaps he does not know.*

People who could so eloquently ponder the riddle of how the universe was born — and philosophically admit that even their supreme deity might not know the answer — were obviously a sophisticated breed of invader.

They were, it is true, a race of warriors. Far from conquering through barbarity, however, they awed and overwhelmed the indigenous tribes by the sophisticated efficiency of their battle skills — especially their employment of fast, light, spoke-wheeled chariots, never seen before in this part of the world. It is also true that for centuries after arriving in India they built neither cities nor national political structures; instead, they enjoyed a pastoral life and developed an elaborate system of spiritual ideas that would suffuse the character of the subcontinent and reverberate throughout the world for thousands of years to come. And although they at first had no writing, they demonstrated impressive intellectual powers by producing and preserving, through the spoken word alone, a stunningly rich body of poetry that served as a repository for their religious ideas. Moreover, these illiterate immigrants introduced the language, Sanskrit, in which the unique culture of India would be embodied.

They called themselves Aryas, which meant "noble of birth and race." These proud, tall, fair-skinned people, with their great herds of lowing cattle and high-spirited chestnut horses, their flocks of sheep and goats and packs of yapping, frisking dogs, had migrated from their ancestral homeland on the Eurasian Steppes to the Iranian plateau sometime around 2000 BC. (Others of the same stock, all speakers of languages derived from the same Indo-European roots, had moved from the Steppes into Europe, where their descendants became the Greeks, Celts, Latins, and Teutons.) From Iran some of the Aryans moved westward, melding their culture, at times violently, with old civilizations of the Middle East. Concurrently, those who later would be known as Indo-Aryans gradually wended their way east through the passes of the Hindu Kush.

They came in tribal groups of varying sizes over a period of hundreds of years.

At night on the trail, dressed in wool and hides to protect themselves against the high-country cold, eating beef and drinking a beerlike beverage called *sura* around their fires, they must have talked of the land they left behind and the prospects that lay before them. As they emerged from the foothills into the fertile valleys of the Indus River and its tributaries — a region they called *Sapta Sindhu,* or "the land of seven rivers" — they probably thanked the nature gods they worshiped for their good fortune. Here was a land to be cherished, spacious and flat, well-watered and ripe with promise, a bountiful land where they could graze their herds, plant crops, and build villages.

This inviting territory was not vacant, however. Others were already living there, including a dark-skinned people — possibly the Dravidians, who in later eras would be found primarily in southern India. In some instances, groups of the newcomers used force to dominate the local populations. But they also mixed with those populations, culturally and racially. The Indo-Aryan language, Sanskrit, would come to incorporate many words and pronunciations traceable to Dravidian tongues. Aryan spiritual concepts would blend with beliefs of the earlier inhabitants to evolve into the multicreed religion and way of life called Hinduism. And, in spite of Aryan racial intolerance, which relegated many of the indigenous people to the lower rungs of a rigid class ladder, intermarriage over the centuries would erase the pure Aryan strain.

Other peoples would bring their own exotic cultural ingredients to the subcontinent at a later point. Each in its turn would be absorbed by the unique society the Aryans helped to create, but none would actually change it. By the time the Aryans had been there for a thousand years or so, the basic elements that make

During the second millennium BC, bellicose Indo-Aryan tribes pushed southward through the passes of the Hindu Kush range to occupy land along the upper Indus River and its tributaries. These invaders were bound together by a powerful religious tradition, summed up in cycles of sacred verses known as Vedas; in time Vedic culture spread southeast along the Ganges River. In China, meanwhile, the various clans of the Yellow River region were dominated by the Shang, a proud line who offered human lives in tribute to their ancestors. The dynasty occupied several capitals during its tenure, among them Anyang, where a wealth of finely wrought bronzes and inscribed bone oracles was later uncovered. Around 1100 BC, the Shang gave way to the Zhou, who extended the scope of Chinese civilization southward to include much of the Yangtze River valley.

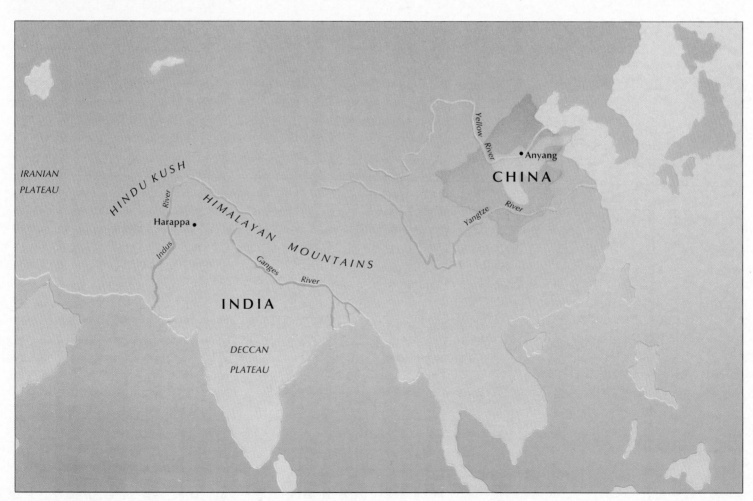

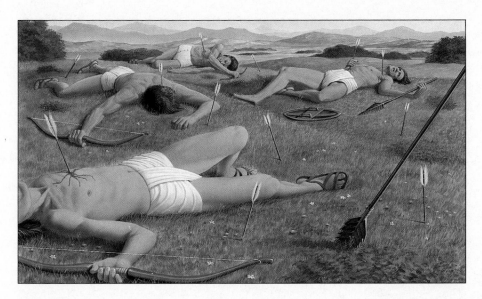

The bow ruins the enemy's pleasure; with the bow let us conquer all the corners of the world. . . . Once shot, fly far away, arrow, sharpened with prayer. Go straight to our foes, and do not leave a single one of them there. — from the Rig Veda

up the world of Hindu India were in place, and they would remain, in every fundamental respect, immutable thereafter.

At the same time that the venturesome Aryans were expanding and consolidating their domain in northern India, a strikingly different but equally enduring culture was taking shape some 2,000 miles to the northeast, in China. On the north China plain, along the banks of the Yellow River, the outlines of a distinctively Chinese civilization were becoming clear. During this era the land and society that would comprise the core of China were first controlled by a line of rulers known as the Shang dynasty and later by a different people, called the Zhou. But in spite of the change in power, China remained basically the same: an organized land of farming villages and walled towns, inhabited by people who worshiped their ancestors, made human sacrifices, developed an elaborate writing system, and created beautiful works of art in bronze and jade. Already the Chinese were self-contained, tightly governed, intellectually and artistically sophisticated — characteristics by which they would be recognized throughout subsequent ages.

The Aryans who settled in northwest India were organized in tribes, each headed by a chieftain and a priest. An Aryan man's principal allegiance was to his tribe, and he was called on regularly to demonstrate his loyalty in battles, both with other Aryan tribes and with bands of non-Aryans. (A common source of friction between tribes was cattle stealing, which the Aryans practiced frequently and with zest.) Despite their undeniable taste for combat, however, the Aryans' most extraordinary legacy was not military but spiritual.

From their early years in India onward they produced a steady flow of religious poems, or hymns, which were passed on orally from one generation to the next. Although this remarkable sacred literature would not be written down until many centuries later, it remained true to its original wording, because the priests who had been charged with preserving the hymns made certain that no changes crept in. The verses were strictly metered and easily committed to memory. In their schools, Aryan children would sit for hours echoing hymns back to the priests line for line, sounding — according to one mildly irreverent poem — like nothing so much as a chorus of croaking frogs.

The verses were practically the only source of information that the Indo-Aryans would leave behind about themselves, since they built no temples or monuments, left no artwork, no grave goods, no written records or seals. They later collected the verses in anthologies known as Vedas, or ''books of knowledge,'' which would in time give their name to the entire period of Aryan domination in ancient India — the Vedic age.

Of these books, the only one to contain historical information is the oldest and richest, the Rig Veda. Between 1500 and 900 BC, Aryan poets collected and com-

posed its 1,028 hymns, which were intended to be sung at sacrificial rites. Despite their sacred purpose and formal poetic style, the Rig Veda hymns give a frequently lively and sometimes vividly detailed account of the Aryans and their way of life.

As numerous references in the Rig Veda indicate, the land was the center of the Aryans' universe, especially because it provided pasturage for their herds of sheep, goats, horses, and cattle. An Aryan landsman measured his worth by the size of his cattle herd, identified by distinctive nicks cut in the animals' ears. In the absence of a monetary system, the cow was the standard unit of trade. Sanskrit was rich in special words denoting the individual characteristics of different cattle — a "cow with a strange calf," for instance, and "a cow barren after calving." In their prayers, Aryans asked for "the cow that is easily milked." They also beseeched their gods for "wealth in cows, sheep, chariots, and well-nourished and strong women."

An Aryan cattleman's animals played a key part in his life. His cows were milked three times daily. Fresh milk and ghee — butter clarified of milk solids, which would spoil too quickly in the heat — were a prominent part of the Aryans' diet. They also consumed beef, mutton and goat meat, cucumbers, oil that had been pressed from sesame seeds, fruit, including bananas, and cakes made from their chief grain, barley. And they discovered in India a food plant of truly exciting properties: sugar cane. The western world would not know sugar until the fourth century BC, when Alexander the Great's soldiers would return from India to Greece marveling over a "miraculous reed" that yielded honey without the help of bees.

The Aryans cooked in earthenware and metal pots; they used special caldrons for important feasts. One hymn sensuously celebrated "the trial-fork of the flesh-cooking caldron, the vessels out of which the broth is poured, the warming pots, the covers of the dishes.'' In addition to milk, the Aryans drank sura, which was probably brewed from barley. It was strong enough to merit censure for ''leading people to crime and godlessness.'' Sura was intended for everyday consumption. The Aryans reserved for their religious ceremonies a more potent, hallucinogenic concoction called soma, which was made from the juice of a plant — or perhaps a fungus — blended with milk or with a grain paste.

They worked the fields with ox-drawn plows in a temperate climate that provided them with two crops a year. They cut the grain with a knife or sickle and then probably threshed it with flails and winnowed it by tossing it into a breeze that would blow the chaff away. Their bulky wooden plows were pulled by teams of two to eight oxen. The accepted wisdom was that only an eight-ox plow was capable of working an entire day, and that a two-ox team was good for only a quarter of a day's work. They apparently practiced some form of irrigation, probably by channeling river water into the fields, and they seemed to understand the concept of soil erosion, as evidenced by a Rig Veda reference to rivers as ''corroders of their banks, like armies destructive of their foes.''

This bronze figurine of a man driving a chariot — accompanied by his dog, which stands on the shaft — is thought to be the product of an Indian civilization that reached maturity long before the Aryan invasion. Probably made around 1500 BC at Daimabad in central India, the work reflects the cultural influence of the sophisticated Harappans, who lived in cities along the Indus River. Although the Harappans fell into decline about 1800, the skills they cultivated survived in villages such as Daimabad and formed an important legacy for Aryan India.

They were huntsmen as well as farmers; dogs were used in boar hunting, though not in herding. Aryan hunters used snares as well as arrows to bag their prey. They captured boars and lions in snares and antelopes in pits; they trapped birds in nets stretched between pegs. Although they did not use iron until about 1000 BC, from the beginning their bronze tools and weapons were superior to those of the region's natives. Aryan dwellings were probably rectangular wooden structures with thatched roofs and several small rooms. The central hearth, where household religious rites were performed, was the focal point.

The Aryan society was strongly patriarchal. In the household, the father was in undisputed command. Men of the warrior class usually had several wives, sons were regarded as more desirable than daughters, and wives by custom were held to stricter standards of morality and fidelity than were their husbands.

But women were allowed a great deal of freedom in the choice of a mate. Although some marriages were arranged, the wonder and power of love was a recurrent motif in Vedic hymns, and Aryan girls probably were able to pick their own husbands. An Aryan wedding began with a feast at the bride's house. Bride and groom pledged themselves to each other by joining hands and walking around a ceremonial fire; then they departed for their new home in a special cart or chariot. Widows were permitted to remarry, and women were free to attend social affairs — the Rig Veda describes "fair ladies flocking to festive gatherings." Women also were active in religious affairs. The girls attended Vedic schools just as the boys did. Females composed several Vedic hymns and even became sages.

This was a society of people who liked to dress well; their religious books included a phrase that meant "well clad." The basic outfit consisted of a "lower garment" and another worn loosely over it; both were commonly made of either wool or deerskin. Both sexes wore gold jewelry on their ears, necks, or arms, and women sometimes decked themselves out in gold-embroidered gowns and ornamental headdresses. Women carefully combed and oiled their hair, which they arranged in long braids. Although the practice of shaving was known, men generally wore beards and moustaches.

Aryans also seem to have had a gift for enjoying themselves. They liked music and dancing, had a taste for alcoholic drink, derived enormous pleasure from chariot races, and had a weakness for gambling. Apparently, both men and women danced — whether together or separately is not known — and a typical musical ensemble included drums, flutes, cymbals, and at least two kinds of stringed instruments, one resembling a lute and the other more like a lyre or harp.

Chariot races were particularly suited to the boisterous Aryan style. The contestants thundered to a marker on a course, careered around it, and roared back to the starting point, where the winner collected his prize. Aryans may have bet on the races, but their favorite game of chance involved rolling nuts toward a depression in the ground. The object of the game is not clear, but there is no doubt that money in some form changed hands. One of the most poignant of the Rig Veda hymns is a classic bettor's lament, a timeless tale of addiction ending in the perennial vow to reform: *The gambler goes to the meeting hall, asking himself "Will I win?" and trembling with hope. But the dice cross him and counter his desire. . . . The dice goad like hooks and prick like whips; they enslave, deceive, and torment. They are coated with honey. . . . The deserted wife of the gambler grieves, and the mother grieves for her son who wanders anywhere, nowhere. . . . This is what the noble Savitr shows me: "Play no longer with the dice, but till your field, enjoy what you possess. . . . Let someone else fall into the trap of the brown dice."*

Savitr was only one of a remarkable assemblage of gods that Aryans viewed as magnified, heroic, and immortal versions of themselves. The thirty-three gods in the Vedic pantheon fall into three broad and sometimes overlapping categories: Celestial gods were rulers of the heavens and sky. Atmospheric divinities were responsible for storms and wind and the mysteries of weather. Terrestrial gods were in charge of fire and harvests and other earthly phenomena. Taken together, the gods, including a few goddesses, were nature given human form, with no fixed hierarchy or seniority — a sort of democracy of the divine.

In seeking favors from their gods — a bountiful harvest, a successful cattle drive, a happy marriage — Aryans believed that the deities, like humankind, expected to receive something in return. Therefore, in exchange for godly dispensations, they sacrificed to the accompaniment of prayerful chants and hymns. The sacrificial ceremonies were supervised by priests who apparently were remunerated by the supplicant with cattle or with gold. Sometimes the price was steep: One passage mentions a fee of 1,000 cows. Fire played a significant part in sacred rites, as did offerings of soma, the gods' favorite beverage. At least one allusion in the Rig Veda indicates that, in addition, human sacrifice might have been practiced at one time.

The racehorse has come to the slaughter, pondering with his heart turned to the gods. The goat, his kin, is led in front. . . . Go happily to the mares who long for you. Go happily to fame and heaven; go happily to the first orders and truths, go happily to the gods, go happily to your flight. — from the Rig Veda

But animals, generally killed with one stroke of an ax that severed the head, were the primary sacrifice. A special ritual called the horse sacrifice was particularly significant. A white stallion was released to wander freely for a year while a detachment of warriors followed behind. All the land roamed by the horse was claimed by the king. Rival chieftains could either accept the king's claim or fight. Finally, when claims to territory had been settled, the stallion was sacrificed. First, its feet were fettered and it was lowered onto its side on a cloth. The Rig Veda vividly describes what happened next: "The ax cuts through the thirty-four ribs of the racehorse who is the companion of the gods." A priest dedicated portions of the butchered animal to various deities.

The most frequently summoned god was Indra, an earthy, tawny-bearded being whose appetites were as great as his prowess. Indra was "he without whom people do not conquer, he whom they call on for help when they are fighting, who shakes the unshakable." Like Zeus, the king of the Greek gods, Indra carried a thunderbolt in his hand. Perhaps because he was beseeched with such regularity, the ever-victorious god appears to have had a more recognizably human personality than other deities: He ate, drank, and lived with tremendous gusto. And of course he lived forever: "The circling years, which wear away all else, to thee bring no

133

decay; thou bloomest on in youthful force while countless ages run their course."

Varuna, lord of justice and king of universal order, differed from most other gods in his relatively stern temper. Most divinities in the generally optimistic Aryan religion were good-natured and high-spirited; Varuna was more of a scolding taskmaster.

When an Aryan died, the corpse was either buried or cremated. Though cremation eventually predominated, a funeral rite described in an early hymn depicts a burial at which the priest asks the earth to be gentle with the departed, to "wrap him up as a mother wraps a son in the edge of her skirt." Death was the province of the god Yama, who permitted the good to cross a bridge that led them to a blissful paradise where joy and light were everlasting. The Aryans viewed heaven as a realm where earthly pleasures — food and drink, music and friends — could be enjoyed eternally. They perceived hell as a kind of bottomless darkness, an abyss where "evil, false, and untruthful men" ended up, though its specific terrors, if any, were not cataloged.

In their prayers as in everything else, the Aryans dwelled in the present; they were a practical people more concerned with the business of living than with the uncertainties that lay beyond the grave. Their hymns are often pleas for good health and long life, victory and contentment. But their belief in heaven and hell was a recognition that their destiny was to some degree determined by the way they conducted themselves on earth. Some forms of behavior were clearly regarded as sinful or immoral — witchcraft and excessive drinking, for example, and, despite its popularity, gambling. Adultery, incest, and abortion were also noted with disapproval in the Vedas. A virtuous Aryan was honest, faithful to the gods, courageous, and generous. *The man who is truly generous gives to the beggar who approaches him thin and in search of food. He puts himself at the service of the man who calls to him from the road,* one hymn asserts. *That man is no friend who does not give of his own nourishment to his friend. . . . The man who eats alone brings troubles upon himself alone.*

The chieftains of the tribes reigned in some splendor, but certain restraints were imposed on their power. An Aryan king customarily bequeathed his throne to his eldest son, but in extenuating circumstances the people of a tribe were allowed to select another member of the king's family, or a person of nobility, as their leader. The regal privileges could include the use of a palace, such as the royal residence with a thousand pillars and a thousand gates described in the Rig Veda, which probably exaggerates. Without a doubt, a king received tribute from both his conquered foes and his loyal subjects. Gifts to the monarch, apparently presented at regular intervals, may have been a form of de facto taxation.

The king's authority, though formidable, was subject to further restrictions. One limitation on his power was a high priest called the *purohita*. He was the ruler's most important minister, a political and spiritual adviser who conferred frequently with the king, summoned the gods on his behalf, and even accompanied him into battle. So impor-

The human-shaped figure above and the harpoon blade at right were among the copper implements mysteriously stashed away in hoards across a broad area of northern India during the second millennium BC. Although many of the items were weapons, they were apparently intended for ceremonial use only. The blade, for example, would have been impractical for hunting. Perhaps such objects were tokens dedicated to the gods.

tant was this official's support that grateful monarchs often showered the purohitas with gifts such as cows, horses, gold, chariots, and female slaves.

Aryan rulers were also obliged to consult with their subjects at assemblies that were at least superficially democratic. Political bodies identified as the *sabha* and *samiti* were mentioned in the Rig Veda. The sabha probably was a council of elders or nobles, whereas the samiti was an assemblage of all heads of families. The king apparently presided over meetings of the samiti and sought the support of its members, which suggests that their support counted. The importance attached to harmony between the ruler and his subjects is reflected in a hymn exhorting the citizenry to "assemble, speak together; let your minds be all of one accord."

It is at least possible, too, that some tribes in the early Vedic period were organized on republican principles without a hereditary monarch; and toward the end of the Vedic age — the seventh and sixth centuries BC — several states were republics, with the governing authority vested in popular assemblies. In extreme circumstances an aroused public would topple a king from his royal perch. A late Vedic text tells of a King Karala, who was deposed and executed for assaulting a young woman of the brahman, or priestly, class. The outraged populace of that tribe proceeded to abolish the monarchy permanently and replace it with a republic.

In general, however, Aryan tribal kingdoms were organized on monarchical principles. Each was composed of one or more villages, usually built on rising ground and protected by fortified stone enclosures. Each village was an administrative unit probably consisting of several houses, with a single extended family living in each home. The chain of obedience apparently flowed from the family head to a village chief and then to the nobles and the king. The monarch's most important deputy besides his priest-adviser was a military commander, who in peacetime wielded civil authority. The Rig Veda also contains an intriguing reference to spies, presumably royal informers assigned to keep an eye on troublemakers.

Warfare, of course, was a king's primary and most costly business. Most wars among Aryan tribes were motivated by nothing more complicated than a desire for a neighbor's cows; the Rig Veda's term for conflict translates as "search for cattle." The elite troops — the king or warlord and his nobles — thundered into combat aboard battle chariots, shooting from their bows deadly arrows tipped with metal or poisoned horn. A bowman's wrist was protected by a leather guard, and he also wore a helmet and coat of mail. For combat in close quarters, Aryan foot soldiers depended on lances, swords, and axes. On the offensive, Aryan infantrymen marched alongside the chariots and charged just behind the vehicles. Under siege they dug in behind stone ramparts and palisades made of stakes or thorns, which their enemies attacked with fire.

In one notable conflict that occurred around the twelfth century BC, the warriors of the most powerful Aryan tribe of the time took on the soldiers of ten other tribes in an engagement known as the Battle of the Ten Kings. The battle grew out of the resentment felt by a priest who had been dismissed by Sudas, king of the mighty Bharata tribe. To gain revenge the humiliated priest organized a confederation of ten other tribes and led them against the Bharatas. King Sudas and his men, surrounded at first, managed to break free and then to outflank their foes. They carried the day and thus consolidated Bharata supremacy. (Even today, the Sanskrit name for India is Bharat.) Three of the ten kings and six thousand other warriors were said to have died in this clash.

The religious texts provide few details about the workings of law and justice in Vedic India, although the emphasis appears to have been on compensating the victims of crime. Cattle theft was a common misdeed, along with burglary, highway robbery, and cheating at dice. The family of a murdered person received a financial settlement, but the Rig Veda tells nothing about how accused murderers were tried and how those found guilty were subsequently punished. Criminals and debtors were at times bound to stakes, and a debtor worked off the obligation by laboring for the man owed.

Fire and water ordeals were sometimes used to test guilt. In one such rite the accused had to carry a red-hot metal ball in his hands, which were protected only by fig leaves, while walking slowly over a specified distance. If he dropped the ball he had to start over; if he burned his hands he was deemed guilty. A similar ordeal judged a person guilty if his hand was injured while plucking an object from boiling water.

The later phase of India's Vedic age, roughly between 1000 and 600 BC, was a time of enormous change and upheaval in almost every aspect of Aryan life. The Aryans spread east and south to the great valley of the Ganges River and beyond, clearing forests with fire, whenever necessary, to create space for their settlements. Their chronically feuding little states evolved into fewer and larger kingdoms and republics with permanent capitals and sprawling bureaucracies. (A major war between rival factions, probably fought in the tenth century BC, came to be celebrated in a long heroic poem called the *Mahabharata,* India's national epic and — at 100,000 couplets — the longest poem known.) The economic emphasis shifted from stock raising to agriculture; rice, which was native to eastern India, supplanted barley as the staple crop.

The population increased rapidly, and toward the end of this period, cities appeared. By the beginning of the seventh century BC, there were sixteen large Aryan states in a broad swath of territory that stretched from the upper reaches of the Ganges Valley all the way across northern India and down into the Deccan, the high, dry plateau that divides the subcontinent's north from the coastal areas of the south. Aryan merchants probably traded with the southerners, largely less-advanced people, and with Mesopotamia. The fact that commerce flourished probably means that in this period the Aryans had some kind of writing, but they would leave no hard evidence of a script behind.

Of all the changes that transformed Aryan life in these years, the most dramatic was the elevation of the priesthood. Priests earlier had been advisers to the kings, but they now became, in the eyes of the people, greater than the kings — indeed, greater even than the divinities they professed to serve. This power stemmed from the increasingly complex rituals through which Aryans communicated with their gods. As the priests made sacrifices and other rites more and more complicated, they became, in essence, masters of mysteries that no other people, not even the king, were able to understand. And kings, like everyone else, deferred to them. The priests' knowledge of magic and incantations made them omnipotent in the eyes of the faithful. It was partly in reaction to the power of the priests that reclusive holy men began the spiritual quests that resulted in the enunciation of several important tenets of early Hinduism.

As priests grew more ambitious, so did kings. Notions of imperialism teased the imagination of ambitious Aryan monarchs, called rajahs: They were exhorted by religious commentaries to attain "preeminence and supremacy over all kings" and "paramount rule, encompassing all." Now richly robed sovereigns ascended their thrones with elaborate ceremonies in which the king set his foot on a tiger skin, symbolically acquiring the beast's power. The congresslike assemblies continued to operate, but the royal retinue expanded. In addition to his spiritual and military counselors, the king now had a staff that probably included a treasurer, a tax collector, and a royal commissioner of dicing. As might be expected, priests were exempt from taxation.

The division of society into castes became an immutable fact of life after the move into the Ganges region. The caste concept sprang from the Aryans' extreme race consciousness: The very word they used for "caste" meant "color." They called the dark-skinned Indus Valley people *dasas,* a word that subsequently came to mean "slaves," and condemned them as heathens. The beginnings of a caste system were elucidated in a Rig Veda hymn, which proclaimed that each of the four classes stemmed from different parts of a primeval male body in descending order — the priests, or brahmans, from his mouth; the rulers and warriors, or kshatriyas, from his arms; the farmers and merchants, or vaishyas, from his thighs; and menial workers, or sudras, and slaves from his feet. The indigenous dasas were consigned to the rank of sudras.

Late in the Vedic age, strict rules solidified the social order. Membership in any of the castes was hereditary and permanent, with certain exceptions: Males in the priest and warrior classes could take lower-caste women to be their wives, but men in the lower two castes could not marry above their stations. Religious texts called Brahmanas composed during this period decreed that sudras lacked property rights, were "fit to be beaten," and could be "slain at will." The texts specified funeral mounds of differing sizes — the higher the deceased's caste, the bigger the mound. Later, occupational subcastes developed, with delicately shaded gradations among them.

A list of trades ticked off in a late Vedic text illustrates the richness that Aryan social and economic life had now achieved. The compilation includes dancer, dancing master, drummer, clown, accountant, goldsmith, engraver, potter, carpenter, bowstring maker, dog keeper, tanner, elephant keeper, butcher, rope maker, investigator, physician, stargazer, and woman who makes scented oils. Whatever the calling, the average Aryan had a yen for material things, a Vedic hymn suggests: "The (metal) smith seeks all his days a man with gold," it declares. "I am a poet, my father is a physician, and my mother a miller with grinding stones. With diverse thoughts we all strive for wealth, going after it like cattle."

Despite the materialistic urges, the most profound change in the late Vedic era was the emergence of a new religious attitude set forth in a series of teachings called the Upanishads. The literal meaning of upanishad, "to sit in front of," suggests the origin of these meditations. Disenchanted with Vedic ritual, religious thinkers began wandering the north Indian countryside around the beginning of the eighth century BC, leading hermitlike lives in quest of wisdom and truth. Eventually they each acquired disciples, who absorbed the revolutionary ideas by sitting before the teacher and repeating the doctrine in ceaseless incantation. The dialogues and thoughts of these ascetic sages were later collected in the 108 Upanishads that have survived.

Many principles that ultimately became a part of Hindu doctrine were first expressed by these remarkable holy men. The Upanishad sages speak of a single universal spirit that animates all life and is present within each individual—instead of the pantheon of nature gods described in the Rig Veda. ''There is a light that shines beyond all things on earth, beyond us all,'' one passage declares. ''This is the light that shines in our heart.'' Another dialogue compares the universal spirit to salt that has been dissolved in water, ''an invisible and subtle essence'' pervading the whole.

According to the Upanishads, a seeker discovered truth not through conventional learning but through intuition and self-denial. The discipline of yoga prepared one for the search. The goal was to liberate oneself from worldly desires and concerns. The human body, the Upanishads taught, is no more than an ''ill-smelling, insubstantial'' amalgamation of bone and muscle and fluids that humanity must learn to transcend. This sentiment was a long way from the Rig Veda's Indra and his hearty, rollicking joie de vivre.

The Upanishads also introduced the idea of transmigration of souls, which maintained that death and rebirth were part of an endless cycle called samsara, and that one's collective deeds, or karma, determined the form that a person would assume in the next life. Even a miserable sudra could take some solace in the knowl-

edge that through proper and dutiful behavior he could be reborn as a brahman. Sacrifices to acquisitive gods and the earthly desires that motivated such offerings were irrelevant; a believer who attained bliss rejected the sundry vanities of the material world.

The Upanishads were the climactic expression of an extraordinary era of intellectual ferment. The restless and dynamic Aryans finally appeared ready to settle down, to refine their culture, and to blend peaceably with their neighbors in the subcontinent. In the Upanishads, their wisest men composed an eloquent overture to what would be one of the world's great religions, Hinduism.

The Chinese culture that began to blossom during this era had grown from roots in its own soil and not, as was the case in Aryan-dominated India, those imported from elsewhere. The Shang and Zhou peoples who were dominant in China from the eighteenth to the third centuries BC had lived in that part of the world during the preceding, prehistoric age, when, according to legend, a dynasty called Xia ruled the land. The Shang and the Zhou dynasties inherited and built upon elements of economic and social life that were established during that dimly perceived period. But it was during the Shang and Zhou periods that a true Chinese civilization developed, a distinctive culture marked by institutions and ideas that ever afterward would be identified as Chinese.

Their dominion was distinguished by impressive cultural and political advances. During this period the Chinese developed a form of writing completely different from the scripts of the Middle East. It would become one of the world's two major systems of writing, and for thousands of years the prevalent one: Until about AD 1800, more than half of all books published were in Chinese characters. The Shang and Zhou Chinese left behind no books, but they did preserve an immensely valuable written archive in the form of inscriptions on bronze vessels and on the oracle bones that they used for divination. These people made significant gains in science as well and produced a glorious body of artwork that would continue to command admiration three millennia later.

They created a centralized political structure designed to govern a widely scattered people. They also developed a world view that would abide with the Chinese for ages to come — the belief that theirs was the supreme civilization, to which all others were unquestionably inferior. Almost all peoples, as a matter of course, have embraced some version of this attitude. But few would make it such a controlling tenet of their relationships with other nations as did the Chinese, who for long periods would be isolated from many foreign influences that might taint the purity of their culture.

Shang political control stretched over a large expanse of north China, possibly some 40,000 square miles. Most of the Shang territory was concentrated in the flood plain of the Yellow River, centered in what is now the province of Henan.

The Zhou peoples, who conquered the Shang and became the ruling dynasty around 1100 BC, came from the Wei River valley on the western edge of the Shang domain. At various times the Zhou peoples extended their cultural and political sphere well beyond what are thought to have been the limits of Shang territory, reaching the Yangtze River valley in the south and the shore of the Yellow Sea in the northeast.

The ancient Chinese capitals were surrounded by feudal domains governed by loyal

This ornate bronze water buffalo, cast in China in the tenth century BC, held wine for ritual functions: The catlike creature perched atop the vessel swung back on a hinge so that the wine could be poured in, while the mouth of the water buffalo served as a spout. Water buffalo proved endlessly useful to the Chinese, providing them with power for hauling, meat for eating, and bones for divination.

lords, whose preserves formed a buffer zone between the walled towns and the marauding tribesmen roaming the country beyond — "the people in the four directions all around." This led the Shang and Zhou Chinese to think of the areas under their direct control as "the Middle Kingdom" — the center of the world and the seat of order and regularity.

Wealth flowed from the land, and from the masses of illiterate peasants who made a meager living by working it, to the elite in the towns. All the land in the Middle Kingdom was regarded as the king's property. "Everywhere under heaven," a Zhou poem declared, "is no land that is not the king's." The underclass, known as the *zhong ren*, cultivated millet, barley, soy, and wheat and raised pigs and chickens, probably turning over any surplus beyond their subsistence needs to the state. Prisoners of war sometimes shared the lot of the peasants, working beside them as slave laborers in the fields beyond the town walls. A peasant who refused to fight under his king's banner was liable to be enslaved, although the resulting difference in his status was apparently slight. Besides this human muscle, domesticated water buffalo were used for farm power.

Ironworking was unknown in China at the beginning of this era, and bronze was so rare that it was used only to make ritual pieces and decorative objects for the wealthy, not tools. Spades, sickles, and many other implements were made of stone. The peasants probably prepared the earth for planting with primitive scratch plows, perhaps tree branches tipped with stone.

Such tools were essential in the cultivation of rice, a grain that became more important to the Chinese economy as Zhou influence extended south into the Yangtze River basin. Rice growing depended on a large and reliable supply of water so that the diked cultivation areas, or paddies, could be flooded regularly. The Yangtze and its tributaries provided the water, and Zhou political power provided the stability needed to build and maintain extensive systems of irrigation canals that fed the paddies. Chinese farmers also produced oranges and peaches, and they grew hemp and cotton for textile fibers and tended silkworms.

The elite dressed themselves in colored silk for public outings and had cotton clothing for use at home. Peasants wore a long, undyed hemp-fiber or cotton shirtlike garment that would remain the standard garb for China's common people until modern times.

While the aristocracy in this sharply divided society lived in spacious wood-and-earth houses with gabled roofs, the peasants inhabited shallow, cellarlike pit dwellings with walls that protruded only a few feet above the ground. For protection, most of the towns were probably ringed by earthen walls as high as twenty-five feet and as thick as fifty feet. Shops and foundries where workers in stone, bone, jade, bronze, and other materials practiced their crafts clustered both inside and outside the walls.

At all levels, Chinese society was a network of extended families, or clans, bound by the cult of ancestor worship. Parents and grandparents, uncles and cousins lived together and shared whatever they had. A person's principal obligation was to respect ancestors and to produce future generations who would offer their ancestors the same reverence. In a peasant family, the man's job was working the fields, fishing, and hunting, whereas women were probably responsible for weaving, silk culture, and making rice wine or beer. Peasant girls were treated as inferiors and sometimes sold into servitude or concubinage. Rare,

Casting a Masterpiece

The bronze marvels of the Shang dynasty, such as the elegantly masked ceremonial cooking vessel below, were made possible by an ingenious casting technique evolved by Chinese smiths. The artisan evidently began his work by fashioning a model of the vessel he intended to make. Around the model, clay was packed to form a mold. Such a cast could not be removed whole, so when the clay was firm but still pliable the mold was cut into sections and lifted off; the artisan could then embellish the segments with fine details. Next, the sections of the mold were fired and reassembled around the model, from which a thin layer had been shaved corresponding to the desired thickness of the finished object. Molten bronze was then poured into the gap between the mold and the shaved-down model. Once the metal had cooled and set, mold and model were removed, and the masterwork emerged.

bright interludes amid the pervasive bleakness of peasant life were the semi-annual festivals marking the beginning and end of the agricultural season. These were joyful celebrations that included singing and dancing competitions among children from various villages.

The king, declaring himself to be "the One Man" and "the Son of Heaven," was the supreme political, military, and religious figure in the Chinese state. He was believed to possess divine qualities and a special gift for communicating with the gods. The royal line was drawn from the dominant clan in the dynasty, the succession passing sometimes from brother to brother and on other occasions from father to son. A Shang or Zhou monarch was expected to have physical strength as well as wisdom. A king could take as many wives as he wished — a Shang ruler named Wu Ding had at least sixty-four. Disputes over succession could be taken before a council of high-ranking nobles.

From all evidence, the king attended to much of the business of his realm personally. He stood at the summit of a ruling pyramid that comprised his family, the feudal lords and their clans, and an aristocracy of gentlemen and their ladies. He himself dispensed justice, which could involve harsh penalties such as the mutilation of a nose or an ear, eye piercing, and castration. Routine affairs of state, such as tax collecting, making armaments, religious practices, and recordkeeping, were overseen by a cadre of bureaucrats, always an important element in Chinese life. The multilayered civil service included a functionary designated assistant tiger retainer, a master of bells, and an assistant runner of horses.

The feudal system inaugurated by the Shang dynasty and later expanded by the Zhou rulers allowed the king to reward his relatives and loyalists while surrounding his

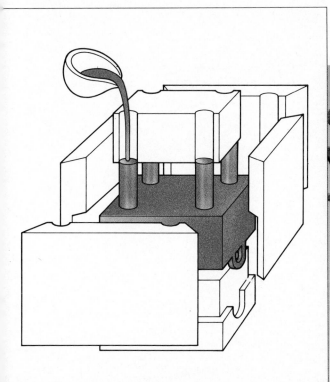

OFFERINGS OF JADE AND BLOOD

For splendor and savagery, the last rites accorded China's ruling elite in the late days of the Shang dynasty have seldom been surpassed. The proudest of patriarchs in a culture that worshiped ancestors, Shang rulers were accorded lavish funerary offerings — tribute paid not only with vessels of bronze and jade but with lashings of human blood.

The somber rites were conducted in huge pits, up to forty feet deep, dug by work gangs near the capital of Anyang. At the bottom of a burial pit the laborers framed a chamber, its wooden walls inlaid and lacquered. The floor of one such chamber was consecrated by the sacrifice of nine armed guards, interred with watchdogs, apparently to protect the tomb's royal occupant against evil spirits.

Once the chamber was prepared, the coffin was carried in and deposited with the grave goods. Then the bloodletting began. Most of the victims were prisoners of war, who were led down the ramps as the pit was being filled in and decapitated by the score. In the royal grave housing the nine guards, more than sixty skulls were later recovered.

Middle Kingdom with a network of allies commanding forces of their own. Each feudal lord was both a political chieftain and his territory's sole property owner, who controlled the land and its peasants from a walled headquarters and supplied military aid to the monarch upon request. During the early Zhou period there were hundreds of these fiefdoms.

As it was for the Aryans, war was a way of life for the people of the Middle Kingdom. Both the Shang and Zhou leaders achieved sovereignty by forcibly ousting their predecessors from power. According to legend, the Shang overthrew the Xia dynasty in about 1750 BC and held sway, despite chronic warfare and turbulence, for more than 600 years. The Zhou people, who succeeded them around 1100 BC, controlled an expanded territory through the calculated dispensation of feudal fiefs. Throughout both dynasties, there were coup attempts, clashes between rival domains, and wars with the outlying barbarian peoples.

In armies numbering as many as 13,000 men, Shang warriors raced into battle in horse-drawn chariots, manned by archers and lancers, to the accompaniment of waving flags and drums and tinkling bronze bells. Five chariots made up a squadron and five squadrons a company. Foot soldiers may have been divided into companies of 100 men, with three companies forming a regiment. They fought with bows, lances, battle axes, and hatchets. The cost in lives was often high: The casualty figure for one engagement was recorded as 2,656.

Shang power apparently began to wane when Shang leaders grew soft and self-indulgent. "Enjoying ease from their birth," said a Chinese commentator, "they did not know the painful toil of sowing and reaping. They sought for nothing but excessive pleasure." The downward spiral climaxed during the cruel and corrupt reign of King Di Xin, the last Shang sovereign. When one adviser displeased him, Di Xin was said to have ordered his heart cut out. The king raised taxes and dissipated the royal treasury on wine-soaked orgies. His nobles were particularly outraged by his mistress Da Ji, who devised ingenious instruments of torture for punishing disloyal subjects. In one notably sadistic ordeal called a grill roasting, the accused was forced to walk a greased metal pole laid across a pit of burning charcoal. It amused Da Ji to see the victim slip onto the coals and burn to death.

The Zhou engineered the end of the Shang dynasty during Di Xin's reign by forming alliances with neighboring peoples. Led by King Wen (called "the Civilized King") and his son and successor Wu (known as "the Military King"), the Zhou overthrew Di Xin, who committed suicide, and proclaimed a new ruling dynasty. Many of the Shang warriors were said to be so disaffected with their monarch that they readily capitulated.

The favorite peacetime diversion of Shang and Zhou kings and their nobles was large-scale hunting expeditions, which reinforced their class solidarity while putting meat on the nobles' tables. The tally for one extended hunt

Reading an Oracle Bone

To chart their future, the Chinese consulted ancestral spirits, who spoke to the living through the bones of animals. The oracle bone shown here — a tortoise's breastplate, from the time of the Shang dynasty — was first polished. Grooves were then hollowed out on the back of the shell and scorched. This process yielded fine cracks on the front, interpreted by the diviner as the oracle's response to a repeated query. That done, the diviner's name was inscribed on the object, together with the date and the nature of the query.

As outlined at right, the cracks produced on this shell were read by the diviner Bin on Xinyou, the fifty-eighth day of a sixty-day cycle. The question concerned a man named Chu Hua, from the region of Cha, who contemplated action against "X": an unknown person or place symbolized by two sticklike hands holding a horn (top left and center right). Here, as on other oracle bones, the question appears in two forms, one positive and the other negative. Perhaps the question was inverted as a precaution, enabling the diviner to confirm his reading before revealing his findings.

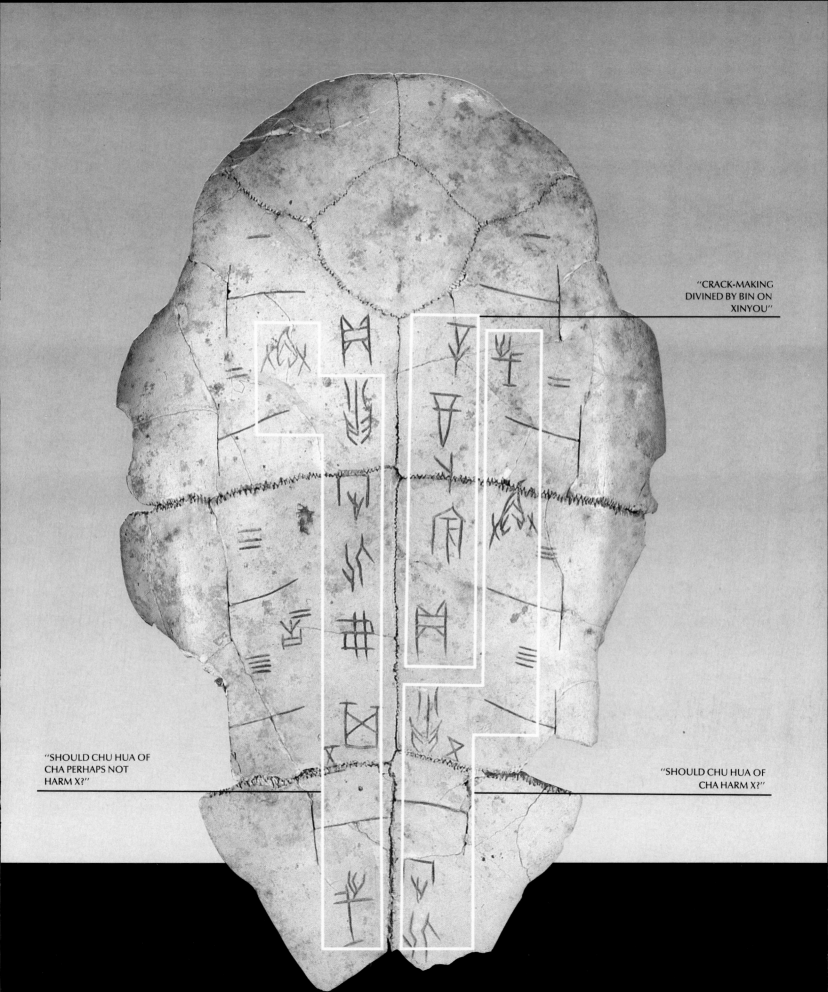

"CRACK-MAKING DIVINED BY BIN ON XINYOU"

"SHOULD CHU HUA OF CHA PERHAPS NOT HARM X?"

"SHOULD CHU HUA OF CHA HARM X?"

was one tiger, 164 foxes, and 199 deer of various species. In the autumn years of the Shang dynasty, the gentry spent fully half their time in pursuit of game.

But at the same time the Shang enjoyed their sport, they also launched intellectual quests — with fruitful consequences. Some of the learned people came up with a unique form of written communication. Writing systems unknown to the Chinese had included the Egyptian hieroglyphic and the Mesopotamian cuneiform scripts, the symbols of which at first represented objects or ideas and later stood for particular syllabic sounds. The symbols of the sounds could be combined to make different words.

In Chinese writing, each character represented a word, and most of the words were each a single syllable, so a combination of the characters could express a multisyllabic idea. Each character represented a specific sound, but in time there would be no standard pronunciation. Thus in later eras Chinese people speaking many different dialects could read the same text — although, if they read it aloud, they might be uttering completely different sounds to express the same meaning. All the principles that characterized later Chinese writing were present in this early script. Children of the upper class learned the writing system along with archery and the rudiments of their religion.

The Shang religious expression tended toward violence. They sacrificed humans and animals in order to seek help and guidance from their ancestral spirits and the gods

This huge bronze ax blade, measuring more than fourteen inches long, was probably wielded by an executioner of the Shang dynasty to dispatch designated victims during ceremonies of ritual sacrifice. Cast in the likeness of a half-human, half-animal face, the blade was left near the entrance of a tomb not far from the remains of forty-eight victims.

of nature. They left behind royal tombs containing as many as 300 skeletons, some decapitated and others on their knees with their hands behind their backs. Prisoners of war were apparently favored as sacrificial victims, but Shang citizens were not exempt: When a Shang king died, his deputies, concubines, and servants sometimes followed him into the grave. Royal tombs were also strewn with ritual vessels, jewels, food, weapons, and even chariots complete with horses and charioteer. The erection of one Shang building — presumably a palace or a temple — was consecrated by the ritual slaughter of 600 people.

In addition to revering their ancestors, the Shang worshiped a supreme god they called Di, who ruled both heaven and earth; they also paid homage to numerous lesser deities associated with nature. When a king died, he was thought to join the gods and to assume their powers. Sacrifices were offered at the change of seasons — or at the outset of a military campaign. The gods were beseeched for rain during droughts; a shaman-rainmaker attempted to summon rain by dancing on a pile of burning timbers, and if he failed, he died. Young girls were sacrificed to placate the god of the Yellow River.

The same feudal and militaristic overlords who ruled China ruthlessly also patronized gifted artists and craftsmen, who created some of the world's most enduring masterpieces in jade and bronze. Bronzesmiths, whose workshops in the palace complexes indicated their superior status to peasants, produced a variety of decorative objects and ritual vessels. They created two-sided symmetrical works by using molds pressed back to back, and complex pieces with several curves and projections by combining a number of molds. Handsome goblets and other vessels flowed out of the bronzeworkers' shops. Among upper-class warriors, bronze was used sparingly for more utilitarian purposes, such as for arrowheads and helmets. The Shang also carved art objects from marble and jade with the assistance of drills and rotary saws.

The beautiful bronze and jade work was only one reflection of an intellectually sophisticated culture. The Chinese developed a calendar of twenty-nine-day and thirty-day months, with extra months added periodically to produce a year of 365 days. They kept records of eclipses of the moon, recognized the summer and winter solstices, and used a sundial to tell time.

They were also musically adept. One lyrical account of a Western Zhou concert lists the instruments — bells, clappers, flutes, "musical stones" (probably chimes), and several different kinds of drums — and concludes that "solemn and harmonious they blend their notes."

The belief that China was a realm surrounded on all sides by unenlightened barbarians pervaded Chinese civilization. In their art as in their politics and religion, the Chinese viewed their society as an island of order, structure, and constancy in a sea of chaos. Their two-tiered social system, with an elite class born to privilege and an underclass sentenced to a life of unbroken toil, was in their minds a reflection of the natural order. The self-contained domain of the Son of Heaven was the hub of the universe.

To some degree this world view reflected a practical imperative: Disorderly barbarians did indeed swarm around their borders, and social or political unrest within the dynasty threatened its stability. But in the eyes of the Chinese the notion that their culture was the center of life also became an ideal that persisted for many centuries.

AWAKENING IN THE AMERICAS

6
The peoples of the Americas, separated from Eurasia and Africa by vast oceans, found their own way to civilization, and at their own pace. Ziggurats encircled by crowded cities dotted the plains of Mesopotamia, great stone pyramids loomed above the Nile, and the Indus Valley buzzed with sophisticated urban life while many early Americans still followed a pattern of existence based on the nomad's seasonal rounds. The people moved purposefully with the advancing year, now reaping the bounty of the river basins, now that of the fog-drenched hills, timing their migrations to the ripening of the wild crops and, in some cases, to good hunting or fishing seasons.

Once in a while, bands of wanderers encountered one another. They may have fought on occasion, but probably not often. So small was each band — most likely about twelve to twenty people — and so interdependent its members that the loss of even an individual or two in a fight could be calamitous. The little groups instead most likely exchanged goods and stories at their meetings, arranged marriages between their young men and women, and celebrated occurrences such as changes of seasons. The celebrations might take the form of religious ceremonies honoring whatever higher powers were believed responsible for the food plants and game that kept these hunter-gatherers alive. Gradually, the seasonal encounters led to the establishment of ceremonial centers at sacred places where supernatural significance clung to certain natural features such as springs or caves: The latter may have been considered wombs of the earth. The centers in turn attracted more small bands of people who came to worship, socialize, and trade.

Sometime after 4000 BC, a few of them had begun to settle in more or less permanent locations. During the third millennium, early Americans gave up the nomadic life in increasing numbers, especially in the highlands and coastal valleys of Peru and along the coasts of Mesoamerica, the region that stretches from the Valley of Mexico south into Honduras. Forming small villages, they experimented with the cultivation of plants and with the domestication of animals. As they learned to produce and store food, the villagers began to organize their labor more efficiently over the course of the year, mustering workers to join with those from other villages on common projects during periods when crops did not require attention. In this fashion, they were able to construct bigger and better monuments to their gods.

By the second millennium BC, the emerging pattern of society in the Mesoamerican and Andean regions was clear: Scattered villages and hamlets, located near fields cultivated by their inhabitants, supported ceremonial centers and groups of shamans, or holy people. The villagers visited the centers regularly to participate in the religious rites performed by the shamans, who later evolved into an elite body of learned priests. The centers grew in power and prestige, forming the bases of the first American civilizations: those of the Olmecs in Mesoamerica and of the Chavín in the Andes.

Civilization came first to Peru, a land of extremes like no other on earth. There, side by side, lay the world's richest fishing ground — just offshore in the Pacific Ocean, the Humboldt Current pulled up deep, cold waters full of fish-attracting plankton — and a coastal desert so dry that some parts of it had gone hundreds of years without receiving rain. Inland from this desert stood the hemisphere's most awesome mountain chain. Second only to the Himalayas of Asia, the Andes rose along the Pacific flank of the South American continent and approached their full majesty in Peru, where several peaks soared above 22,000 feet. To the east, the mountains plunged precipitously into the rain-forest basin of the world's largest and mightiest river, the Amazon.

Rivers that ran down the western slopes of the Andes eventually cut across the coastal desert to the Pacific. When the rains came in the highlands, the rivers swelled, nourishing subtropical oases along their banks. The early inhabitants of the region learned that these river corridors in the desert could support plants and animals, and therefore human life. And they discovered that for seven months each year, mists billowed up from the cold Humboldt waters and rolled inland from the coast to cover the low hills lying just beyond the desert. The moisture was not sufficient for farming, but supported plants that could absorb water from the atmosphere and that provided food for all manner of small game.

Below the mountain peaks but above the timberline, at about 12,000 feet, lay highland plateaus. Parts of this area, although quite dry, were covered with immense natural pastures for deer and American cousins of the camel — llamas, vicuñas, and guanacos — that variously provided meat, textile fiber, and beasts of burden for the region's people. Other parts of the highland plateaus received considerable rain, and in those places much richer pastures developed, along with great swamps and thickets around large lakes. The swamps were home to numerous species of wildlife, and contained a profusion of edible plants and roots in addition to strong reeds that could be used for building houses or boats.

Just below the plateaus, the highest valleys of the rivers that descended toward the coast proved excellent for growing potatoes, squash, beans, and certain grains. Later, corn would be grown in the valleys midway down the slopes. Corn flourished in the lower valleys as well, but those lands were even better suited for cotton, fruit trees, and coca bushes. (The early Peruvians found that if they chewed coca leaves mixed with lime produced by burning seashells, the alkaloidal stimulant effectively countered the fatigue humans often experience in thin, high-altitude air.)

Waters coursing down the east side of the Andes encountered a heavily wooded transition zone at about 11,000 feet, from which they gradually dipped into the Amazonian floodplain and a rain forest whose 100-foot-high canopy was in some places so impenetrably thick that no vegetation grew in the gloom below. When Andean people ventured into either of these wooded environments, they probably were awed by the incredible array of birds and animals there, and most of all by the mighty jaguar, the largest great cat in the Americas.

Considering the plenty, it was only natural during the third millennium BC for Andean people to give up their migratory life and settle in order to concentrate on the bounty of one particular place. They built small, rude houses, often set halfway into the earth, using whatever materials might be available locally — stone, clay, reeds. The old trails of the seasonal rounds became trade routes through the river valleys. Before long, central Peru was the scene of a thriving exchange among the settlers who lived on the marine-rich coast and in the agricultural valleys, the pasturelands of the mountains, and the tropical forests lying to the east. The trade began as an exchange of food between fishermen and farmers. Inhabitants of Peru's coastal desert harvested the ocean for their primary food: anchovies. In small boats, they put out to places near shore where billions and billions of the tiny fish swarmed to feed on the plankton in the Humboldt Current. The fishermen scooped up the anchovies with fine mesh nets, dried them, and ground them into fish meal, a commodity easily stored and transported. (The same basic activity, albeit with improved equipment, would still be the foundation of the region's economy 4,000 years later.) The coastal people, who had very little arable land, traded the protein-rich fish meal for inland root crops — sweet potatoes, white potatoes, and other tubers — that were high in carbohydrates. Thus both communities acquired the balance of foodstuffs they needed.

In the valleys, the farmers grew and traded cotton as well as their food crops. The species of cotton they cultivated was a wild American cotton plant crossbred with a domesticated variety from Asia, a fact that would intrigue and puzzle botanists and historians when it was discovered through chromosomal studies four millennia later. For their raw cotton, the inland villagers received such exotic goods as lustrous red Pacific seashells and brilliantly hued Amazonian bird feathers, which they bestowed on their leaders and used in rituals. In the coastal settlements the cotton fibers were twisted into yarn with hand-held spindles and made into textiles by techniques that vaguely resembled crocheting and macramé, requiring no looms. The cloth makers sometimes painted their fabrics and sometimes used dyed yarns to create elaborately patterned textiles. The designs included birds, human figures, serpents, and fish, all expressed in stylized geometric forms.

Now the early Peruvians were sufficiently prosperous and numerous to expand the ceremonial centers that in earlier centuries had marked the junctions of their nomadic rounds. The inhabitants of the villages, both on the coast and in the valleys, could celebrate their good fortune by building large temple complexes of stone and adobe at the centers. Most of the temples were constructed in the same basic pattern. Atop a rectangular mound of earth faced with stone — which ranged from twenty feet to sixty feet in height and up to 1,500 feet in length — stood the temple building itself. In its principal, white-walled chamber was a ritual hearth, a pit for the sacred fire, often situated in the middle of a sunken area. In front of the temple, at the foot of the mound, was a rectangular forecourt surrounding a circular sunken court that might be as deep as fifteen feet. Stairways connected the different levels.

Worshipers apparently entered the complex at the far side of the forecourt, facing the

By 1200 BC, distinct cultures were evolving in two disparate regions of the Americas. Inspired by a religion that recognized jaguars and other jungle predators as gods, the Chavín of the lofty Peruvian Andes built massive stone pyramids at ceremonial complexes such as Chavín de Huantar, Cerro Sechín, and Kotosh. Some 3,000 miles to the north, a similar cult took root in the sweltering rain forests along the Gulf Coast of Mesoamerica. There the Olmecs carved colossal stone heads and piled up high temple mounds of clay at the religious centers of San Lorenzo, La Venta, and Tres Zapotes.

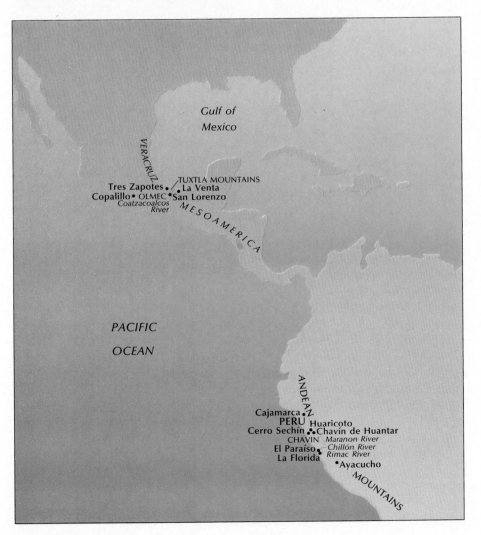

Gulf of Mexico

VERACRUZ

TUXTLA MOUNTAINS
Tres Zapotes • / • La Venta
Copalillo • OLMEC • San Lorenzo
Coatzacoalcos River

MESOAMERICA

PACIFIC OCEAN

ANDEAN

Cajamarca •
PERU Huaricoto
Cerro Sechín •• Chavín de Huantar
CHAVIN Maranon River
El Paraíso • Chillón River
La Florida Rimac River
• Ayacucho

MOUNTAINS

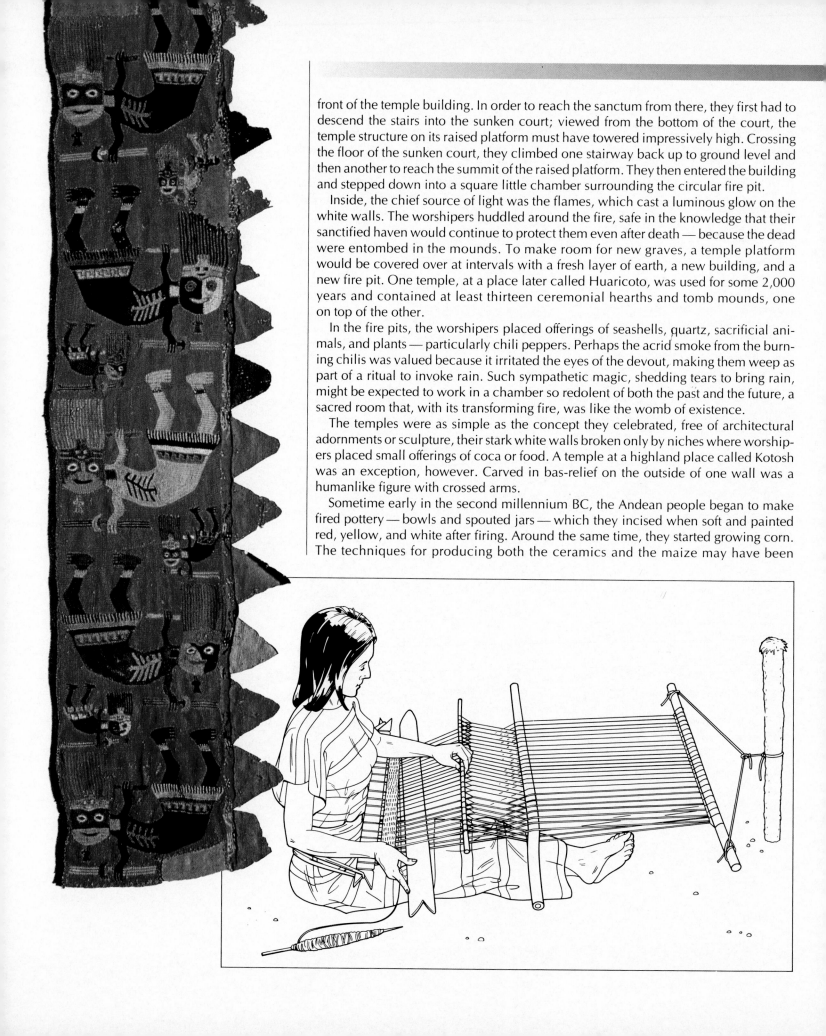

front of the temple building. In order to reach the sanctum from there, they first had to descend the stairs into the sunken court; viewed from the bottom of the court, the temple structure on its raised platform must have towered impressively high. Crossing the floor of the sunken court, they climbed one stairway back up to ground level and then another to reach the summit of the raised platform. They then entered the building and stepped down into a square little chamber surrounding the circular fire pit.

Inside, the chief source of light was the flames, which cast a luminous glow on the white walls. The worshipers huddled around the fire, safe in the knowledge that their sanctified haven would continue to protect them even after death — because the dead were entombed in the mounds. To make room for new graves, a temple platform would be covered over at intervals with a fresh layer of earth, a new building, and a new fire pit. One temple, at a place later called Huaricoto, was used for some 2,000 years and contained at least thirteen ceremonial hearths and tomb mounds, one on top of the other.

In the fire pits, the worshipers placed offerings of seashells, quartz, sacrificial animals, and plants — particularly chili peppers. Perhaps the acrid smoke from the burning chilis was valued because it irritated the eyes of the devout, making them weep as part of a ritual to invoke rain. Such sympathetic magic, shedding tears to bring rain, might be expected to work in a chamber so redolent of both the past and the future, a sacred room that, with its transforming fire, was like the womb of existence.

The temples were as simple as the concept they celebrated, free of architectural adornments or sculpture, their stark white walls broken only by niches where worshipers placed small offerings of coca or food. A temple at a highland place called Kotosh was an exception, however. Carved in bas-relief on the outside of one wall was a humanlike figure with crossed arms.

Sometime early in the second millennium BC, the Andean people began to make fired pottery — bowls and spouted jars — which they incised when soft and painted red, yellow, and white after firing. Around the same time, they started growing corn. The techniques for producing both the ceramics and the maize may have been acquired from a neighboring culture, or they may have been developed by experimentation in the region. Whatever their origin, once pottery making and corn cultivation became widespread, the ritual use of fire declined.

Perhaps this was because of fire's expanding utilitarian role. Using fire to prepare life-sustaining meals was somewhat akin to employing it for sacrifices to the gods. But using it to make pots, and a bit later to work metal, may have undermined its sacred appeal. Concurrently, the many virtues of newly domesticated corn made people think not of fire but rather of arable, well-watered land.

Fresh religious notions focusing on water gradually developed along the coast, leading the people there to turn their backs on the smoke-filled temples. Between 1800 and 1600 BC, coastal villagers either abandoned or modified the old ceremonial centers with their sunken circular courts. They replaced them with new complexes that consisted of a series of large mounds, shaped like pyramids with flattened tops and arranged in a U pattern. In some cases the pyramidal mounds that formed the sides of the U were joined like arms to the larger, dominant mound at the U's closed end. At other complexes each mound was separate. In every instance, however, the vast courtyard embraced by the U, which could be as large as 150 feet square, was carefully leveled, and had some form of irrigation system fed from a nearby river. And the courtyards invariably opened to the northeast, because there the Andeans saw the sun climb out of the mountains that sent down the rivers — the mountains that were givers of water and therefore keys to the planting season and to the harvest.

The new U-shaped complexes were built in valleys throughout the region, each on a trade route and close to a river. Like the old centers, the new temples had stark white walls free of architectural sculpture or other decoration. Among the earliest built was a temple at a place later named El Paraíso, by the mouth of the Chillón River. It encompassed an area of more than 120 acres. Its six truncated pyramids, constructed mainly of cut stone set with clay mortar, stretched for 350 yards around the U. A strong, stable political power must have been established in the valleys, since it obviously took more than one generation to build such monumental structures.

Water was the driving force behind the advancing social and political organization. More and more of the fishermen now seemed bent on becoming farmers, and to support an increased agricultural population the villagers had to make better use of the rivers. As early as 2400 BC, some residents of the coast had been diverting small amounts of river water to their fields. But the new religious centers marked the introduction of large-scale canal irrigation. At a temple later named La Florida, built around 1750 BC in the lower Rímac Valley ten miles from the ocean, the villagers constructed a canal two-and-a-half to four miles long that more than quadrupled the amount of arable land previously available. La Florida became the largest settlement in the entire region, home to perhaps several thousand people, and dominated a trade network that included parts of both the Rímac and Chillón valleys. Most of the religious centers were, like La Florida, surrounded by irrigated farmland, and their irrigated courtyards apparently were planted with sacred orchards and fields.

The new temples and the large-scale agriculture that developed at the same time were causally intertwined with a major shift in population patterns. More and more

The ancient people of the Andes worked at simple, portable looms *(left)* to produce textiles of extraordinary quality and beauty. To use these so-called backstrap looms, the weaver fastened one end to a stationary object such as a post and leaned back against a waist strap to maintain tension on the lengthwise threads, or warps. Then she wove in the crosswise threads, or wefts, from a bobbin. Such a procedure resulted in the cotton-and-alpaca-wool border shown at far left, decorated with a procession of figures that appear to be falling through the air. Above, a Chavín god with prominent fangs and a headdress of snakes glares menacingly from a piece of woven cotton fabric.

Chiseled onto the wall of a temple in Peru, a Chavín warrior *(far left)* holds a battle-ax at the ready. The severed heads beside him testify to the grim fate of Chavín captives: dismemberment in bloody rituals. The prisoner depicted above has been cut through at the waist.

people moved away from the ocean and up the interior river valleys until, by 1400 BC, Peru's whole central region from coast to mountains had become culturally integrated. The trade networks, for instance, offered vastly more variety in food than the basic bargain of protein for carbohydrates. Llama caravans arrived in the coastal area carrying coca, sweet maniocs, and peanuts from the east. Corn, cucumbers, potatoes, and beans became staples of both highland and coastal diets.

This integration was reflected in the spread of a new cult across the entire northern half of Peru. Beginning as a local sect, it evolved into a brilliant synthesis that melded many social, religious, and artistic elements — including some traditions from the sunken-court and U-shaped temple complexes — into a cohesive and coherent whole. Twentieth-century scholars would call its practitioners the Chavín, after a religious center established in a remote valley on the eastern slopes of the Andes, near where the town of Chavín de Huantar would be built much later. There, at a venerable junction of trails from the coast, the highlands, and the jungle, the elite priestly class of the Chavín temples took the most complex images of the day and fashioned from them the first great style of American art and architecture, a style that would eventually spread across much of Peru and serve to cement the New World's first civilization.

The cult did not originate at Chavín de Huantar, however. It was born farther north, in some unknown village, and gradually spread southward. By about 1000 BC, its influence reached as far south as central Peru, close to where the city of Lima one day would rise.

Initially, the Chavín appeared to establish themselves by conquest. At the first complex they took over, a place later called Cerro Sechín, they carved stone reliefs depicting beheaded, mutilated, and castrated victims of violent combat, as well as heads taken as trophies in battle and scenes of ritual human sacrifice. Carved stone warriors marched triumphantly across the temple walls, and two stone plaques that apparently celebrated a victory stood at the main entrance.

Eventually, however, the Chavín probably came to rely more on the intimidating power of their images and the force of their ideas than on war. Moreover, they were flexible and clever enough to incorporate local themes and symbols into their rituals, which helped them to enlist popular support for their movement.

Still, once the Chavín influence arrived at an old religious center, the architecture at the site changed dramatically. The Chavín merged features of the U-shaped complexes with those of the still-older structures marked by circular sunken courts. However, they often ignored the northeast orientation of the old complexes, built the circular courts much larger than their predecessors had, and altered the U design to suit themselves. They often closed off the open end of the U with a colonnade, for instance. Their flat-topped pyramids were lower than those of earlier temple builders. They created symmetrical plazas in the middle of their complexes and decorated the walls surrounding them with huge stone relief carvings. They apparently wanted to create balanced backdrops for their dramatic sculpture and their undoubtedly dramatic rituals. They saw architecture not only as art but as symbol, a statement in stone of the social and spiritual power of their priestly elite and the gods they served.

The merging of styles that made these symbols was evident in the fifty-foot-high temple building at Chavín de Huantar, constructed over a period of 500 years beginning in the ninth century BC. It contained several levels of interior galleries with ceilings of beamlike stone blocks, partially supported by stones cantilevered from the

walls. The masons cut niches into the stone walls and built vents to carry air to interior rooms. The temple faced out over a large, square, sunken plaza. Long angular mounds stretching from the temple along both sides of the plaza gave to the whole a semblance of the ancient U shape. Two staircases led down from the temple to a circular court that was sunk into the plaza and lined with carvings of jaguars and anthropomorphic figures.

Chavín imagery came chiefly from creatures of the tropical forest. The sculptors at Chavín de Huantar drew on the lush woods of the eastern Andean slopes in carving ferocious stone monsters that combined features from humans, hawks, eagles, snakes, jungle cats, and caimans. Worshiped above all animals were the jaguar and the caiman, a crocodilelike South American reptile: The Chavín placed the fangs of one or the other in the mouths of virtually all their statuary, even carvings of birds and humans. In Chavín ideology, the caiman probably represented the lord of rivers and the jaguar the forest rain god.

It is no surprise, then, that a ceremonial complex dominated by the two animals focused powerfully on the ritual manipulation of water. A system of canals and conduits carrying water from the glacially fed Huachecsa River ran through and under the complex. The galleries reverberated to the thunderous roar of rushing water. A visitor would stand in awe, transfixed by the sound. And there was more: In the temple's most ancient section, two galleries intersected to form a cross. A worshiper approaching the junction through the dark arms of either gallery saw a massive, thirteen-foot-high stone sculpture of a snarling, anthropomorphic jaguar stuck like a knife in the middle of the floor, bathed in sunlight from openings above and virtually filling the sacred space at the intersection of the cross. The creature was clearly meant to intimidate, with its right forelimb raised and its left slung alongside, its digits terminating in claws, its mouth curled back at the corners to reveal two formidable fangs protruding over a lower lip, and its eyebrows and hair rendered as snakes.

The Chavín carvings are all the more impressive because the artists reduced their figures to a combination of straight lines, simple curves, and scrolls, probably because chiseling stone with simple cutting devices was difficult. This simplification encouraged them to treat anatomical features geometrically and to adopt geometric repetition as a way of creating a special symmetry. Chavín sculptures were perfectly balanced within the space available to each carving; many of the sculptures could be turned upside down or on either of their sides and still be seen as upright. The perfect balance and invertibility of the Chavín style underscored the basic dualism at the heart of the Chavín religion. It was a cult based on the pairing, interaction, and reconciliation of opposites, such as good and evil, black and white, up and down, day and night, north and south, summer and winter, sky and earth, male and female.

The people of Chavín de Huantar were ruled by priests who lived on wide terraces surrounding the temple. They used hallucinogenic cacti and stimulating coca in the rituals they performed. They wore headdresses of gold (perhaps adorned with exotic bird feathers), gold earrings, gold nose ornaments, gold mouth masks, and capes as well as kilts. From their homes, they could look up at the outside walls of the temple, constructed of finely worked stone in rows of alternating sizes, and see jutting out from the surface large stone heads — some of them humanlike, others fantastic beasts. Though clearly supernatural, the heads may have symbolized ritual sacrifice — a grim reminder of priestly power over the people whose homes stretched along the valley below.

Against a backdrop of the snowcapped Andes, a team of Chavín goldsmiths works at a furnace. Three smiths blow through reed pipes to keep the wood fire white-hot, while a fourth holds a sheet of gold over the flames. Soon he will place the softened metal on the flat surface behind him and hammer it into the desired form — perhaps an elaborate pectoral ornament. The hammered and soldered spoon above may have been used by Chavín priests for dipping snuffs made from hallucinogenic plants. The horn blown by the figure on the spoon's handle is formed from a silver conch shell.

The common folk dressed in cotton tunics and loincloths, worked their farmland, and paid tribute to the priests. Throughout the year, the priests would call on the villagers to labor in temple construction and to tend the sacred orchards. A group of craftsmen and artists resided in Chavín de Huantar itself, creating sculptures, tanning hides, weaving textiles, and manufacturing items of obsidian, copper, silver, and gold for the priestly elite's adornment: mirrors, beads, necklaces, pendants, and spool-shaped ear baubles sometimes so large that they grotesquely distended the earlobes through which they were worn.

In addition to their other skills, the Chavín became expert metallurgists. Gold had been worked in the Andes since at least 1500 BC, but by 800 BC Chavín goldsmiths were turning out impressively intricate pieces that fostered a greatly increased demand for the precious metal. The Chavín found the gold in the alluvium-rich rivers of the highlands or in mines that had already been worked for quartz. Using blowpipes to puff up the temperatures of charcoal fires, they smelted the gold in portable furnaces and crucibles, then beat it into thin sheets with hammers, made from bronze or meteoric iron, over cylindrical stone anvils. An important trade item for the Chavín, the gold was symbolically associated with the sun and agricultural rebirth.

The Chavín spread their culture all the way to the south coast beyond Lima not long after they founded the complex at Chavín de Huantar. Despite the great distance from the hub of Chavín life, they apparently penetrated southern coastal society without simplifying or distorting their ideology. The same was not true of the central Peruvian coast, where the old U-shaped ceremonial complexes yielded little to Chavín style. Some areas resisted Chavín proselytizing altogether for hundreds of years.

Then, during the fifth century BC, a period of devastating weather with calamitous floods and starvation apparently convinced a desperate people to embrace the new religion. By about 400 BC, the Chavín religious influence stretched from what came to be Cajamarca in the north to Ayacucho in the south, and from the edge of the Amazon basin to the rim of the Pacific.

When it was at the apogee of its power, the Chavín world began to dissolve. No clues were left to tell future generations why this first American civilization ended, or what happened to the Chavín themselves. But they profoundly influenced all the subsequent civilizations in that part of South America: Every major Central Andean deity from then till the coming of the Europeans bore a resemblance to the glowering god in the temple at Chavín de Huantar.

In Mesoamerica, the great journey toward civilization followed a path similar to that in the Andes, but for reasons not understood reached an equivalent level of complexity at a later date. The Mesoamericans had developed corn, a hybrid of wild grasses, around 4000 BC. They apparently learned to cultivate the grain along with beans, squash, chili peppers, avocado, and tomato — all vegetables unknown outside the Americas. It was not until about 2000 BC, however, that they gave up their seminomadic ways and became more or less settled farmers, with ground corn meal as a staple of their diet.

They gathered in relatively independent little villages not unlike the hamlets that had existed in Sumer about 5,000 years earlier. They developed extensive trade routes, akin to those in central Peru, but seem to have exchanged valuable materials such as precious

This Olmec ceremonial mask, carved of greenstone, combines the facial features of man and cat. It could have been used at rituals to convince worshipers that the priest who wore it was a werejaguar, a powerful forest spirit able to change at will from human to feline form.

stones rather than foodstuffs. Gradually developing most of the neolithic arts, they built cramped shelters of cane wood and thatch, grew their corn and other crops, made crude pottery, wove cultivated cotton into cloth, and plaited wild plant materials into baskets. They worked stone by grinding and chipping, and modeled little female figures in clay. Their leaders and elders lived and dressed much as other villagers did, and local shamans performed the all-important religious rites invoking rain and bountiful harvests.

Then, commencing around 1400 BC, Mesoamerica experienced a sudden surge of energy and imagination that produced a swift flowering of monumental art and architecture; of ceremony, trade, and technology; of the whole complex structure of society. At sacred sites in the midst of the rude little hamlets rose extensive ceremonial centers, with pyramids built around spacious plazas. Fine sculpture and painting appeared where only cottage crafts had been practiced before. In the ceremonial centers, shamans evolved into sophisticated priests, the region's first full-time intelligentsia, who presided at elaborate rituals and developed a knowledge of the heavens, mathematics, and engineering, as well as a method of recording events that became a system of writing in the later Maya culture.

The people who performed this feat of civilization were the Olmecs, or "dwellers in the land of rubber," so described because rubber trees abounded in the rain-drenched forests of their heartland near the Gulf of Mexico. Their origins are unclear. Perhaps they came from the highlands of southwestern Mexico or the lowlands along the Gulf Coast. They subjugated other peoples, but it is unlikely that they forged what could be called an empire, at least not in the sense of controlling a large geographical region through a centralized administration. They apparently had no large standing army to enforce an imperial will. They may have been organized as a number of strong and militaristic chiefdoms, whose leaders governed with the consent of elite families that produced both chiefs and priests. Or the leaders may have been the priests themselves, controlling a theocratic society that brought large areas under its spell.

However they organized themselves, the Olmecs were responsible for the rise of the first complex society in North America. Wherever they went, they created magnificent public works and a highly advanced style of monumental art. As it was among the Chavín, the jaguar was an important symbolic being for the Olmecs. It appeared often in the stone that they carved in the round, achieving an extraordinary realism unknown to the Peruvians. They also fashioned small images in precious stone — jade and jadelike serpentine.

To depict their leaders they sculpted immense stone heads, some weighing as much as twenty tons each and standing nine feet tall. The portraits are of strong, thick-lipped, broad-nosed men, wearing helmets that may have been headgear for a ritual game the Olmecs played with a rubber ball. These colossal visages appeared around 1200 BC, near the coast in the tropical lowlands along the Gulf of Mexico. Eventually, Olmec influence would reach from central Mexico 1,250 miles south to the land later called Costa Rica.

They must have been daunting to their enemies, these Olmecs — a people who claimed to be related to jaguars, who sacrificed human beings to their gods, who practiced ritual cannibalism and may have taken the heads of conquered foes. They evidently believed that, in the distant past, a being who could appear in the form of a jaguar or of a man had copulated with a woman, fathering a child. The infant combined the features of man and jungle cat and could take the shape of either — it was, in effect, a werejaguar, analogous to the Greeks' god Zeus, who could transform himself into a range of animals and objects, or the werewolf of European folklore. The Olmecs never tired of portraying this being. With its chubby limbs and baby face, it remained a perpetual infant, yet its toothless mouth snarled with the ferocity of the jaguar. Perhaps the Olmecs venerated this deity as the ancestor of their people and patron of their elite families.

The jaguar imagery probably had its roots in an older, pre-Olmec belief that shamans were the jaguar's alter egos and that even common human beings had animal alter egos whose fates closely paralleled their own, so that if the animal died, so would the person, and vice versa. These animals were later called naguals. For the Olmecs, the jaguar may have been the nagual of chiefs and priests: In one tomb of an Olmec ruling family, mourners buried the body of an infant alongside the corpses of two jaguars, probably the child's naguals.

It was the jaguar's connection to the ruler that assured its prominence in Olmec art. Olmec rulers commissioned monumental stone images of a seated figure, sometimes female, cradling a werejaguar baby, as well as small finely sculptured jade and serpentine werejaguars. In one cave, in southwestern Mexico, early Olmecs painted a portrait of their leader, his rank apparent by his headdress of long tail feathers from a quetzal bird, shown entwined with a jaguar. On forty-ton basalt slabs that might have been used as ceremonial podiums, a carved representation of the genealogical cord connected the ruler to his ancestors and, ultimately, to the werejaguar.

These chieftains ruled a society of accomplished builders. In 1250 BC, the Olmecs created a large ceremonial center of clay and wood at a place later named San Lorenzo, in the tropical rain forest of Veracruz on the Gulf Coast. Painstakingly piling up basket after basket of soil, they constructed a broad clay platform 150 feet high, probably buttressing its flanks with great logs. Atop this artificial plateau, their engineers raised tall mounds of earth clustered around rectangular courtyards aligned roughly on a north-south axis. Mirror symmetry lay at the heart of their design: A feature on one ridge would be duplicated on its counterpart. Perhaps to please the eyes of gods above, Olmecs sometimes worked to achieve an overall design that

These chubby figurines, modeled in white clay by Olmec potters, represent infant werejaguars. Pointed, catlike ears sprout from the baby on the upper left, while a stylized paw print marks the head of the child in the center. The lips of the standing figure have begun to curl back into a feral grimace. The androgynous statuettes were probably dressed in male or female costumes. Their owners may have revered them as household gods.

could only be comprehended from an aerial viewpoint. San Lorenzo may have been intended to look, from the heavens, like an enormous bird flying east.

San Lorenzo was a well-chosen site for an urban center. The surrounding lowland savannahs, forests, and rivers were a veritable cornucopia, flourishing with fruits and flowers and animal life including deer, monkeys, tapir, peccaries, opossums, armadillos, partridges, turkeys, turtles, and fish. The Olmecs even discovered there a kind of jungle toad that caused hallucinations when ingested and used it in their rituals. And the area's abundant rain ensured two harvests a year.

San Lorenzo soon became the center of Olmec civilization. It was here that the people first erected the colossal stone heads of their leaders, at least seven of them in what may have been a dynastic succession between 1200 and 900 BC. They painted them a garish purple with dye that they extracted from a mollusk — related to the Phoenician murex — that lived in the waters off the Gulf Coast. It was here, too, that they placed their gigantic basalt slabs decorated with fantastic animal and humanoid carvings.

The amount of labor involved in producing these monuments was staggering. The Olmecs quarried the rock in the Tuxtla Mountains, fifty miles to the north as the eagle flies. Because they possessed neither the wheel nor draft animals, they had to wrestle stone from the quarry by means of human muscle power. They dragged the huge blocks down to navigable rivers and floated them on great balsa rafts to the Gulf of Mexico, then along the shore and up the Coatzacoalcos River. On arrival at San Lorenzo, the blocks had to be hauled up the side of the platform. The Olmecs used stone not only for monuments and thrones but to construct a drainage system to empty San Lorenzo's ceremonial pools, which were filled by rainfall that measured 180 to 200 inches a year.

There was nothing egalitarian about the society at San Lorenzo. The majority of the people under Olmec domination were corn farmers, who probably raised their two crops a year on communally held upland soils where the rainy-season floods could not reach. The Olmec elite appropriated for themselves the rich river-bottom lands, where they harvested bumper crops after the summer floods had subsid-

The face of a werejaguar child snarls from this jade ornament, carved by an Olmec artist about 1000 BC. Holes drilled in the flanges on either side of the face served, perhaps, as eyelets for a necklace cord. Unfamiliar with gold, the Olmecs favored jade as a raw material for jewelry and religious art, prizing it so highly that pieces of the rare green stone were sometimes recycled. Centuries after the Olmec jaguar cult had faded into oblivion, a Maya artist engraved the reverse side of the ornament shown here with a design honoring his king.

ed, like the ancient Egyptian pharaohs who exploited the "Gift of the Nile."

From San Lorenzo, this restless people spread their influence north and south. The natural fecundity of the Gulf Coast led to a growth both in population and in the wealth of the Olmecs, providing impetus for their expansion. In some regions they apparently were content to trade instead of conquer, operating a form of commercial consulate through which they imported natural materials and exported their art and jewelry. Yet these descendants of jaguars could never be described as strictly peaceable merchants: In most cases, Olmec trade seemed to go hand in hand with military prowess. The Olmecs may have begun their expansion first by pacific means — by trade or marriage alliances. If they met with resistance in a particular village, however, they would resort to force. From that village, they would set up a trade network and exact tribute from the surrounding villages. From San Lorenzo, they continued successfully practicing this sort of commerce — backed by armed might — for possibly 300 years. But in time, the harshness of Olmec rule and exploitation, along with the pressure of rising populations, apparently led to rebellion and catastrophe.

Around 900 BC, what seems to have been a peasant revolt — coupled perhaps with a dynastic war among the Olmec elite — utterly destroyed San Lorenzo. The rebels ruthlessly toppled the monuments and defaced them. The huge carved stones were ritually buried in piled-earth ridges running down the sides of the mounds. There they would lie for centuries as the jungle reclaimed the forsaken place. Much later, natural erosion would cause a few of the big heads to tumble out and roll down the plateau into the grasslands below, causing people of another era to gaze in awe and wonder.

The destruction of San Lorenzo did not signal the decline of the Olmecs. A vigorous new dynasty soon sprang up at a place later named La Venta, on an island in a swamp near the Tonalá River, eighteen miles inland from the Gulf Coast. The new rulers had more colossal heads erected and built the greatest of all the Olmec sites, a two-square-mile complex dominated by a 103-foot-high, vertically ridged cone, made of earth and perhaps shaped to resemble a volcano.

About the same time, the Olmecs established a number of other new temple sites. At a place later known as Copalillo in the mountains of southwestern Mexico, far distant from La Venta, they constructed what may be the first stone temple in Mesoamerica. For this project they used huge blocks of travertine marble, which they finished so carefully that the blocks fitted flush against one another without mortar. The temple had an aqueduct, a stone drainage system, and an interior courtyard where the Olmecs played their favorite game, in which a ball was propelled through the air by an elbow, hip, or some type of bat. The game was a religious ritual and was used to divine the future.

From La Venta, Copalillo, and other centers, Olmec merchants traveled throughout southern Mexico and perhaps even to Guatemala, El Salvador, and Costa Rica to barter their stunning figures and axheads of jade, serpentine, or schist. Olmec missionaries and bands of warriors took the same trails to spread their religion and political power.

A stratified society like that of the Olmecs could not have existed without a surplus of food, but the surpluses were never great enough to support many large, truly urban concentrations of people. Aside from La Venta, most of the ceremonial centers probably housed no more than 1,000 aristocrats, priests, retainers, and full-time artisans each. But La Venta was a special place, for its era a magnificent urban center. The

In this depiction of a traditional Olmec odyssey, laborers haul on ropes that control a giant stone ceremonial head as it drifts down the Tonalá River in southeast Mesoamerica. The head, which weighs about 50,000 pounds, is floating on a raft constructed of large dugout canoes decked over with rough planking. The destination of the sculpture — the pyramid complex of La Venta, an important religious center on an island — can be seen in the distance.

Monuments of this sort were carved — probably in the likeness of Olmec rulers — at quarries in the volcanic Tuxtla mountains, some fifty miles west of La Venta. Sculptors squared and flattened features such as ears, nose, and lips, presumably to protect them from damage during the journey to the temples in the swampy Olmec heartland. From the quarries, the heads had to be pulled as far as twenty-five miles overland to the nearest navigable streams.

At least four of the gargantuan heads stood at La Venta, which was destroyed around 400 BC. San Lorenzo, an earlier Olmec center abandoned about 900 BC, boasted nine of the massive sculptures.

THE OLMECS' STONE COLOSSI

center and surrounding villages were home to perhaps 10,000 people, many of whom probably labored for decades to construct the complex. To build the great cone itself they had to pile up some 3,500,000 cubic feet of clay. Nearby, in the linear layout typical of earlier sites, they raised a number of huge earthen platforms using different colors of clay — red, yellow, and purple — to face the sides, which were buttressed with wood and cut stone. On the platforms they erected temples with walls of cane or wattle and daub, and floors of colored clays. Spacious plazas stretched out from the temples and were adorned with stone altars, large stone bas-reliefs, and, of course, the colossal heads.

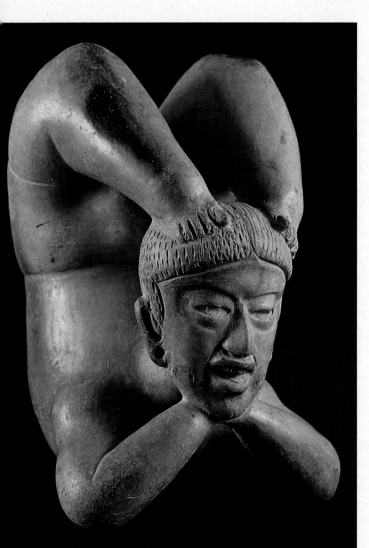

Olmec society at this time may have directly influenced the lives of some 350,000 Mesoamericans, most of them common folk who in the tropical climate probably wore only minimal clothing, perhaps cotton breechcloths. The men of the ruling elite, their retainers, and the merchants and artisans of La Venta and other centers sometimes wore breechcloths that formed short skirts, held in place by belts, and occasionally donned tunics or mantles. Women wore only skirts and belts. Clothes were made of cotton and other vegetable fibers, such as those of a cactus called the century plant. On ceremonial occasions, most of the citizens wore simple turbans; in contrast, priests and chiefs sported extraordinarily complicated headdresses apparently fabricated of cloth and leather over frameworks of reed and held on their heads by chin straps. Some instead wore straw hats decorated with tassels or hanging beads, which perhaps represented seeds.

Indeed, the Olmecs paid much more attention to adornment than to their basic clothing. They wore ornaments of jade and other colored stones, and they pierced their earlobes and the septums of their noses to wear intricately carved jade earrings and beaded, tubular nose pins. They also loved bracelets, anklets, necklaces, and pendants. Olmec artisans produced articles decorated with both abstract and extremely realistic motifs, including parts of the human body — hands, legs, fingers, ears — the jaws of animals, and the tails of stingrays. The priests and chiefs wore as pendants concave magnetite mirrors, remarkable pieces of precision-polished stonework. The wearers may have used the concave mirrors to start fires in ritual ceremonies by focusing the rays of the sun, a trick that would certainly have left the populace impressed with their leaders' magical powers.

The Olmec elite possessed other special skills and knowledge that in all probability were not understood by the masses. They knew enough about astronomy to calculate the length of the year and the lunar month, and to devise the first calendar in the Americas, which was most likely as accurate as any in use elsewhere during the period. The calendar enabled priests and chiefs to schedule seasonal ceremonies and to direct farmers in the timing of agricultural activities, abilities that doubtless enhanced the leaders' power over their subjects. The Olmecs could keep chronological track of more than just the passing year: Like

This vase of terra-cotta, crafted in the Olmec style around the year 1000 BC, may represent a shaman performing a ritual somersault intended to magically transform him into a jaguar. The vessel contained liquid, which could be poured from an opening in the left knee. Priests may have used the vase for libations offered during ceremonies honoring the rain god or some agricultural deity.

that of the later Maya, their calendar measured time in a continuous count from some seminal occurrence in the distant past, perhaps the birth of the gods. They memorized the dates of significant events, enabling them to pass on to future generations a chronologically correct sequence of their history. The importance of this form of calendar — which people in the twentieth century AD would take for granted — can be seen by comparing the Olmec dating system to that used by the Aztecs a millennium and a half later. The Aztecs did not use what scholars would one day call the "long count" of the Olmecs and could ascribe dates only within a fifty-two-year cycle, which was as extensive a period as their calendar covered. It was as if modern people could differentiate between years but not between centuries: Would "It happened in '49" mean 1949, 1849, or even 1549?

Obviously the Olmecs could not maintain a calendar without some system of writing and numbering. Like the ancient Egyptians, they used pictorial symbols, but they did not leave many examples of their hieroglyphs for scholars of the future to study, probably because most of their inscriptions were carved into wood that rotted away in the humid heat when the jungles eventually reclaimed Olmec land.

While that conquest by nature would not be complete for another 700 years or so, the Olmec world began to crumble much sooner. The ceremonial center at Copalillo was abandoned around 600 BC. Two centuries later, La Venta, like San Lorenzo before it, was deliberately and violently demolished; twenty-four of its forty major monuments were mutilated and ritually buried, perhaps by vengefully triumphant rebels. A complex at a site later named Tres Zapotes apparently somehow escaped destruction, and Olmecs hung on there until about 200 BC. But they were a faded reflection of their vigorous, glorious ancestors. They ceased to produce colossal heads and reduced their ambitions to mere commercial enterprise, living off the old trade routes and the Olmec reputation for fine crafts.

As the Chavín culture had for Peru, the Olmec society served as a foundation upon which other Mesoamerican civilizations would build. The Maya adopted and improved the Olmec calendar; they also developed Olmec hieroglyphs into a more flexible, mixed semantic-phonetic script. And the Aztecs, who many hundreds of years later established an immense military-mercantile empire in Mexico, would write poetry about a legendary "land of rain and mist" called Tamoanchan on the eastern sea. There, long before the founding of the Aztec capital, "in a certain era, which no one can reckon, which no one can remember, there was a government for a long time." Tamoanchan might have been the name that the Olmecs gave to their land.

Though desolate and covered with weeds, neither Copalillo nor La Venta ever lost its significance as a holy shrine. For centuries, through all the civilizations that followed, the Indians in the mountains of southwestern Mexico and the jungles of the Gulf Coast traveled to the sites, bringing with them their offerings, now in a Maya, now in an Aztec, now in a colonial vessel. Even in the twentieth century, archeologists examining the ruins would observe Indians coming in the night to make their offerings and pray in ancient tongues. These worshipers may not even have known they were praying to strange, forgotten gods who were once the secret forces behind a great civilization that never discovered the wheel, never harnessed a beast of burden, never codified a system of laws on stone or paper, but endured for a thousand years.

1500 BC	1400 BC	1300 BC	1200 BC	1100 BC
	Hittite king Suppiluliuma I creates an empire that includes most of Asia Minor.	Long-standing hostilities between the Hittites and the Egyptians erupt into the Battle of Kadesh.	Invasion of the Sea Peoples puts an end to the Hittite empire.	
Assyria becomes a vassal of the Mitanni for eighty years.	Under Adad-narari I and his son Shalmaneser I, Assyria expands into an internationally recognized power.	Assyrian governors rule Babylon as Babylonia enters a period of political instability.	Nebuchadnezzar I takes charge in Babylonia and restores national morale. Tiglath-Pileser I of Assyria defeats the Mushki in the north and wages continuous war against the Aramaeans, who are finally subdued around 900 BC.	

MIDDLE EAST

Tuthmosis I campaigns in Nubia and in Syria. Hatshepsut is crowned ruler. Amun is elevated to the national god and his priesthood acquires great wealth and control throughout Egypt. Tuthmosis III becomes pharaoh. His fifty-four year reign and those of his son and grandson pave the way for Egypt's golden age.	Amenhotep IV, with his queen, Nefertiti, establishes the Aten as the sole and supreme god of all Egypt. He moves the capital of Egypt to Amarna and changes his name to Akhenaten (spirit of the Aten). Tutankhaten becomes pharaoh and reinstates Amun and other gods, whose temples reopen.	Egyptians under Ramses II fight the Hittites under Muwatalli in the Battle of Kadesh. Egypt loses face in the eyes of Syria and Palestine, and many city-states throw off the Egyptian yoke. The Hebrews take flight from Egypt in the Exodus. Pharaoh Merneptah turns back Libyans and allied tribes, who try to settle in Egypt.	Sea Peoples attempt to invade Egypt by sea and by land, but are repelled by Ramses III, the last strong ruler of Egypt.	

EGYPT

Canaanite cities become vassals of Egypt. A tidal wave destroys Minoan ports.			Mycenaeans attack Troy. Invasion of the Sea Peoples destroys Phoenician coastal towns.	The fortress of Mycenae falls to the Dorians.

MEDITERRANEAN

Aryans compose and compile Vedas during the next 600 years.			Battle of the Ten Kings is fought in India.	Zhou dynasty begins in China.

ASIA

San Lorenzo is settled in the Olmec heartland.				La Venta is founded.

AMERICA

Time Frame: 1500-600 BC

Esarhaddon of Assyria marches into Egypt and captures Memphis.

Double monarchy exists in Assyria: Shamash-shumi-ukin reigns over Babylonia while Ashurbanipal controls the rest of the empire.

Nabopolassar becomes king of Babylonia.

Assyria begins harrassment of the Phoenicians.

The city of Nineveh falls and the Assyrian empire begins to dissolve.

Israelites defeat the Philistines under King David.

Sargon II of Assyria builds the city of Khorsabad and takes the throne in Babylonia.

With the accession of Nebuchadnezzar II, Babylonia enters a period of grandeur.

Shabako of Kush invades Egypt, which is now splintered into eleven provinces. The Kushites become recognized overlords of the land.

Assyrians overrun Egypt and take Memphis.

Libyan kings rule Lower Egypt.

Psamettichus I of Egypt restores unity to the country.

Neccho II encourages Phoenician circumnavigation of Africa.

Sparta annexes Laconia.

Rome is founded.

The alphabet reaches Greece.

The first Greek coins are minted in Lydia in Asia Minor.

Phoenicians develop alphabetic writing system while establishing trading routes and settlements in the Mediterranean.

Etruscan city-states begin to take form.

Homer composes the *Iliad* and the *Odyssey*.

First Greek settlement in Italy is established at Pithecusae (Ischia).

Sparta attacks Messenia.

Lycurgan reforms are enforced in Sparta. The Corinthian tyrant Cypselus overthrows the aristocratic clan of Bacchiadae.

Carthage is allied with the Etruscans against the Greeks. Phoenicians circumnavigate Africa. Etruscan power reaches its height.

Phoenicians build temple of Solomon in Jerusalem.

Carthage, a Phoenician colony, is founded on the African coast.

A Greek colony is founded at Syracuse.

First Etruscan, Lucius Tarquinius, ascends the Roman throne.

Aryans migrate from the Indus region eastward to the Ganges Plain.

First republics form in India.

San Lorenzo is razed.

Chavín de Huantar is built in Peru.

Olmecs occupy Tres Zapotes.

ACKNOWLEDGMENTS

The editors wish to thank the following individuals and institutions for their valuable assistance in the preparation of this volume:
England: Dunsford — Reynold Higgins. London — Carol Andrews, Department of Egyptian Antiquities, British Museum; Richard Blurten, Department of Oriental Antiquities, British Museum; Peter Connolly, Institute of Archaeology, University College; John E. Curtis, Department of Western Asiatic Antiquities, British Museum; Samuel Eilenberg; Robert Knox, Department of Oriental Antiquities, British Museum; Anne Millard; T. C. Mitchell, Keeper of Western Asiatic Antiquities, British Museum; Peter J. Parr, Department of Western Asiatic Archaeology, Institute of Archaeology, University of London; Julian E. Reade, Department of Western Asiatic Antiquities, British Museum; Robert Skelton, Keeper of the Indian Department, Victoria and Albert Museum; Brian A. Tremain, Photographic Services, British Museum. Oxford — Fiona Strachan, Griffith Institute, Ashmolean Museum; Michael Vickers, Department of Antiquities, Ashmolean Museum.
Federal Republic of Germany: Aachen — Michael Jansen, Gesellschaft zur Förderung der Forschung in Süd-Asien, RWTH. Berlin — Joachim S. Karig, Ägyptisches Museum, Staatliche Museen Preussischer Kulturbesitz; Heidi Klein, Bildarchiv Preussischer Kulturbesitz; Jürgen Settgast, Direktor, Ägyptisches Museum, Staatliche Museen Preussischer Kulturbesitz; Marianne Yaldiz, Museum für Indische Kunst, Staatliche Mu-

seen Preussischer Kulturbesitz. Bonn — Stephan Seidlmeyer, Ägyptologisches Institut, Universität Bonn; Paul Yule. Cologne — Ulrich Wiesner, Museum für Ostasiatische Kunst. Hildesheim — Bettina Schmitz, Roemer- und Pelizaeus-Museum. Karlsruhe — Michael Maasz, Badisches Landesmuseum. Munich — Irmgard Ernstmeier, Hirmer Verlag; Dietrich Klose, Staatliche Münzsammlung; Dietrich Wildung, Direktor, Staatliche Sammlung Ägyptischer Kunst. Stockdorf — Claus Hansmann. Stuttgart — Gerd Kreissl, Klaus-Joachim Brandt, Linden Museum. Tübingen — Helmut Brunner, Emma Brunner-Traut.
France: Paris — Michel Amandry, Conservateur au Cabinet des Médailles; Daniel Arnaud, Directeur d'Etudes, E.P.H.E.; François Avril, Curateur, Département des Manuscrits, Bibliothèque Nationale; Christophe Barbotin, Conservateur du Département des Antiquités Egyptiennes, Musée du Louvre; Laure Beaumont-Maillet, Conservateur en Chef du Cabinet des Estampes, Bibliothèque Nationale; Catherine Bélanger, Chargée des Rélations Extérieures du Musée du Louvre; Jeannette Chalufour, Archives Tallandier; Béatrice Coti, Directrice du Service Iconographique, Editions Mazenod; Antoinette Decaudin, Documentaliste, Départément des Antiquités Orientales, Musée du Louvre; Michel Fleury, Président de la IV Section de l'Ecole Pratique des Hautes Etudes; Marie-Françoise Huyghes des Etages, Conservateur, Musée de la Marine; Françoise Jestaz, Conservateur, Cabinet des Estampes, Bibliothèque Nationale; Marie Montembault,

Documentaliste, Département des Antiquités Grecques et Romaines, Musée du Louvre; Françoise Nader, Office du Tourisme Libanais; Marie-Odile Roy, Service Photographique, Bibliothèque Nationale; Jacqueline Sanson, Conservateur, Directeur du Service Photographique, Bibliothèque Nationale.
German Democratic Republic: Berlin — Liane Jakob-Rost, Direktor, Vorderasiatisches Museum, Staatliche Museen zu Berlin; Hannelore Kischkewitz, Ägyptisches Museum, Staatliche Museen zu Berlin; Evelyn Klengel-Brandt, Vorderasiatisches Museum, Staatliche Museen zu Berlin; Wolfgang Müller, Ägyptisches Museum, Staatliche Museen zu Berlin.
Israel: Tel-Aviv — David Ussishkin, Department of Archaeology, Tel-Aviv University; Shelly Wachsman, Supervisor of Underwater Archaeology, Department of Antiquities and Museums, Ministry of Education and Culture.
U.S.A.: California: Berkeley — Frits Staal, Department of Philosophy, University of California at Berkeley. Connecticut: New Haven — David W. Goodrich. Maryland: Gaithersburg — Janet Palmer Mullaney. New York: Corning — David Whitehouse. Cornwall-on-Hudson — John R. Elting. New York City — Deanna Cross, Metropolitan Museum of Art. Virginia: Alexandria — Camille Fallow. Washington, D.C. — Ann Pollard Rowe, The Textile Museum.

The index for this volume was prepared by Roy Nanovic.

PICTURE CREDITS

nasty, 1550-1291 BC, Trustees of The British Museum, London (Kurt Flimm, Karlsruhe); Musicians, facsimile painting, tomb of Djeserkarseneb, Egyptian, Eighteenth Dynasty, 1550-1291 BC, Egyptian Expedition of The Metropolitan Museum of Art, Rogers Fund, 1930 (30.4.9). **40, 41:** Kohl pot, glass and gold, Egyptian, Eighteenth Dynasty, 1550-1291 BC, Trustees of the British Museum, EA 24391; Nefertari, wall painting, Egyptian, Eighteenth Dynasty, 1363-1349 BC, Thebes West, Valley of the Kings (Hirmer Fotoarchiv, Munich); Mirror, silver disk, gold handle, Egyptian, Eighteenth Dynasty, 1460 BC, The Metropolitan Museum of Art, Fletcher Fund, 1920 (26.8.98); Hair curler, bronze, Egyptian, Eighteenth Dynasty, 1550-1291 BC, Roemer- und Pelizaeus-Museum, Hildesheim. **42:** Ointment spoon, wood, Egyptian, Eighteenth Dynasty, 1300 BC, Trustees of the British Museum, EA 5965; Comb, wood, Egyptian, Nineteenth Dynasty, 1291-1185 BC, Photo Réunion des Musées Nationaux, Paris; Container in shape of the god Bes, faience, Egyptian, The Norbert Schimmel Collection. **46:** The royal family, bas-relief, Egyptian, Eighteenth Dynasty, 1345 BC, Ägyptisches Museum, Staatliche Museen Preussischer Kulturbesitz, Berlin (West) (Margarete Busing). **47:** Akhenaten, cut-relief, Egyptian, Eighteenth Dynasty, 1364-1347 BC, The Egyptian National Museum, Cairo (Kodansha Ltd., Tokyo). **48:** Serpent, gilt on wood with quartz inlay, Egyptian, Eighteenth Dynasty, 1333-1323 BC (Lee Boltin). **49:** Anubis, wall painting, Egyptian, Nineteenth Dynasty, 1291-1185 BC, Thebes West (Kurt Flimm, Karlsruhe). **50:** Sarcophagus of Tutankhamen, art by Roger Stewart, Surrey. **52, 53:** The Hypostyle Hall at Abu Simbel, Egyptian, art by Robert Hynes, inset Abu Simbel (© Farrell Grehan/Photo Researchers, Inc.) **55:** Detail, priest, bronze, Egyptian, Twenty-first Dynasty, 1000 BC, Musée du Louvre, Paris (Erich Lessing, Culture and Fine Arts Archives, Vienna). **56:** Altar of Tukulti-Ninurta I, stone, Assyrian, thirteenth century BC, Staatliche Museen zu Berlin, Vorderasiatisches Museum, Berlin, GDR; Priest, bronze, Egyptian, Twenty-first Dynasty, 1000 BC, Musée du Louvre, Paris (Erich Lessing, Culture and Fine Arts Archives, Vienna); background (West Light); Man with jaguar baby, jade, Olmec, 1500-600 BC, The Brooklyn Museum, L.47.6, loaned by Robin B. Martin; Male worshiper, bronze, Greek, 1500-600 BC, Herakleion Museum, Crete (Ekdotike Athenon Athens). **58, 59:** Akhenaten and Nefertiti, stone, Egyptian, Eighteenth Dynasty, fourteenth century BC, The Egyptian National Museum, Cairo; background (© Stockphotos Inc.); Supporters of the Winged Sun Disk, Tell Half, Assyrian, Aleppo Archeological Museum, Syria (G. Dagli Orti, Paris) — Sun goddess, gold, Hittite, The Metropolitan Museum of Art, lent by Norbert Schimmel (L.1983.119.3). **60, 61:** Harsaphes, silver, Egyptian, 900-700 BC (private collection, FRG); Goddess Thoueris, silver, Egyptian, Twenty-sixth Dynasty, 640 BC, The Egyptian National Museum, Cairo (Barry Iverson); fertility goddess, ivory, Phoenician, fourteenth century BC, Musée du Louvre, Paris (Lauros-Giraudon, Paris); background (© Tony Stone Worldwide/Masterfile); Signet ring, gold, Mycenaean, 1550-1200 BC (Vicky Kalliora, Athens); Pretty lady figurine, pottery, Tlatilco, Mexico (Peter T. Furst). **62, 63:** Jaguar shaman, jade, Olmec, 1000-900 BC (Michael Latil, courtesy Department of Pre-Columbian Studies, Dumbarton Oaks, Washington, D.C.); background (© Stephen Green-Armytage 1979/The Image Bank) — Tiger, bronze, Chinese, Zhou dynasty, 1100-600 BC (Courtesy of the Freer Gallery of Art, Smithsonian Institution, Washington, D.C.) (Acc.no. 35.22R); Lioness Sekhmet, gilded wood, Egyptian, Nineteenth Dynasty, thirteenth century BC, The Egyptian National Museum, Cairo (Kodansha Ltd., Tokyo); Lion, stone, Assyrian, 865 BC, Trustees of the British Museum, London, WA 118895. **64, 65:** Stela of Baal, stone relief, Phoenician, nineteenth-eighteenth centuries BC (Jean Mazenod, *Art of Ancient Near East*, Editions Mazenod, Paris); Figure of Baal, bronze, Phoenician, fourteenth-thirteenth centuries BC, Musée du Louvre, Paris (Erich Lessing/Culture and Fine Arts Archives, Vienna); background (© William James Warren/West Light); Stela of the god TeHub, basalt, Babylonian, eighth century BC, Musée du Louvre, Paris (Erich Lessing/Culture and Fine Arts Archives, Vienna); Demon Pazuzu, bronze, Assyrian, 1500-600 BC (Photo Réunion des Musées Nationaux, Paris). **66, 67:** Funeral procession, clay plaque, Etruscan, 530-520 BC, Musée du Louvre, Paris (Bulloz, Paris); Tombstone, Hittite, 700 BC, Adana Archeological Museum, Turkey (G. Dagli Orti, Paris); background (Photo Daniel Faure, Paris); Tutankhamen, carved wood and bronze coated with gesso and gilded, Egyptian, Nineteenth Dynasty, thirteenth century BC, The Egyptian National Museum, Cairo (Kodansha Ltd., Tokyo). **68:** Detail, throne room of Mycenae, art by Dante Kristoff. **70:** Maps of Mediterranean, drawn by Alfred T. Kamajian. **71:** Trojan horse, from amphora, clay, Greek, seventh century BC, Archeological Museum, Mykonos (Ekdotike Athenon, Athens). **72, 73:** Citadel of Mycenae, art by Dante Kristoff, from sketch by Fred Holz, based on books *Mycenae: Rich in Gold*, by George E. Mylonas and *Mycenae: An Archeological History and Guide*, by Alan J. B. Wace. **74:** Throne room of Mycenae, art by Dante Kristoff, based on *Mycenae: Rich in Gold*, by George E. Mylonas, and reconstruction drawings by E. Olympios contained therein, and reconstruction drawing of throne room of Pylos by Piet de Jong. **76:** Death mask (mask of Agamemnon), hammered gold, Mycenaean, sixteenth century BC, Musée du Louvre, Paris (© Erich Lessing/Culture and Fine Arts Archives, Vienna). **77:** Diadem, thin sheets of embossed gold on leather or fabric, Mycenaean, sixteenth century BC, National Archeological Museum, Athens (Mauro Pucciarelli, Rome). **78, 79:** Lion's-head rhyton, gold, Mycenaean, sixteenth century BC, National Archeological Museum, Athens (Ekdotike Athenon, Athens); Signet ring bezels, gold, Mycenaean, sixteenth century BC, National Archeological Museum, Athens (Nimatallah/Art Resource); Decorative garment disks, gold repoussé, Mycenaean, sixteenth century BC, National Archeological Museum, Athens (Mauro Pucciarelli, Rome); Necklace of small beads in form of birds, gold, Mycenaean, sixteenth century BC, National Archeological Museum, Athens (Ekdotike Athenon, Athens); Earrings embellished with granulation, gold, Mycenaean, sixteenth century BC, National Archeological Museum, Athens (Ekdotike Athenon, Athens). **80:** Pomegranate-shaped pendant, gold, with superfine granulation detail, Mycenaean, fourteenth century BC, Trustees of the British Museum, London, GR.623; Capture of wild bull from Vaphio cup, embossed gold, Greek, c. fifteenth century BC, National Archeological Museum, Athens (T.A.P. Service, Athens). **82:** Detail from base of three hoplites in combat, paint on terra-cotta, Corinthian, c. 625-600 BC, Musée du Louvre, Paris (André Held, Ecublens, Switzerland). **84:** Armorer working on a helmet, bronze, Greek, c. 700 BC, The Metropolitan Museum of Art, Fletcher Fund, 1942 (42,11.42); Statuette of warrior, bronze, Greek, 550-540 BC, Olympia Museum (Vicky Kalliora, Athens), **85:** Statuette of man carrying a ram, bronze, Greek, second quarter of seventh century BC, Antikenmuseum Staatliche Museen Preussischer Kulturbesitz, Berlin (West) (Ingrid Geske); Statuette of youth running, bronze, Greek, c. 530 BC, National Archeological Museum, Athens (T.A.P. Service, Athens); Statuette of horse and rider, bronze, cast separately, Greek, second quarter of sixth century BC (Jean Mazenod, *L'Art Grec*, Editions Mazenod, Paris). **86:** Verso of ancient coin, electrum, Miletus, Asia Minor, c. 580 BC, Staatliche Münzsammlung, Munich. **87:** Recto of ancient coin, solid silver, Lydian, sixth century BC, Bibliothèque Nationale, Paris — Recto of ancient coin, electrum, Miletus, Asia Minor, 620-580 BC, Staatliche Münzsammlung, Munich — Recto of ancient coin, electrum, Lydian, beginning of sixth century BC, Bibliothèque Nationale, Paris — Recto of ancient coin, electrum, Ionian, first half of sixth century BC, Bibliothèque Nationale, Paris — Recto of ancient coin, electrum, Teos, Asia Minor, c. 580 BC, Staatliche Münzsammlung, Munich — Recto of ancient coin, electrum, Miletus, Asia Minor, 620-580 BC, Staatliche Münzsammlung, Munich; Recto of ancient coin, electrum, Lesbos, first half of sixth century BC, Staatliche Münzsammlung, Munich. **89:** Detail, Battle of Lachish, art by Lloyd K. Townsend. **90, 91:** Battle of Kadesh, art by Lloyd K. Townsend. **92, 93:** Battle of Sea Peoples, art by Lloyd K. Townsend. **94, 95:** Battle of Lachish, art by Lloyd K. Townsend. **96, 97:** Battle of Greek phalanx, art by Lloyd K. Townsend. **98:** Antefissa, painted terra-cotta, Etruscan, 550 BC, Museo Nazionale di Villa Giulia, Rome (Hirmer Fotoarchiv, Munich). **100:** Maps of Phoenicia, drawn by Alfred T. Kamajian. **101:** Canaanite prisoner of war, faience glazed tile plaque, Egyptian, 1198-1166 BC, courtesy The Egyptian National Museum, Cairo (Barry Iverson). **102:** Core-formed glass, art by Fred Holz; Head-shaped pendant, glass, Phoenician, fifth-fourth centuries BC, Badisches Landesmuseum, Karlsruhe. **103:** Necklace with earplugs and amulets, glass, Egyptian, Eighteenth Dynasty, 1400-1350 BC, The Corning Museum of Glass, Corning, New York: Vase, Phoenician, Trustees of the British Museum, London, GR 259. **104:** Cosmetic vessel, glass, Egyptian, Eighteenth Dynasty, 1350 BC (Lee Boltin). **106, 107:** Lion mauling slave boy, carved ivory plaque, inlaid with lapis lazuli, carnelian, gold, lead, and diamond, Phoenician, eighth century BC, Trustees of the British Museum, London, WAS 349 H (Michael Holford, Loughton, Essex). **108:** Mask, terra-cotta, Phoenician, 700-500 BC, Museo Nazionale (Scala/Art Resource). **109:** Death mask, clay, Nazca, Peru, 1500-600 BC (Michael Latil, courtesy Department of Pre-Columbian Studies, Dumbarton Oaks, Washington, D.C.); anthropoid sarcophagus, clay, Canaanite, twelfth-eleventh centuries BC, Israel Museum, collection of Israel Department of Antiquities exhibited and photographed (David Harris). **110:** Urn head, clay, Etruscan, seventh century BC, Museo Archeologico, Chiusi (© Mauro Pucciarelli, Rome). **111:** Mask, jadeite, Olmec, 900-800 BC (Peter T. Furst). **114:** Inkwells, bucchero pottery, Etruscan, seventh-sixth centuries BC, The Metropolitan Museum of Art, Fletcher Fund, 1924 (24.97.21ab). **115:** Map of Italy, drawn by Alfred T. Kamajian. **116:** Female dancer, painting, Tomb of Triclinium, Etruscan, 470 BC, National Museum, Tarquinia; Flutist, painting, Tomb of the Leopards, Etruscan, fifth century BC, National Museum, Tarquinia (Mauro Pucciarelli, Rome). **117:** Female dancer, painting, Tomb of Giocolieri, Etruscan, sixth century BC, National Museum, Tarquinia (© Mauro Pucciarelli); Male dancer, painting, Tomb of Triclinium, Tarquinia, Etruscan, 470 BC (Nimatallah/© Artephot-Ziolo). **118:** Male dancer, Tomb of the Augers, Etruscan, 530 BC, Museo Nazionale, Tarquinia (Hirmer Fotoarchiv, Munich). **119:** Map of Phoenician sea trade routes, drawn by Alfred T. Kamajian. **120, 121:** Phoenician ships at sea, art by Jim Deal. **122, 123:** Phoenicians at trade port, art by Jim Deal. **124, 125:** Phoenicians returning to home port, art by Jim Deal. **126:** Detail, Shang dynasty burial, art by Lloyd K. Townsend. **128:** Map of India and China, drawn by Alfred T. Kamajian. **129:** Painting based on quote from Rig Veda hymn "To Arms," art by Don Ivan Punchatz. **130, 131:** Statue of man and dog on ox-drawn chariot, bronze, India, c. 1500 BC, The Museum of Western India, Bombay (Dirk Bakker, courtesy National Gallery of Art). **133:** Painting based on quote from Rig Veda hymn "The Horse Sacrifice," art by Don Ivan Punchatz. **134:** Anthropomorphic figure, copper, India, second millennium BC (Samuel Eilenberg, London). **135:** Harpoon blade, copper, India, second millennium BC, Museum für Indische Kunst, Staatliche Museen Preussischer Kulturbesitz, Berlin (West). **138:** Water buffalo-shaped wine vessel, bronze, China, late Shang, early Zhou dynasty, tenth century BC (Leo Hilber, Fribourg, Switzerland). **141:** Bronze casting, art by Damon M. Hertig/Giraffics; Cooking vessel with moon-shaped face, bronze, China, second millennium BC (Hubert Josse, Paris). **142, 143:** Shang dynasty royal burial, art by Lloyd K. Townsend. **145:** Oracle bone, tortoise breastplate, China, middle of second millennium BC, Institute of History and Philology, Academia Sinica, Taipei. **146:** Ceremonial ax, bronze, China, c. 1300-1030 BC (© 1987 Seth Joel). **148:** Detail, transporting an Olmec colossal head, art by John Ross. **151:** Map of the Americas, drawn by Alfred T. Kamajian. **152:** Textile, woven wool, Paracas, Peru, 1000-600 BC, Dumbarton Oaks Research Library and Collections, Washington, D.C.; Backstrap weaving loom, art by Fred Holz. **153:** Textile, painted cotton, Chavín, Peru, 1000-600 BC (© 1985 Justin Kerr, courtesy Edward H. Merrin Gallery, Inc.). **154, 155:** Los Danzantes, stone, bas-reliefs, Cerro Sechín, Peru, 1000-600 BC (© 1982 Johan Reinhardt, Peru). **156:** Chavín goldsmith, art by Robert Hynes. **157:** Spoon, gold, Chavín, 1000-600 BC (Michael Latil, courtesy Department of Pre-Columbian Studies, Dumbarton Oaks, Washington, D.C.). **159:** Mask, incised serpentine, Panuco, Mexico, 600-400 BC, The Peabody Museum of Archaeology and Ethnology, Harvard University (Hillel Burger copyright © 1987 Pres. and Fellows of Harvard College, all rights reserved). **161:** Jaguar babies, kaolin pottery, Olmec, 1500-600 BC (© Justin Kerr) (3). **162:** Flanged pectoral ornament, quartzite, Olmec, 1500-600 BC (© 1985 Justin Kerr). **164, 165:** Transporting an Olmec colossal head, art by John Rush. **166:** Vase, pottery, Tlatilco, Mexico, Olmecoid, 600 BC, National Museum of Anthropology of Mexico City (Kodansha Ltd., Tokyo).

INDEX

BIBLIOGRAPHY

BOOKS

Aldred, Cyril, *The Egyptians.* London: Thames and Hudson, 1961.

Allchin, Bridget, and Raymond Allchin:
The Birth of Indian Civilization: India and Pakistan before 500 B.C. Harmondsworth, England: Penguin Books, 1968.
The Rise of Civilization in India and Pakistan. New York: Cambridge University Press, 1982.

Altekar, A. S., *Education in Ancient India.* Varanasi: Nand Kishore & Bros., 1965.

Amiet, Pierre, *Art of the Ancient Near East.* Transl. by John Shepley and Claude Choquet. New York: Harry N. Abrams, 1980.

Austin, M. M., and P. Vidal-Naquet, *Economic and Social History of Ancient Greece: An Introduction.* London: B. T. Batsford, 1977.

Boardman, John, *Pre-Classical: From Crete to Archaic Greece.* New York: Penguin Books, 1978.

Casson, Lionel, *Ships and Seamanship in the Ancient World.* Princeton: Princeton University Press, 1971.

Ceram, C. W., *Gods, Graves, and Scholars.* New York: Alfred A. Knopf, 1968.

Chadwick, John, *The Mycenaean World.* New York: Cambridge University Press, 1976.

Chandra, Pramod, *The Sculpture of India: 300 B.C.-1300 A.D.* Washington, D.C.: National Gallery of Art, 1985.

Chang, Kwang-chih:
The Archaeology of Ancient China. New Haven: Yale University Press, 1977.
Shang Civilization. New Haven: Yale University Press, 1980.

Connolly, Peter, *The Greek Armies.* Morristown, N.J.: Silver Burdett, 1985.

Creel, Herrlee G., *The Western Chou Empire.* Vol. 1 of *The Origins of Statecraft in China.* Chicago: University of Chicago Press, 1970.

Davies, Nigel, *The Ancient Kingdoms of Mexico.* Harmondsworth, England: Penguin Books, 1983.

De Bary, Wm. Theodore, ed., *Sources of Indian Tradition.* New York: Columbia University Press, 1964.

Donnan, Christopher B., ed., *Early Ceremonial Architecture in the Andes.* Washington, D.C.: Dumbarton Oaks, 1982.

Doty, Richard G., *Coins of the World.* New York: Ridge Press, 1976.

Edey, Maitland A., and the Editors of Time-Life Books, *The Sea Traders* (Emergence of Man series). Alexandria, Va.: Time-Life Books, 1974.

Edwards, I.E.S., *The Cambridge Ancient History:*
Vol. 2, Part 1, *History of the Middle East and the Aegean Region.* Cambridge: Cambridge University Press, 1973.
Vol. 2, Part 2, *History of the Middle East and the Aegean Region.* Cambridge: Cambridge University Press, 1975.

Elisseeff, Danielle, and Vadime Elisseeff, *New Discoveries in China: Encountering History through Archeology.* Transl. by Larry Lockwood. Secaucus, N.J.: Chartwell Books, 1983.

Fairservis, Walter A., Jr., *The Roots of Ancient India.* Chicago: University of Chicago Press, 1975.

Fong, Wen, ed., *The Great Bronze Age of China: An Exhibition from the People's Republic of China.* New York: Metropolitan Museum of Art and Alfred A. Knopf, 1980.

Garraty, John A., and Peter Gay, eds., *The Columbia History of the World.* New York: Harper & Row, 1972.

Gernet, Jacques, *Ancient China.* Transl. by Raymond Rudorff. Berkeley: University of California Press, 1968.

Glubok, Shirley, *Discovering Tut-ankh-Amen's Tomb.* New York: Macmillan, 1968.

Grant, Michael:
The Ancient Mediterranean. New York: Charles Scribner's Sons, 1969.
The Etruscans. New York: Charles Scribner's Sons, 1980.

Gurney, O. R.:
The Hittites. Harmondsworth, England: Penguin Books, 1952.
Some Aspects of Hittite Religion. Oxford: Oxford University Press, 1977.

Hamblin, Dora Jane, and the Editors of Time-Life Books, *The Etruscans* (The Emergence of Man series). New York: Time-Life Books, 1975.

Hammond, N.G.L., *A History of Greece to 322 B.C.* London: Oxford University Press, 1984.

Harden, Donald, *The Phoenicians.* Vol. 26 of *Ancient Peoples and Places.* New York: Frederick A. Praeger, 1963.

Hibbert, Christopher, *The Emperors of China* (The Treasures of the World series). Chicago: Stonehenge Press, 1981.

Hicks, Jim, and the Editors of Time-Life Books, *The Empire Builders* (The Emergence of Man series). New York: Time-Life Books, 1974.

Higgins, Reynold, *Minoan and Mycenaean Art.* London: Thames and Hudson, 1985.

Homer:
The Iliad. Transl. by Richmond Lattimore. Chicago: University of Chicago Press, 1971.
The Odyssey. Transl. by Robert Fitzgerald. New York: Doubleday, Anchor Books, 1963.

Hopfe, Lewis M., *Religions of the World.* Encino, Calif.: Glencoe, 1979.

Hopkins, Edward Washburn, *The Religions of India.* New Delhi: Munshiram Manoharlal, 1970.

Hopper, R. J., *The Early Greeks.* New York: Harper & Row, Barnes & Noble, 1976.

Hucker, Charles O., *China's Imperial Past.* Stanford: Stanford University Press, 1975.

Humble, Richard, *Warfare in the Ancient World.* London: Cassell, 1980.

Keightley, David N., ed., *The Origins of Chinese Civilization.* Berkeley: University of California Press, 1983.

Keith, Arthur Berriedale, *The Religion and Philosophy of the Veda and Upanishads.* Vol. 2. Westport: Greenwood Press, 1977.

Keller, Werner, *The Bible as History.* Transl. by William Neil. New York: William Morrow, 1956.

Knauth, Percy, and the Editors of Time-Life Books, *The Metalsmiths* (The Emergence of Man series). New York: Time-Life Books, 1974.

Levenson, Joseph R., and Franz Schurmann, *China: An Interpretive History.* Berkeley: University of California Press, 1969.

Li, Chi, *Anyang.* Seattle: University of Washington Press, 1977.

Linecar, Howard, *Coins and Coin Collecting.* New York: Hamlyn, 1972.

Littauer, M. A., and J. H. Crouwel, *Wheeled Vehicles and Ridden Animals in the Ancient Near East.* Netherlands: E. J. Brill, 1979.

Loud, Gordon, and Charles B. Altman, *Khorsabad.* Vol. 40 of *University of Chicago Oriental Institute Publications.* Chicago: University of Chicago Press, 1938.

Lumbreras, Luis G., *The Peoples and Cultures of Ancient Peru.* Transl. by Betty J. Meggers. Washington, D.C.: Smithsonian Institution Press, 1974.

Macneish, Richard S., Thomas C. Patterson, and David L. Browman, *The Central Peruvian Prehistoric Interaction Sphere.* Vol. 7 of *Papers of the Robert S. Peabody Foundation for Archaeology.* Robert S. Peabody Foundation: Andover, Massachusetts, 1975.

Macqueen, J. G., *The Hittites and Their Contemporaries in Asia Minor.* London: Thames and Hudson, 1986.

Mahajan, Vidya Dhar, *Ancient India.* Delhi: S. Chand, 1968.

Majumdar, R. C., ed., *The Vedic Age.* London: George Allen & Unwin, 1952.

Marrou, H. I., *A History of Education in Antiquity.* Transl. by George Lamb. New York: Sheed and Ward, 1956.

Mascaró, Juan, transl., *The Upanishads.* Harmondsworth, England: Penguin Books, 1985.

Mookerji, Radha Kumud, *Ancient Indian Education.* Delhi: Motilal Banarsidass, 1969.

Moscati, Sabatino:
Ancient Semitic Civilizations. New York: G. P. Putnam's Sons, Capricorn Books, 1960.
The World of the Phoenicians. Transl. by Alastair Hamilton. New York: Frederick A. Praeger, 1968.

Moseley, Michael E., *Pre-agricultural Coastal Civilizations in Peru.* Burlington, N.C.: Carolina Biological Supply, 1978.

Murnane, William J., *The Road to Kadesh.* Chicago: University of Chicago, 1985.

Mylonas, George E., *Mycenae: Rich in Gold.* Athens: Ekdotike Athenon S.A., 1983.

Oates, Joan, *Babylon.* London: Thames and Hudson, 1979.

O'Flaherty, Wendy Doniger, transl., *The Rig Veda.* Harmondsworth, England: Penguin Books, 1984.

Picard, Gilbert C., *Carthage.* Transl. by Miriam and Lionel Kochan. London: Elek Books, 1964.

Piggott, Stuart, *Prehistoric India to 1000 B.C.* New York: Barnes & Noble, 1962.

Pritchard, James B., *Recovering Sarepta, a Phoenician City.* Princeton: Princeton University Press, 1978.

Randhawa, M. S., *Beginning to 12th Century.* Vol. 1 of *A History of Agriculture in India.* New Delhi: Indian Council of Agricultural Research, 1980.

Rawlings, G. B., *Ancient, Medieval, Modern Coins and How to Know Them.* Chicago: Ammon Press, 1966.

Reade, Julian, *Assyrian Sculpture.* Cambridge, Mass.: Harvard University Press, 1983.

Redford, Donald B., *Akhenaten: The Heretic King.* Princeton: Princeton University Press, 1984.

Roberts, J. M., *The Pelican History of the World.* Harmondsworth, England: Penguin Books, 1980.

Roux, Georges, *Ancient Iraq.* Harmondsworth, England: Penguin Books, no date.

Rowe, John Howland, *Chavin Art: An Inquiry into Its Form and Meaning.* New York: University Publishers, 1962.

Saggs, H.W.F.:
Everyday Life in Babylonia & Assyria. New York: G. P. Putnam's Sons, 1965.
The Might That Was Assyria. London: Sidgwick & Jackson, 1984.

St. John, Jeffrey, and the Editors of Time-Life Books, *Noble Metals* (The Planet Earth series). Alexandria, Va.: Time-Life Books, 1984.

Sandars, N. K., *The Sea Peoples: Warriors of the Ancient Mediterranean 1250-1150 B.C.* Vol. 89 of *Ancient Peoples and Places.* London: Thames and Hudson, 1978.

Schwartzberg, Joseph, ed., *A Historical Atlas of South Asia.* Chicago: University of Chicago Press, 1978.

Sealey, Raphael, *A History of the Greek City States ca. 700-338 B.C.* Berkeley: University of California Press, 1976.

Sinnigen, William G., *Ancient History from Prehistoric Times to the Death of Justinian.* New York: Macmillan, 1981.

Starr, Chester, *The Economic and Social Growth of Early Greece.* New York: Oxford University Press, 1977.

Steindorff, George, and Keith C. Seele, *When Egypt Ruled the East.* Chicago: University of Chicago Press, 1942.

Taylour, Lord William, *The Mycenaeans.* London: Thames and Hudson, 1983.

Tê-K'un, Chêng, *Shang China.* Vol. 2 of *Archaeology in China.* Cambridge: W. Heffer & Sons, 1960.

Trigger, B. G., B. J. Kemp, D. O'Connor, and A. B. Lloyd, *Ancient Egypt.* New York: Cambridge University Press, 1983.

Vermeule, Emily, *Greece in the Bronze Age.* Chicago: University of Chicago Press, 1964.

Wace, Alan J. B., *Mycenae.* Princeton: Princeton University Press, 1949.

Warmington, B. H., *Carthage.* New York: Frederick A. Praeger, 1960.

Wertime, Theodore A., and James D. Muhly, *The Coming of the Age of Iron.* New Haven: Yale University Press, 1980.

White, J. E. Manchip, *Ancient Egypt.* New York: Thomas Y. Crowell, 1953.

Wolpert, Stanley, *A New History of India.* New York: Oxford University Press, 1982.

Yadin, Yigael, *The Art of Warfare in Biblical Lands.* Vol. 1. New York: McGraw-Hill, 1963.

PERIODICALS

Crossley, Mimi, "Ancient Olmec Site Unearthed in Mexico." *The Washington Post* (Washington, D.C.), April 26, 1986.